The High Life

Qualitative Studies in Crime and Justice,
Volume 2

The High Life

Club Kids,
Harm & Drug Policy

Dina Perrone

LYNNE
RIENNER
PUBLISHERS

BOULDER
LONDON

To my mom, dad, and brother
for all their love and support

Published in the United States of America in 2010 by
Lynne Rienner Publishers, Inc.
1800 30th Street, Boulder, Colorado 80301
www.rienner.com

and in the United Kingdom by
Lynne Rienner Publishers, Inc.
3 Henrietta Street, Covent Garden, London WC2E 8LU

ISBN: 978-1-881798-46-0 (pb : alk. paper)

First published in 2009 by Criminal Justice Press.
Reprinted here from the original edition.

Printed and bound in the United States of America

The paper used in this publication meets the requirements
of the American National Standard for Permanence of
Paper for Printed Library Materials Z39.48-1992.

5   4   3

CONTENTS

LIST OF FIGURES AND TABLES

ACKNOWLEDGMENTS

First and foremost, this book would not have been possible without the club kids. They gave me direct access into their lives and shared their deepest experiences. Thanks to them, we are all a bit more knowledgeable.

I give my heartfelt thanks and warmest affections to the following people for their consideration, time, and support. They have been incredibly helpful providing places to read, write, relax and have fun. They have also been very valuable as mentors, editors and friends. They were instrumental to the completion of the research, the writing of the book, and the sanity of the author:

Rich Allinson, Adi Avivi, BST, The Baigorri Family, The Barnabas Family, Laura Bishop, Christie L. Bowles, Mel, Sal and Fausto Cavaleri, Stacy Caveleiro, Ko-lin Chin, C. Chip Cookie, Jim Finckenauer, Earl Grey, Pamela Heard, Galma Jahic, Ricardo Janvier, Bruce Johnson, Marissa Levy, Satenik Margaryan, Moira O'Brien, Robert Pandina, Katie, Lenore, Pat and Pasquale Perrone, Phyllis Schultze, Sasha Selimotic, Steve Sifaneck, Mercer Sullivan, Jenn, Vonn and Mable Sumner, Rebecca Tiger, Melissa, Vince, Gabriella, and Amy Tricomi, Penny Tyson, Lalo Valdez, and Richard Wright.

I cannot stress how grateful I am for all your guidance, assistance, encouragement, patience, and love.

ABOUT THE AUTHOR

Dina Perrone is assistant professor of criminal justice at California State University, Long Beach. She received her M.A. and Ph.D. in criminal justice from the School of Criminal Justice at Rutgers University-Newark. There, she received a University Grant for her dissertation project on the New York City club kids, on which this book is based. She has published on this research in the journal *Substance Use & Misuse* and in Bill Sanders's edited book entitled *Drugs, Clubs and Young People*. Dina was a National Institute of Drug Abuse, Behavioral Sciences Training, Pre-Doctoral Fellow at the National Development Research Institute, Inc.

While she has written various articles within the criminal justice field – topics including the privatization of prisons and self-control theory – her primary areas of research interest include drug use, drug policy and deviance. Throughout her career, she has sought to dissect the drug user stereotype through understanding patterns of use, drug experiences and mitigating factors of harm. She is currently the principal investigator on a Bridgewater State College grant-funded study of *salvia divinorum* users. Dina is interested in collaborating with other researchers investigating drug use in other cities, cultures, and nations to illuminate the nature of drug use patterns and harms, and to inform drug policies.

FOREWORD

Mercer L. Sullivan
Series Editor

I am pleased to present Dina Perrone's study of club-drug users as the second volume in this series of *Qualitative Studies in Crime and Justice*. This fascinating and timely piece of research follows in a long tradition of field studies of deviant behavior. Field methods are uniquely valuable for this kind of subject matter for at least two enduring reasons. First, there is the practical difficulty of studying "hidden" populations and behavior. Unlike the socially marginalized drug users who are studied more often, these "club kids" are hiding in plain sight. They play mainstream social roles and maintain conventional social relationships. Their extensive drug use, however, is the hidden deviant behavior of ostensibly conventional people. It is hard to imagine a way of finding out a great deal about this behavior through random sample surveys of the general population.

This research does indeed find out a great deal, and that is the second enduring reason that field methods are invaluable for studying deviant behavior. When some people do things that most others do not, we inevitably want to know more about what is going on than the vague, distal predictors of who the deviants are likely to be. We want to know: Why would anyone want to do that? What actually happens? Why are they not afraid? Are there any consequences and, if so, what? This study delivers all of that, in detail.

The methods employed here are traditional for this kind of study. The field researcher gets approval from a human subjects review board; goes through a frustrating period of trying to gain trust from the people she wants to study; observes and writes field notes; interviews and transcribes; sorts the data into conceptual categories; and pulls it all together in a written analysis. This much is easy to describe schematically, difficult to accomplish.

The innovative and illuminating aspect of this study is the wide-ranging array of theoretical perspectives brought to the material. At risk of oversimplification, we might venture that qualitative research in recent years has been pulled between two poles. One of these is interpretive, concerned above all with meaning and sometimes, unfortunately in my view, disdainful of positivist and empiricist aspirations. The other pole hews closer to the positivist and empiricist paradigm that is hegemonic in social science, sometimes at the expense of grappling fully with the complexities of the lived making of meaning.

Dina Perrone here works both sides of that continuum, comfortably and productively. She begins with meaning, culture, spectacle, the "emic." She draws the reader into the lived experience of the club kids. Then she moves to "etic" questions: What kinds of harm result? How is harm regulated and controlled? How does participation in this lifestyle evolve over the life course? Pulling it all together, she looks outward, to the social policies currently designed to deal with the harms of drug abuse. Her critique of those policies is harsh, but it is evidence-based. I expect that some will agree with her point of view. Others will not and some may well be outraged. Everyone, however, will know a lot more about the behavior in question. Close readers from all sides will probably rethink the questions.

INTRODUCTION[1]

At club Birdland[2] it was a "Welcome to the Jungle" themed party, and DJ Alex was spinning tribal instead of house music. Birdland was decorated in a jungle theme with butterflies and monkeys hanging from the ceiling, and trees shading areas of the dance floor. Two guys who were shirtless, wearing straw skirts and elaborate masks danced on the stage. The masks resembled a tribal member depicted in an old film. Osiris was "already fucked-up from 'G.' " I started to dance with Osiris's friend, who consumed mushrooms earlier . . . Bebek was dancing while pounding his walking stick on the floor. Since it was quite hot, everyone was sweating. Bebek's face make-up was dripping off his face. Suddenly, DJ Alex blew the horns and a cold breeze gusted on the crowd followed by thick smoke; it was the freeze blast . . . Sweating profusely the other part of the time was almost worth the cool air now. It was cold and quite exhilarating. (July 31, 2004; field note)

While drug use has long been a part of American culture, it has consistently been construed as problematic and a menace to society. Historically, drug users have been portrayed as a threat to normal life and a strain on both the welfare and criminal justice systems. The media have predominantly portrayed the typical drug user as an individual who craves drugs, engages in other criminal activities (such as theft) to support the drug habit, depends economically on public assistance and is chronically unemployed. Academic studies have also played a role in the production of this stereotypical image of the drug user. In general, criminological literature focuses on the criminality of less powerful segments of society, mainly the young and the poor,[3] and other studies of drug use tend to be based on survey methods focusing on causes of drug use and identifying differences between drug users and non-users. Both media depictions of drug use and academic research on drug users have pathologized drug users and emphasized how destructive these drugs can be.

This has fueled a response to address the drug problem in the U.S. that relies primarily on the criminal justice system. Over the past 20 years, the U.S. government has adopted a great amount of legislation, enforcement practices, and sentencing policies to eliminate or curb drug use and drug trafficking. Moreover, the U.S. government has exponentially increased its drug control budget from about $1 billion in 1981 to approximately $12 billion in 2004. About two-thirds of that ($8 billion) is allocated to domestic and international enforcement and interdiction.[4] Arrests and incarcerations of drug offenders – disproportionately people of color[5] – have increased at a very large scale. Incarcerations in state and federal prisons for drug offenses have risen over 1100% since 1980. The majority (60%) of these drug-offending inmates were incarcerated for possession offenses. Seventy-five percent of inmates incarcerated for drug offenses were convicted of non-violent crimes, and 58% of them had no history of violence.[6] Between 1988 and 2004, the average length of the sentences for drug crimes increased by 17%, while other sentences increased on average by 8%.[7]

Despite numerous efforts to eliminate or even curb illicit drug use and illicit drug trafficking, many Americans continue to have access to, and consume, illicit substances. The drug war has massive flaws. Criminal justice-based drug policies have not effectively accomplished the drug war's goals.[8] This can largely be attributed to two flawed assumptions underlying this drug policy: (1) that the individual has a pathology, which is the sole cause of the "drug problem," and (2) that all illicit drug use will lead to harm. The problems and harms resulting from drug use are much more complex, and this becomes clearer when different populations of drug users – such as hidden, White, middle-class, educated and employed users, like those presented in this book – are investigated. These users demonstrate how their broader social context – including settings of use, ties to family and work, and levels of capital (skills, networks, wealth) both influence use decisions and mitigate drug-related harms.[9]

The culture and capital of the user and the social environment in which the drugs are used greatly influence use, abuse, and harm. How the individual uses drugs, where he/she uses them, and the norms and rituals surrounding drug use all influence decisions about whether and which drugs to use. These factors can also exacerbate or curtail negative drug experiences – including trips to the emergency room and drug arrests. A user's social embeddedness (responsibilities and obligations) can encourage users to control, reduce or cease use. Above all, social and economic privileges can shield users from police drug busts and, therefore, arrest, as such tactics mostly target visible, street drug users in poor, socially excluded communities. The pharmacological properties of the drug do not solely determine its effects or whether its use is pleasurable or harmful.

Since the war-on-drugs policy neglects to address how those cultural factors, social settings and user norms affect drug use and the drug experience, it continues to fail. The drug war policy seeks to impact users' behaviors with very little knowledge about the population of users these policies are targeting. An improved understanding of the social and cultural meanings of drug use can deconstruct the stereotype of the drug user and inform our understanding of how drug-related harms actually happen. Drug policy could be more effective if it shifted from an abstinence-only, criminal justice-based strategy to a more balanced approach focusing on the health and lifestyles of these users.

CLUB DRUGS

Club drugs are drugs that are used primarily in venues where dancing takes place. Most studies and news reports in the United States on club drugs – particularly MDMA (ecstasy, E), crystal methamphetamine (crystal, crystal meth, tina), cocaine (coke, larry), ketamine (K, Special K) and GHB (G) – have focused on the prevalence, trends and risk factors of their use,[10] and the harms associated with use.[11]

Epidemiological research, which is based primarily on self-report surveys, indicates that the highest prevalence of club drug use occurs among Whites from suburban areas between the ages of 17 and 25.[12] Furthermore, these surveys, as well as other studies of club drug users, show that club drug use predominantly occurs within dance club settings, where individuals use one or a variety of club drugs at intervals throughout the night, along with licit substances, such as tobacco and alcohol.[13]

In addition to displaying images of young, White club drug users, the media depict these users as childish and irresponsible. The media have portrayed many club drug users as ravers, who frequent legal and illegal all-night parties or raves. Often these ravers are wearing sun-visors and baggy clothes, sucking on lollipops or pacifiers, and carrying glowsticks.

The media have also reported stories on club drug use as destructive and harmful. For example, the Home Box Office (HBO)[14] repeatedly aired *Small Town Ecstasy*, a documentary about a divorced father's use of ecstasy at raves with his children. The Public Broadcasting System's (PBS)[15] former weekly television series *In the Mix* broadcast an episode entitled "Ecstasy," in which teens in rehabilitation programs or prisons as a result of their ecstasy use were interviewed to discuss their harmful drug experiences.

Similarly, the drug GHB has been portrayed as a facilitator of date rape, and was headlined in the New York Times as the "New Drug [that] Can Induce Coma or Death. . . . "[16] Newsweek gave crystal methamphetamine the "America's Most Dangerous Drug" award,[17] and a headline in the New York Times read "Cocaine Users Face Greater Risk of Aneurysm."[18]

Partially in response to the negative attention given to the harmful effects of clubs drugs, the government has implemented punitive policies to eradicate club drug use.[19] For instance, the federal Food and Drug Administration added the club drugs ketamine and GHB to the schedule of controlled substances, making them illegal. In 2001, the federal Sentencing Commission increased the penalties for ecstasy possession.[20] In 2003, Congress enacted the Illicit Drug Anti-Proliferation Act to punish establishment owners — i.e., club owners — for use of drugs in their venues.

While depictions of club drugs are somewhat accurate to the extent that they can be harmful and destructive, and some users fit the image of the raver, such depictions are not representative of all club drug users. The patterns, settings, rituals and triggers of harm associated with club drug use are multifaceted. Both the current representation of drug users and the response to drug use ignore this complexity, and take a simplistic approach to understanding and addressing club drug use. The studies and the media portrayals lack the contextual information associated with drug use – the experiences of clubbing (going to dance venues) and club drugs. A few research projects have gathered in-depth knowledge on club drug users, but they have focused primarily on men who have sex with men.[21] The factors associated with club drug use, especially within the heterosexual population, are explored in this book.

Without understanding the cultural and situational elements associated with club drug use, it is likely that the very people these policies are intended to target will ignore the prevention efforts.[22] Most importantly, the drug war's policies will fail to help the users avoid harms or reduce or desist from use – and may cause harm to these users.[23] However, as depicted in this book, these club drug users are able to largely escape the war on drugs.

This book presents the cultural and situational context in which club drugs are used. It dissects the stereotype of the club drug user (White, young, raver), investigates the patterns of use, and explores the harms that the users experience. The research provides a view into the lives of various club drug users with whom I spent 15 months (March 2004 – June 2005) as they "partied" in a variety of venues along the east coast of the U.S. By entering the dance clubs, observing the club drug users' behaviors, and asking them questions, I learned about why and how club drugs are used. I was also able to understand the social settings of their use and the factors associated with their use that have mitigated or exacerbated the harmful effects of those substances. I discovered the norms, meanings, rituals and significance attached to their use of drugs, and observed how these norms, meanings and rituals helped them to escape the war on drugs.

The club drug users on whom this book is based are identified here as the "club kids"[24] — the label that George, an informant, used to describe those who go to dance venues and use drugs. The "club kids" title is actually a misnomer. I am not talking about idle kids here. Rather, these drug users, at the time of the study, ranged in age from 22 to 33. Most had college degrees and were employed full time in professional careers. They did not have criminal records, even though they had been using "hard" drugs (e.g., ecstasy, cocaine, LSD or ketamine) for at least eight years. Their adult responsibilities led most of them to engage in drug-using rituals that minimized the harms they experienced. They tried to ensure they safely met their obligations and avoided arrest or emergency room visits. Contrary to societal expectations, their drug use had not prevented them from becoming successful, taxpaying members of society. Their drug use had neither caused them to engage in crimes to support their use, nor resulted in any arrests. The club kids continued to be dedicated family members and employees. Through the club kids' culture of drug use (e.g., rituals and norms) and their connectedness (e.g., employment), these users were able to both engage in moderate (i.e., controlled) drug use and escape being ensnared in the drug war.

ORGANIZATION OF THIS BOOK

This book begins with a description of how I met the club kids and ways in which data on this group were obtained. It also provides many glimpses into the lives of these fairly affluent and well-educated club drug users. The subsequent chapters are then divided into two parts: (I) Club Kids' Dance Culture and (II) Drug Use among the Club Kids. The first part embarks on an exploration of the club kids as a subcultural group with particular rituals, styles, tastes, and cultural norms. The club kids are situated in a historical context. I assess how they fit within the subculture literature,[25] and how they compare to other subcultures, such as those of the hippies and the mods and the rockers. Next, the emergence of the club kid culture and the clubbing experience are analyzed using theories of consumption, commercialization, and globalization.[26] Here, the club kids' perceptions of the importance of clubbing and the appropriateness of using drugs in these settings are discussed.

The second part of this book investigates the club kids' patterns of drug use. First, I describe how three factors – the drugs used, the individual's mindset at the time of use, and the setting of use[27] – shape drug experiences and decisions. I especially focus on how drug knowledge[28] and peer norms influence which drugs to use and which drug combinations to avoid. Next, I explain that the club kid's capital – economic capital, life and job skills (human capital), and social networks (social capital) protect them from the harms of drug arrests, emergency room visits, and overdoses.[29] As the club kids get older, they slowly move from the emerging adulthood to adulthood stage of their lives. This progression over their life-course[30] has increased their levels of capital, shaped their drug use experiences – both negatively and positively – and affected their patterns of use. In this section of the book, special attention is given to the steps these club drug users have taken to maintain productive lifestyles and prevent negative effects and harmful behaviors that could have led to emergency room visits, employment problems and/or death.[31]

The absence of a discussion of the effect of criminal justice policies is notable. Moderation, desistance, and harm avoidance occurred without consideration of legal polices and criminal justice tactics. Instead, the club kids' cultural norms and socio-economic statuses were the predominant influences on their drug use and experiences.

The book concludes with an in-depth discussion of the implications for the dialogue surrounding drug use and drug policy. In the U.S., criminal justice perspectives dominate drug policy, with an emphasis on punishment and interdiction. Accordingly, responses to drug use are crafted in ignorance of culture, including the possibility of controlled drug use and of the impact of social networks and social capital as protective factors. The relationships among culture of use and the harm resulting from drug use demonstrate that the social context of drug use shapes the drug experience. In better understanding these elements, we can redefine the image of the drug user, and we can further demonstrate the importance of prevention, treatment and harm avoidance in drug policy. The focus of drug policy can be shifted from primarily a criminal justice approach – with an abstinence-only strategy – to a policy that incorporates principles from the cultural and health fields that will lead to a more balanced response to drug use.

NOTES

1. Some of the material in this chapter has previously appeared in Perrone, 2006.
2. To ensure the confidentiality and safety of the participants, all names in this document, including names of venues, DJs and people, have been changed. Any chosen pseudonym that is identical or similar to current venues or venues that are no longer in operation was accidental.
3. Whiteacre, 2005.
4. e.g., Inciardi, 2008.
5. e.g., MacCoun and Reuter, 2001; Tonry, 2007.
6. Mauer and King, 2008.
7. Ibid.
8. e.g., MacCoun and Reuter, 2001.
9. e.g., Perrone, 2006; Waldorf et al., 1991; Zinberg, 1984.
10. e.g., Fendrich et al., 2003; Johnston et al., 2005; National Survey on Drug Use and Health [NSDUH], 2005; Pulse Check 2004; Yacoubian et al., 2003; cf., Hunt and Evans, 2003; Kelly, 2006.
11. Altman, 2005; HBO, 2002; Jefferson, 2005; Mitchell, 2001, PBS, 2001, Stout, 1999.
12. Recent studies have shown that club drug use is increasingly prevalent among other populations (e.g., Fendrich et al., 2003; Krebs and Steffey, 2005; Martins, Mazzotti, and Chilcoat, 2005; Maxwell and Spence, 2005; Novoa et al., 2005; Ompad et al., 2005), and among those outside of dance club culture (e.g., Community Epidemiology Group (CEWG), 2003; Fendrich et al., 2003; Krebs and Steffey, 2005; Lankenau and Clatts, 2005; Maxwell and Spence, 2005; Novoa et al., 2005; Ompad et al., 2005).
13. Fendrich et al., 2003; Forsyth, 1996; Hammersley et al., 1999; Hansen et al., 2001; Johnston et al., 2005; Kelly, 2006; Lankenau and Clatts, 2005; Martins et al., 2005; Measham, 2004; NSDUH, 2005; Parker and Williams, 2003; Pulse Check, 2004; Sanders, 2005; Ter Bogtet al., 2002; van de Wijngaartet al., 1999; Yacoubian et al., 2003.
14. HBO, 2002.
15. PBS, 2001.
16. Stout, 1999.
17. Jefferson, 2005.
18. Altman, 2005.
19. Jenkins, 1999.
20. see also Associated Press, 2001; Drug Enforcement Agency, 2002.

21. e.g., Klitzman et al., 2002; Ross et al., 2003.
22. Sifaneck, Kaplan, Dunlap, and Johnson, 2003.
23. see MacCoun and Reuter, 2001.
24. These clubbers borrow this name from the clubbers of the early 1990s, who were associated with Peter Gatien, Michael Alig and the club Limelight. Frank Owen (2003) best explains this phenomenon: "The Limelight in the mid-'90s was one of the most famous clubs in Manhattan . . . Once an Episcopal church with an imposing Gothic exterior and stained-glass windows, this gloomy labyrinth of dark corners and hidden nooks and crannies was a perfect setting to which both sell and consume drugs" (p. 3). Peter Gatien was the club's owner: he owned additional clubs in New York City during that time, including The Tunnel and Club USA. Michael Alig was known as "the king of the club kids" (Owen, 2003, p. 3). He was a party promoter and worked for Peter Gatien. He and the club kids appeared on the Geraldo Show and were featured in People, Time, Newsweek, and The New York Times (Owen, 2003). Alig was later convicted of manslaughter and sentenced to 10-20 years for the murder of a drug dealer. See Owen (2003) and the film "Party Monster" (Bailey and Barbato, 2003) for more information.
25. e.g., Fischer, 1975; Fine and Kleinman, 1979; Hebdige, 1979/2002; Sullivan, 1989.
26. e.g., Baudrillard, 1989; Castells, 2000, 2004; Presdee, 2000; Veblen, 1899/1994.
27. Zinberg, 1984.
28. e.g., Becker, 1973.
29. e.g. Bourdieu, 1986.
30. e.g., Sampson and Laub, 1993.
31. see also Becker, 1963; Grund, 1993; Zinberg, 1984.

1. METHODOLOGY[1]

Research Aims

The goal of this research was to dissect the stereotype of the club drug user and to investigate how the culture and settings of use shape drug experiences and drug harms. Understanding the individual, social, situational and pharmacological factors that shape the emergence of this drug-using and clubbing culture and the patterns of drug use among this group was critical. To do so, it was important to keep the culture situated in the context in which its rituals and drugs of choice are produced and presented. Dick Hebdige, a sociologist,[2] notes that ethnography is the best method to achieve those goals, as the detail gathered in ethnography "can reconstruct the history, can penetrate the skin of style, and draw out its hidden meanings." Unlike self-report surveys, the method most often used to assess risk and patterns of drug use, this study employs qualitative research methods, such as participant observations and in-depth interviews. According to Denzin and Lincoln,[3] qualitative researchers study phenomena in their natural setting, attempting to make sense of, or interpret phenomena in terms of the meanings people bring to them.[4] This method enabled me to obtain "depth and detail" from "direct quotation and careful description."[5] Essentially, I sought to "understand the world as seen by the respondents."[6]

This chapter provides a description of the methodologies used to gain access to, observe the behaviors of, and obtain interviews from the sample. I first discuss how I simultaneously participated in the activities of this group (with the exception of drug use) and carefully observed their behaviors. A discussion of the lengthy interview protocol with the participants is next. I then explain how I used a popular Internet forum frequented by the sample to gain information on events to attend. Throughout this chapter, I also describe the obstacles that were confronted and how the research goals were achieved. This chapter concludes with a discussion of how I analyzed the ethnographic data.

RESEARCH METHODS

Like many drug ethnographers whose own life experiences, such as their living arrangements, conveniently provided them with access to drug users or dealers,[7] my early life experiences supplied me with an entree into the lives of drug users. While studying for a Masters of Arts degree in 2001, I enrolled in a qualitative methods course that required a field research project. At the time, my romantic partner was friendly with two men who frequented the Plant, a New York City dance club, where drug use was prevalent. They suggested that I conduct my class research project at that club. On my first observation, by chance, I met "Mike," who was from the neighborhood where I grew up. After I told him about my course project, he offered his assistance in obtaining participants. When I embarked on my dissertation project two years later, the club Plant had closed. To find venues in which to conduct participant observations and locate potential interviewees, I contacted Mike (a 26-year-old paralegal), who became my first key informant. When he extended an invitation to travel with him and his friends to Miami for a major electronic music event in March 2004, the dissertation project – on which this book is based – officially commenced. During that one week stay in Miami, I met many dance club attendees, who later became participants in the study. I spent nearly every weekend from that point until June 2005 with a variety of club kids. The terms "club kids" and "the sample" are used interchangeably throughout this book.

Over that 15-month period, 45 different participant observations took place in a variety of venues where dancing occurred in Miami, New York City, the Shore region in New Jersey, and the Hamptons in Long Island, New York. At those venues, I engaged in numerous informal conversations with other venue attendees, and employed two sampling methods – convenience sampling (selecting individuals who are conveniently available) and snowball sampling (asking participants to provide names and contact information of others who may participate) – from which 18 individuals agreed to a formal interview.[8]

To ensure the safety of my participants, I took extensive measures. Venues' and participants' true names were kept separate from the data. All recorded data were stripped of personal identifiers. Any chosen pseudonym that is identical or similar to a current venue, or a venue that is no longer in operation, is accidental. I created multiple keys that linked names to contact information and pseudonyms.

PARTICIPANT OBSERVATIONS

Participant observation involves some amount of social interaction with the subjects of the project. The researcher directly observes and participates in the activities of the group under study. Participant observation is an effective strategy for watching, listening, and gaining knowledge about a particular group.[9] During participant observations, the researcher joins in the group's activities. In my study, we danced together, ate together, sometimes carpooled to dance events, and frequently chatted. It is important to note that I never participated in drug use with them, and that they knew I was doing research. I collected a total of 45 participant observations – meaning I went with the participants to 45 different dance/club-related events.

In New York City, I went with the club kids to eleven different venues – ten dance clubs and one lounge. In the Hamptons, we went to four dance clubs, two restaurants and one hotel. We attended dance events at one club along the Jersey Shore and three bars/clubs in Miami. In Miami, I also spent time with them observing their behaviors at two separate hotel pools and in two hotel rooms. The dance clubs, bars and lounges had a minimum age requirement of 21 years, and on Friday nights some of the clubs in New York City permitted those 18 years of age or older to enter.

Spending time with the club kids was expensive and exhausting. The clubs, bars and lounges had a cover charge (a fee for entry) that was rarely less than $15 and sometimes as much as $60. Only one bar in Miami and the lounge in New York City did not require a fee for entry. Most of the clubs were open from 10 pm until 8 am, but it was often possible to locate an open club at any time throughout the weekend. "After-hours" clubs opened around 5 am and closed around 2 pm. Hotel pool parties or outdoor clubs tended to start around noon, and participants' hotel rooms were always open for partying. With such extensive and flexible daily hours of operation, the club kids often danced and consumed drugs continuously for 24 hours. This duration tended to be longer during holiday weekends and vacations.

Because of these hours of operation, a great deal of planning went into attending events for an observation. Preparation for the observation included contacting informants and interviewees who intended to attend that evening's event. I often slept prior to the event, dressed accordingly and took the appropriate transportation (bus, train or, if available, I borrowed a car). Frequently, I met informants prior to entry and we were admitted inside together. When I entered through the general population doors, in contrast to the VIP doors (see Chapter 4), female security officers were often present and responsible for searching both my belongings and my person. Inside the venue, we met with other informants at their typical locations, as most club kids had a favorite spot in each club where they congregated. The following field note exemplifies my preparation process:

> I called Osiris in the afternoon to see if he was going to club Birdland tonight. He already had plans to take someone with him, but would call me if his plans changed. Later, around 8 pm, I called Tina to learn of her plans for the evening. She was in the process of getting ready. She and her friend Sophia were going to a bar in midtown prior to going to Birdland. We planned on meeting at Birdland. She was to call me when they were leaving the bar in route to the club. Osiris phoned around 11:30 pm to see if I needed a ride to the club, as his plans fell through. Since he was leaving around 12:15 am, I decided to meet him there; it was impossible for me to be ready by then, as I still had to shower. Around 12 am, Tina called apologizing for not calling sooner. She was already at Birdland. I told her I would be there in about an hour. I asked if she was in the VIP section, as I would not be able to enter that section without being on a list. She was, and instructed me to call her when I get to the main dance floor . . . When I arrived two extremely long lines led from the entranceway in the center of the block and ended close to the corners on both sides of the street. I asked the bouncer, a big Black male, the difference between the two lines. The one on the right was for the guestlist and the other was for the general population . . . When I finally made it to the front of the line I showed the bouncer my identification and shuffled passed the ropes. Since there was a separate entrance for VIP[s], I called Tina. Because she did not answer, I left her a message. I then walked over to see if she left anything with the VIP doorman for me, but she hadn't. I walked over to the huge crowd forming around the guestlist when someone tapped me on the shoulder. It was Osiris. We both obtained passes from the guestlist bouncers, and I gave Tina another call. Again, she did not answer. However, she quickly returned my call. She was standing on the dance floor near the female performer who had silver stuff in her hair. I told her I would meet her there. Osiris and I entered the club . . . As we approached the square where Tina was, first, Ralph, wearing a fitted t-shirt and jeans and dancing closely with a girl, stopped me to say hello. Then George, wearing jeans and a black button-down shirt – completely unbuttoned – also dancing with a girl said hello to me. Mike followed, wearing black pants and a black

shirt, dancing with a bunch of people. I also said hello to Dan, who was wearing a striped shirt and jeans. I finally found Tina. (May 22, 2004; field note)

While this was a typical night, it was equally common for informants neither to call nor to return my phone calls prior to going out. Some of the reasons for this disconnect were they forgot, or were too high on drugs, or simply refused to call. Running into Mike at club DVS, provides an example:

I was dancing with Timmy and Lori when Mike, Dan, and Julia walked by. Mike said hello to Timmy. He saw me and gave me a kiss hello. I then asked, "why didn't you call me?" He replied, "we were doing pills all night. Sorry." (March 9, 2004; field note)

When this occurred, I went to the venue alone hoping to meet someone I knew; I often did. Clearly, relying on the informants was not always ideal. In addition to plans falling through, often they were late meeting me. During one incident I waited outside the club for almost two hours.

J. Masters bought me a ticket from Bebek; they were $30 a piece for DJ Ibi's event at club NRG. I'd give him the money when I saw him . . . Around 9 pm, I phoned J. Masters [also known here as "J."] asking what time he intended to arrive at NRG. He wanted me to be in the city between 11:30 pm and 12 am. He thought he'd pick me up at Port Authority, but I insisted it would be easier if I took a cab and met him there . . . Around 10 pm, J. phoned to inform me he was running a bit late. J. Masters called me again around 11:30 pm, to remind me of his tardiness. I wondered if I could eat something before I left. He said I had time to eat, since he would not be in the city for at least 30 to 40 minutes. (April 8, 2004; phone conversations)

Around 12:30 am, I took the bus to meet J. Masters at NRG. When I reached Port Authority, I waited for a cab, and called J. to see where he was. Oddly, he did not answer his phone . . . I called him again, but he still did not answer. I began to get worried and decided to call Giustina to see if she's heard from him. Apparently there was a major problem with the number of tickets J. purchased. J. only had one extra ticket meaning he did not buy enough tickets for Giustina, her friends and me. And, J. told her the ticket belonged to me. As a result, Kelly and J. had a huge fight, and when Giustina spoke to him, she hung-up on him. She asked if I wanted to meet at her house, and we'd go to NRG together. She didn't think four to six girls would have a problem getting in. I agreed, but thought I should wait for J, since I owed him $30 for my ticket. She was going to call him one more time, but I thought I should call him first. I called him twice, but he still did not answer his phone. I phoned Giustina who was surprised J. wasn't answering his phone especially since she hung-up the phone with him about ten minutes ago . . . I decided to text message J. around five minutes to 1 am telling him I was in a cab, and wondered what was going on. When he did not respond, I phoned him again, but there was still no answer. I messaged him again at 1:10 am telling him I was at NRG, and wanted to know what was going on. He finally called me at 1:15 am letting me know he was on his way and apologized. I told him that I'd be at NRG waiting for him . . . I waited for about an hour, it was 1:55 am. I decided to cross the street to wait on the opposite side of the club. I text messaged J. again to let him know I was now across the street, to which he quickly responded, again apologizing and letting me know he was in the city. I responded that it was "okay" and I was "still waiting . . . " It was about 2:15 am when I called J. again to see where he was. Martina answered the phone informing me they were on their way. They thought they would meet me in about 20 minutes . . . I was starting to get really cold . . . At 2:35 am I phoned J. again, asking if he was lost. He was walking down the block, and again apologized claiming it was not his fault. He added that it was actually a really funny story that he'll tell me when he gets here . . . He phoned me two minutes later asking where I was, since he did not see me. I was in front of the club still waiting when I finally spotted him. We entered the club by 3 am. (April 8, 2004; field note)

Observations during data collection were initially structured to obtain a sample representative of all persons and events within the venue. Ethnographers Martyn Hammersley and Paul Atkinson[10] explain "that any attempt to represent the entire range of persons and events in the case under study will have to be based on adequate coverage of the various temporal divisions." However, once in the field, I monitored Internet forums and established relationships with various club kids, who instructed me on which places and times would be best to attend (see Table 1.1). Following their suggestions greatly strengthened rapport and trust; this facilitated obtaining formal interviews. While I made strong efforts to attend most events with the club kids, in some instances not having immediate access to a car limited my ability to do so. For example,

When I called Osiris,[11] he informed me that tomorrow was the opening day for both [club] Jockies and Waves. He wanted to know if I was going. Since I did not have a car, I was unable to make it. (April 30, 2004; phone conversation)

Often, I borrowed cars from family members and friends.

Table 1.1: The Observations

	Date	Venue	Time Arrived*	Time Departed*	Informant	Hours Spent
1	03/05/04	Castle Hotel	12:30am	1:30am	Mike	1
2	03/05/04	New Yorker[b]	2:00am	4.00am	Mike	2
3	03/06/04	Castle Penthouse	6:00pm	9:30pm	Mike	3.5
4	03/07/04	Hacienda Hotel	3:30pm	7:30pm	Mike	4
5	03/09/04	DVS[c]	6:00am	8:00am	Mike	2
6	03/09/04	Stars[c]	8:30am	11:00am	Mike	3.5
7	03/14/04	Plant II[c]	6:30am	8:30am	Mike	2
8	04/03/04	NRG[c]	12:30am	2:00am	Osiris	1.5
9	04/03/04	Plant II[c]	2:30am	4:30am	Osiris	2
10	04/15/04	Danceteria[b]	12:00am	2:00am	Internet	2
11	04/25/04	Wax[b]	7:00am	10:00am	Osiris	3
12	05/02/04	Waves[b]	7:45pm	11:00pm	Osiris	2.25
13	05/15/04	NRG[c]	1:00am	4:30am	Osiris	3.5
14	05/22/04	Birdland[c]	1:30am	4:00am	Tina	2.5
15	05/29/04	The Planet[b]	3:00pm	7:00pm	Internet	4
16	05/30/04	Rio[b]	2:30am	5:30am	Paula	3
17	05/30/04	The Planet[b]	5:00pm	8:00pm	Osiris	3
18	05/30/04	Shady Pines Htl.	9:00pm	11:00pm	Internet	2
19	05/31/04	Barroom[b]	3:30am	6:00am	Osiris	2.5
20	06/12/04	Birdland[c]	12:30am	4:00am	Osiris	3.5
21	06/19/04	Live[b]	1:00am	4:30am	Internet	3.5
22	07/25/04	Rio[b]	1:40am	5:00am	Paula	4.5
23	07/30/04	Devils[a]	12:30am	3:00am	Mike	2.5
24	07/31/04	Birdland[c]	1:30am	5:30am	Osiris	4
25	08/14/04	Birdland[c]	1:00am	5:00am	Paula	4
26	08/27/04	Devils[a]	12:00am	4:30am	Angelina	4.5
27	08/29/04	Waves[b]	10:00pm	1:00am	Osiris	3
28	08/29/04	Live[b]	2:00am	5:15am	Bebek	3.25
29	09/04/04	The Planet[b]	3:00pm	7:00pm	Paula	4
30	09/04/04	Mexican Grill	8:30pm	10:30pm	Paula	2
31	09/04/04	Shady Pines	11:00pm	12:00am	Paula	1
32	09/04/04	Copa[b]	12:30am	2:30am	Paula	2
33	09/05/04	Barroom[b]	4:30am	7:30am	J. Masters	3
34	10/02/04	Birdland[c]	3:30am	5:30am	Paula	2
35	10/02/04	NRG[c]	6:00am	9:00am	Pez	3
36	10/16/04	Birdland[c]	3:00am	7:00am	Pez	4
37	10/25/04	Danceteria[b]	4:30am	8:30am	Isaac	4
38	10/29/04	Idol[c]	1:00am	6:30am	J. Masters	5.5

(continued)

Table 1.1: *(continued)*

	Date	Venue	Time Arrived*	Time Departed*	Informant	Hours Spent
39	11/26/04	Birdland[c]	1:00am	7:30am	J. Masters	6.5
40	01/07/05	Ritchie's[b]	1:00am	3:00am	J. Masters	2
41	01/07/05	Savior[b]	3:30am	5:00am	J. Masters	2.5
42	02/11/05	Birdland[c]	1:30am	6:45am	J. Masters	5.25
43	03/04/05	Birdland[c]	3:00am	6:30am	J. Masters	3.5
44	04/08/05	NRG[c]	2:30am	6:00am	J. Masters	3.5
45	04/23/05	Heart[b]	6:00am	9:30am	J. Masters	3.5

*All times are approximations.
[a]Bar/Lounge
[b]Club: 5,000 sq. ft. to 20,000 sq. ft.
[c]Mega Club: Over 20,000 sq. ft.

Inside the Club

Throughout the observations, I canvassed the venue, paying particular attention to individual behaviors and social interactions among the patrons. I made note of the type of music playing, the substances consumed, the layout and design of the dance club, and the patrons' style of dress. I also engaged in informal discussions with dance club patrons. While conducting observations, I was very cognizant of the impression I was giving, attempting to build rapport and trust, and protecting the safety of my participants and myself.[12]

The informal discussions during the events served two purposes:

1. they provided opportunities to ask questions about observed behaviors, since "what an act means is never self-evident,"[13] and,

2. some informal discussions eventually led to formal interviews. For example, while at the Hacienda pool party the DJ stopped the music. I was confused, and was able to ask a club kid about why this occurred:

> DJ Barbuck stopped the music. The crowd was screaming, whistling, and clapping. I asked Dan, "what is DJ Barbuck doing?" Dan replied, he was "fucking with everyone." The music was off for a few minutes. Barbuck started up again, and the crowd was screaming. (March, 2004; field note)

While at the hotel Castle in Miami, I engaged in a conversation with George. During that conversation I asked for an interview, which I obtained once we returned to New York, and that occurred as follows:

> Creda and Mike went to the front desk so they could check in and buy beer. George asked Ralph if he had that CD. George said, "the one that we listened to at –." Ralph interrupted, "yeah, oh let's put it on. Track 10 is awesome." They put on track ten, and were bouncing around to it. Dan then put on another CD. He put on this track that he described as being evil. He said it's what they would play in a movie after you killed someone and were disposing of the body. He said, "listen to it." Thirsty, I asked to make sure the bottle on the table was filled with water rather than GHB, and drank some. We began to talk about where we were from, and where we currently live. Since George is from New Jersey, I asked if he would be interested in participating in an interview when we returned from Miami. (March 6, 2004; field note)

During another observation, an informal conversation with an attendee known neither to the club kids nor to their friends led to the following interview:

> The guy behind me asked if I was still waiting for a drink. I replied that I was. He suggested I act more aggressively. I replied that the bartender knew I was here. He thought perhaps the bartender didn't like girls. I thought that was possible. The bartender walked over to us and asked the guy what he wanted. He ordered himself a drink, and told the bartender what I wanted as well, a plain Red Bull. When we received our drinks, the guy asked to pay for mine. I insisted he didn't, but he paid regardless. I thanked him and introduced myself. He told me about how he does lighting for many clubs . . . He's just known as "the light guy." I asked him about how the lights work wondering if they were computerized and coordinated with music like motion sensors operate. He said, "not really, but it is computerized." He has been doing lights for about 14 years. His name is Isaac, and he's 34.

On average, the observations lasted three hours (see Table 1.1). Since memory is an essential part of the participant observation method, "very long periods of observation . . . become quite unmanageable."[14] A long observational time frame could have had potential negative effects on the accuracy of my data. Furthermore, conducting research during the late evening and early morning hours was difficult, and I quickly learned the necessity of being as alert as possible. Sleeping prior to the observation and consuming one Red Bull® energy drink during the observation proved to increase my wakefulness.

Keeping detailed notes inside and directly outside the venue, while attempted, was also difficult. On one occasion in the Hamptons, while I waited for Paula, I chose to sit in the car to write a few notes before heading to my hotel. The following field notes reveal the consequences:

> While at the club the Planet, I ran into Winston. We said hello. He then told me to be careful about my research, as people are saying that I am from the FBI. I asked him who said it. He replied, "it's irrelevant." He said I should be careful about having a notebook and taking notes in front of everyone. I was confused, and a bit upset. He told me not to worry. (May 30, 2004; field note)

The following day:

> At club Barroom, I spoke to Estevez who was standing by the bar. He said, "hello" and proceeded to tell me that a lot of people are saying that I'm FBI. I was surprised. Estevez directed me to the cubicle to the right of the entranceway to sit down and talk. He repeated that people think I'm FBI. I told him I wasn't. He said, "that night at Waves, Eddie was fucked-up on E, and thought it was funny that I was doing research." Yet, because I kept calling to set-up an interview, Eddie got suspicious and told Estevez to be careful. Then, when they saw me sitting in my car in the parking lot by the Planet, Eddie told Estevez that I was FBI. I had my notebook out and was taking notes. I reiterated that I wasn't FBI. He also stated that it appears like I "just landed in the scene, just showed up." I told him about Mike, George, and Tina. I told him how Mike directed me where to go and who to talk to. I also told him about our trip to Miami. He was there as well, but doesn't remember seeing me. He suggested I say a disclaimer when I meet people. Next time I would. (May 31, 2004; field note)

Impression Management

During the observations, it became clear that my age, gender, personality, class, race and overall appearance greatly determined access to various areas within the club and influenced informal conversations with dance club patrons.[15] Ethnographers Hammersley and Atkinson state: "not only may the female researcher sometimes find it difficult to be taken seriously by male hosts, but other females may also display suspicion and hostility in the face of her intrusions."[16] However, in the predominantly heterosexual male-run industry, being female had some benefits.[17] Since I appeared "unthreatening," I was able to gain access to certain settings with relative ease. In a few instances, I was able to progress to the front of very long lines, and male employees who were interested in more than my research gave me tours of the DJ booth. The following field notes exemplify how I gained access to both enter and tour the clubs:

> Most venues permit couples and females to move to the head of the line. However, tonight club Birdland did not have that policy . . . I decided to ask one of the bouncers if I could cut the line since I was alone. He replied, "of course. Just let me see some ID." I showed him my ID, and he removed the rope allowing me to enter. (May 22, 2004; field note)

> At 4:30 am, Isaac met me at the corner of the block where the club Danceteria was located and walked me to the door of the club . . . A line was already forming outside the place, which opens at 5 am. With Isaac, I walked right in and neither of us was searched . . . Inside, he showed me around the place, the overhead lights were still on so it was easy for me to see. The club was decorated in fluorescent colored ornaments hanging on the walls and the poles. Isaac commented that these were the decorations for the resident DJ who just quit spinning here last weekend. The venue was quite small . . . There were large curtains separating the main room from the back bar and VIP area. Through the curtains was a bar, and to the right of the bar was the roped off VIP area. Isaac asked if I've ever seen the kitchen. I was unaware this club had one. We entered the other side of the ropes and walked through the door. It was a full kitchen equipped with large pizza style ovens, stoves, and large counter areas, which are not used. Isaac said that this is "where it all happens" including drug use and sex. I wondered how you obtain access to the kitchen when the club is open. He thinks you have to be in the VIP area. We headed towards the DJ booth where the light console and the turntables are located. We entered the booth from narrow steps. Both the DJ and the light guy work in this space. Isaac told me that he just put in some new lights and lasers, and hooked up an additional CD player for DJ Ibi. Ibi's manager and another DJ entered the booth. Ibi's manager Richard introduced himself to me. He was setting up all of Ibi's records and threw in a CD until Ibi arrived. Ibi is expected to arrive by 6am. Isaac was called out of the booth to fix a few things and to locate some tape. He returned commenting he was, "very psyched" about the night; he was "ready." (October 25, 2004; field note)

During my participant observations, I was very aware of what Hammersley and Atkinson[18] describe as "impression management." How researchers present their bodies "affects both our own experiences of fieldwork and the nature of the data we collect."[19] My physical appearance, including style of dress and demeanor, influenced how I was perceived. For example, I wore a hat to an observation at club Barroom. When I removed my hat, a club patron dancing near me was surprised to see my short hair:

> A guy behind me asked why I was wearing a hat, and pulled the hat off my head. Surprised to see my short hair, he asked, "where is all the rest of your hair?" I replied, "I cut it." He told me that I am supposed to have long straight hair. I explained that this style was more fitting. He insisted, "You are supposed to have long straight hair." I thought it was odd for him to suggest that, since he didn't know me. He stressed, "that doesn't matter," and walked away. (September 5, 2004; field note)

I was very conscious of the importance of producing a self[20] that adhered to the norms of the club kids. While I refused to grow my hair, I attempted to "dress in a way that [was] similar to the people"[21] I was studying. In many instances I phoned a participant to see what she planned on wearing for the event. The following field note demonstrates this:

> I phoned J. Masters around 11 pm asking if he was still wearing a suit. He never met his client for dinner so he was dressed casually. I wondered if he thought I could wear sneakers. He was curious as to why everyone was concerned about what to wear. I have not been to NRG in awhile, and was afraid that if I wore sneakers, they would not let me in. He didn't think it was a problem. He spoke to Giustina and Kelly and they weren't dressed-up . . . I quickly phoned Giustina to see what she was wearing. She lost her cell phone, so it took her awhile to figure out who I was. Although she said she knew who I was, "tiny with black hair," I reminded her about the macaroni and cheese night. She insisted she remembered . . . I wondered what she was wearing. Apparently, everyone has been calling her curious about what to wear. She was just wearing flip-flops, but now that everyone was calling her, she started to think she should change. I didn't want her to change, since I'd then feel uncomfortable wearing sneakers. She didn't care what anyone thought; she always wears sneakers and will wear flip-flops tonight. (April 8, 2005; phone conversations)

Trust and Rapport

To create trusting relationships in the field, I was conscious of establishing rapport within the field through informal discussions and frequent attendance at events. While on observations, I danced with the club kids, joined them for dinners and breakfasts, and carpooled to events. Furthermore, my honesty and frankness about myself helped me build a high level of trust with my participants. Personally investing in the field is essential for obtaining high-quality data.[22] In one instance, I expressed to an informant the reasons I chose to refrain from conducting an observation that night:

> Osiris phoned to see if I was interested in going to Dunes tonight. I told him I wasn't going out this weekend, since I'm not feeling well. He commented that I'm always sick and not feeling well. I explained that this was a little different; it's more like a sad, depressed kind of not feeling well. He asked if I wanted to talk about it. I didn't. He told me to be happy, and call him later. (April 15, 2005; phone conversation)

Two additional field notes indicate the type of relationships I established:

> J. Masters asked how my Sunday was. I told him I went to a wake, and visited my parents. I told him how on my visit I successfully won a game of a Scrabble against my parents. He believes I am becoming a little obsessed with scrabble, but suggested we play together via an online game. (March 7, 2005; phone conversation)

> Osiris and I chatted a bit about some of our favorite CDs and movies. I told him about the DVDs I recently purchased on clubbing. He thought he may actually be in one of those DVDs. Since I was not completely familiar with the music of the scene, he would make a CD of the classic songs and his favorites. We also discussed the films we have recently seen, and some popular clubbing films, including Go,[23] Party Monster,[24] and 24Hour Party People.[25] He owns a few documentaries that he thought I would like. He is going to copy OutFoxed[26] and Control Room[27] for me. (November 6, 2004; field note)

The time spent in various locations with the drug users provided a high level of rapport and trust with the participants. How the club kids concealed, prepared and consumed substances, as well as their drug experiences were witnessed during observations. An excerpt from an observational field note while in Mike, George and Ralph's hotel room exemplifies this:

> There were a bunch of empty water bottles, a Sprite, a six pack of Corona Light, and water bottles filled with G [GHB] on the table. George was sitting at the table crushing some "tina" [crystal methamphetamine] wrapped in a 20 dollar bill with a Heinz ketchup bottle. As he crushed, he saw a problem. The "tina" was pushing through the small pores of the bill. George explained that the problem with "tina" was it is "too fine." Ralph told George he was incorrectly folding the bill, "it has to be folded in four ways." Ralph showed George how it was done. George said he doesn't "have patience for this shit," and removed himself from the table. Since they were waiting for room

service, Dan placed the microwave dish, holding the once liquid and now powdered K [ketamine], back in the microwave. Ralph took over George's job crushing the tina. He was glad they came-up with a new word to indicate taking a dose of tina, which they called "flicks." It was necessary to distinguish it from "bumps," which are used to speak about taking a dose of K. (March 6, 2004; field note)

Adverse Events

As many researchers of "hidden" and "deviant" populations have experienced,[28] initially, many drug users in the clubbing "scene" felt threatened by my presence, and they spread rumors I was an agent of the Federal Bureau of Investigation (FBI). Because I was unfamiliar with the scene and Mike provided my only entree to the lives of the club kids, most club kids felt, as Estevez explained, that it appeared like I "just landed in the scene; just showed up." Being affiliated with the FBI or the Drug Enforcement Agency (DEA) was the only explanation they could fathom for my presence. Consequently, when one individual among a group of friends distrusted or disliked me, access to that group was blocked. I was ostracized, ignored, and poorly treated by that group. For example, Julia's negative feelings toward me compelled her to throw ice during an observation. I experienced many instances, especially in her presence, when I felt uncomfortable and was harassed. Some prospective male participants asked for sex or nudity as payment for their involvement in the study.[29] For example, I approached one male inside a club to discuss the possibility of an interview, and he stressed that he would only agree to participate in my study if he "saw me in a thong." In many instances, both the people to whom I was talking and the topic of conversation affected the length of time I spent with the individuals and in the situation. If I felt uncomfortable at any point during the observation, or felt my safety was in jeopardy, I exited the situation and sometimes exited the club.[30] For example,

> While at the bar at club Danceteria, I spoke to one guy about my research. He was very excited, and offered to take me around the clubs in Las Vegas. I gave him my card. We walked around a bit, and headed to the dance floor. While on the dance floor, he began to grope and touch my waist and buttocks. I told him to stop. He persisted to touch me in ways that made me uncomfortable. I told him I was not interested, and stopped dancing with him. (April 15, 2004; field note)

These experiences are not uncommon in such settings, nor are they unusual among female ethnographers.[31] Many female researchers experience some form of sexual harassment in the field.[32]

In the tradition of ethnographic research on users and dealers, I also confronted various other issues during the participant observations.[33] For instance, I observed drug deals while hanging out with the club kids, and they also offered me drugs and asked that I temporarily "hold" drugs for them on several occasions. I refused to carry or consume drugs.

On occasion I witnessed the negative effects of drugs, as the following field note at the afternoon pool party at the Hacienda Hotel reveals:

> Sitting at a table in front of the bathroom was one guy passed-out on a chair. A female from the bathroom line was yelling at a male. She was trying to focus his attention on the passed-out guy. A guy with a t-shirt on, shorts, and a black shoulder bag, quickly ran over to him. He was shaking him, and pushing him around. The guy did not wake-up, rather he was sprawled on the chair, head back, and legs stretched forward. His arms were hanging off to the side and the guy shook him again, saying, "wake-up, wake-up." A few other males came to help him out, but there was still no response. The guy with the shoulder bag walked away and returned a few minutes later. He shook the guy once again. He finally awoke, and began to bite and lick his hand. He said he was okay, and moaned a bit. They tried to sit him-up but he couldn't hold himself up. Two other guys, who appeared to be his friends, tried to lift him. He stood up. (March 7, 2004; field note)

Luckily, however, I only witnessed one of the users in my sample experiencing harm:

> When we arrived at [club] Savior, J. was very, very sick vomiting on the floor. Giustina suggested we head back to her house, as J. was too sick to stay out. Kelly, Giustina, Shauna and Pez wanted to go to [club] NRG after Savior. I did not care what we did, although I was very hungry. Giustina said I could eat at her house. J. liked the idea of going back to Giustina's house, and Shauna and Pez decided to go to NRG. We told Shauna and Pez we would meet them later at NRG. J's friend had her car in the parking lot across the street and would drive us to Giustina's, but we decided it would be easier if we just took a cab. (January 7, 2005; field note)

Other reactions to drugs, such as "G"ing out (an adverse effect of overusing GHB) or passing out, never occurred during participant observations.

Other "passed-out" club goers (not members of the sample) were often seen carried by bouncers who walked through the crowd of club kids to a brightly lit room. The closest I came to an alarming encounter occurred when an unconscious man blocked access to my [borrowed] car door:

> There was a Latino man lying on the floor blocking my path to the car. Two uniformed officers and a plain clothed man, apparently an acquaintance of the guy on the ground, stood over him. The acquaintance indicated to the officer he only knew the passed-out guy from the "scene" [i.e., going to clubs and parties]. The officers asked if he knew what the guy consumed this afternoon. It was 7 pm. The acquaintance replied "alcohol," adding he may also have taken some GHB. The cops suspected that GHB was the culprit. The cops repeatedly tried to wake the seemingly unconscious man by pushing the muscles by his clavicle. But the guy didn't budge until they forcefully pushed on his sternum. At that point, the guy popped up for three seconds, and passed out again. The cop placed his foot under the guy's head to keep it from hitting the concrete. The cop complained about the use of substances, explaining that the guy took a drug that was in some household cleaners. A few people exiting [club] Planet walked by and around the commotion. One girl whispered to her friend, "G'd out." The EMS arrived. They checked his heart and blood pressure. Everything was basically normal, but he was unconscious. EMS stated that "the GHB was frying his brain." Since he was wheezing, they placed an oxygen mask over his air passages. They again tried to wake him using the same two methods. Pressure on the sternum worked, but the guy again passed out within three seconds. EMS complimented the cop for use of his foot as a pillow. When the ambulance arrived, the police recapped the story. They checked him again and documented the guy's name, which they obtained from his wallet . . . As they strapped him onto a gurney and carried him into the ambulance, the guy awoke in fright. Since he was strapped down and unable to move, he began to scream. He did not know where he was going or what was happening. (May 29, 2004; field note)

These situations could have had serious ramifications for the research and my safety. It was essential to adhere to the guidance of informants, to place the safety and interests of the participants first, and to use good judgment. Ethnographers have two important ethical responsibilities:

1. we must put the safety and the interests of our participants first, and

2. we must recognize that our informants are more knowledgeable about any situation than we are.[34]

Developing field relations and confronting such dilemmas in the dance club settings were part of a dynamic process – sources of strain, stress and learning. Most importantly, this process facilitated a comprehensive understanding of the realities and experiences of the club kids.

Field Notes

While traveling home from an observational period, usually during a taxi cab ride or a bus or a train trip, I completed the Observation Protocol and made note of key reminders of that evening's occurrences. This included events from the night (in as close to chronological order as possible), and the conversations I'd had with club patrons. Observations were formally recorded within three days. "The longer the time between observation and recording, the more troublesome will be the recall and recording of adequately detailed and concrete descriptions."[35] For further documentation of the events surrounding my study population, I kept an electronic field journal. Within this journal, I documented all interactions that took place outside of an observation with my participants, including phone conversations, e-mails, and impromptu breakfasts. For example, when I did not attend a night out for clubbing, Osiris often phoned to meet him for breakfast, as recorded in the following:

> Osiris phoned me around 4 am to see if I was going to come to Birdland. I was sleeping and told him to call me when he was leaving. I could hear him very clearly so I was wondering if he was still there; he was. He said he'd give me a call later. He phoned me again at 6:20 am to see if I wanted to grab breakfast; I did. He was in his car and would be at my house in twenty minutes. He called me when he was outside my apartment. I asked where he wanted to go for breakfast. He thought a great place for Sunday Brunch would be open, but it was too early; 7 am. The only other option was the diner . . . In route to the diner, I asked how the night was. He stated, the place was still packed when he left and the music was very good. (April 10, 2005; field note)

Engaging in activities outside of the dance venues facilitated trust and rapport, and provided the opportunity to talk to the club kids outside of the loud dance club.

Sampling

The crowd that gathers at dance clubs is both selective and highly regulated by economics and taste distinctions.[36] Some people attend particular venues based on music preferences, peer interests, and finances. Yet, it is largely unknown who attends these clubbing events and uses drugs. As a result, I employed two different sampling methods to recruit participants: convenience sampling and snowball sampling. Three key informants greatly assisted in gathering the total of 18 formal, tape-recorded interviews. The role of the key informants was crucial to establishing trust and rapport, gaining access, and addressing issues in the field.[37] The study originally commenced with one key informant, Mike, who eventually reduced his involvement in the study. Three other key informants emerged: Michelle, J. Masters (also referred to as J. throughout the book) and Osiris. Mike, J. Masters and Osiris advised on which clubs to attend and which club kids would be interested in the study. Participants had to be 18 years of age or older, and they must have attended a New York City dance club at least once. They were either current or former drug users.

The key informants provided a pool of club attendees whom the informant and I separately approached to explain the research project. From those who agreed to participate, I inquired if their peers would also be willing to partake in the project. This fostered the growth of the snowball chain. Snowball sampling is an established procedure for locating participants in research on hidden populations,[38] and I found it was the most effective method in obtaining interviews. Twelve of the eighteen participants were recruited in this manner. George explains the importance of being connected to someone he trusted:

> You came in through a friend, so therefore you're accepted in my book . . . Had I not known you, I'da probably been a dick to you and probably just fuckin' couldn't care less about you, you or your paper. [39]

I made an additional effort to recruit individuals who frequent dance clubs, who appeared quite different from those obtained through the snowball method. During my observations at the dance club, I employed convenience sampling through engaging in informal conversations with certain patrons, who were unknown to the those already in the study or had different styles from those I interviewed. I informed these patrons about my research and asked if they would like to participate in a formal interview at a later date. For those who were interested in volunteering to participate in the study, I provided them with a business card indicating my contact information. This method of sampling was ineffective. I distributed my card to over 50 venue attendees, but I obtained only three interviews in this way. Even those individuals linked through the snowball sampling method who received my business card did not call to arrange an interview. After realizing the ineffectiveness of this recruitment method, I began to obtain cell phone numbers from those who expressed an interest. This proved a much more efficient method than handing out my card. Through obtaining their contact information, I received a total of ten interviews (nine via snowball sampling, and one via informal conversation).

Many possible reasons exist for the low response rate. First, we currently live in a climate in which people are anxious, untrusting, acutely aware of and concerned about threats to their well-being and personal safety.[40] Many feared the risks associated with participating in the research, especially those who thought I was associated with law enforcement. For example, early in the research project, Osiris refused to connect me with his friends:

> I called Osiris. He began to comment that he thought I was an undercover FBI agent or a DT [detective]. I asked why he thought that. He replied that my non-drug using behavior and need for interviews are suspicious. As a result, he could not introduce me to his friends anymore. I asked if there was any way of resolving this. He didn't think so. (June 8, 2004; phone conversation)

> I called Osiris to ask if he still thought I was connected to law enforcement. He replied that he's suspicious of everyone and I should not be concerned. He still would not introduce me to his friends anymore. (June 12, 2004; phone conversation)

Osiris and I eventually established trust. He is one of the informants with whom I still have contact.

Females were much more reluctant than male participants to agree to a formal interview. Those women who agreed to participate either were connected to an individual who had already agreed to an interview (Betty Cool, MaryJane,[41] Lucille, Ariel, and Tina) or knew me through friends or family (Michelle, Monica, and Angelina). The following phone conversation demonstrates one female's concern about the interview:

> I called Jackie and after I reminded her who I was, she expressed interest in helping me out. She thought I could ask her a few questions over the phone. I explained that the interview lasts about two hours, and it's best that we meet somewhere. She lives in the city where she also works and attends college. She is fairly busy and will have school and finals until the middle of May . . . She inquired about the questions, and asked if any were about drug use. I explained that they are, since they are a part of the scene. She wondered if she would have to write or be videotaped. I informed her that I only tape-record if she allows, I pay her, and her responses are confidential. (April 25, 2005; phone conversation)

Jackie never completed an interview. Many club kids, such as Estevez and Paula, also did not agree to an interview. Still, they continued to play a significant role in the research project. While not included in the formal sample (see Table 1.2), their comments from phone conversations and observations are included in this work.

All interviews were conducted outside of the dance club in public settings, such as pizzerias, coffee shops, parks, and food courts. In three instances, the interviews occurred in an apartment. Although I sought to engage in one-on-one interviews, with one interviewer and one interviewee, my most thorough and enjoyable interviews occurred when two or three interviewees were present. These participants suggested this interview structure, to which I did not object. Having peers give an interview together provided higher levels of comfort, while increasing the number of interviewees.

FORMAL INTERVIEWS

The interviews lasted approximately two hours and addressed the participants' clubbing and club drug using histories and experiences, and the methods they employed to address and reduce harm associated with their club drug use. Prior to the commencement of the interview, each interviewee signed an informed consent form and was compensated with a $20 gift card to a department store. Upon completion of the interview, participants and I remained connected through phone conversations and both planned and impromptu meetings during observations.

The $20 compensation was intended to act as an incentive to obtain greater numbers of interviewees. However, during conversations with many potential participants they stressed that they did not want compensation. The following field note provides examples of this:

> While hanging out at the Hacienda, I asked Dan if I could interview him back in NYC. I told him that I'd pay him with a $20 Macy's gift card. He said he doesn't want my money, but took my [business] card. (March 7, 2004; field note)

Despite these comments, each interviewee accepted the $20 gift card.

The informed consent letter described the purpose of this study, the extent of their participation and that he/she would receive a $20 Macys® or Bloomingdales® Gift Card for his/her participation. They were also informed that their participation was voluntary, that their responses were confidential, and that at any time they could refuse to answer a question.

Additionally, the letter asked for the participant's permission to tape-record his/her interview. At the beginning of each interview, I read the letter with the individual and asked if s/he had any additional questions.

At the beginning of the interview, each participant chose a pseudonym, which was used throughout the course of the study. The participant's real name is not associated in any way with the information that s/he shared with me. The participant and I both signed the consent form, and a separate section of the letter in which he/she provided permission to tape-record the interview. Upon completion of the interview, the interviewees were informed that any questions about the research or their rights as a research subject could be addressed by contacting me through e-mail or phone, or by contacting the sponsored program administrator. All of this information is provided on the informed consent form, of which each participant received a copy.

Since this research focuses on a drug-using population, it is possible that the interviewee had consumed some substance prior to the interview. Each interview was prefaced with asking the participants if they felt capable of answer a series of questions about their involvement in the club scene. All interviewees indicated they were capable of completing the interview, and at no point during the interviews did I discern that a participant appeared unable to continue. However, SickKid's[42] interview did come to a halt when his friend arrived at the park where the interview was held. To avoid detection, SickKid stated, "Kill it right now. That's it, my friend's comin'." We stopped the interview.

The Interview Protocol

The interview was semi-structured, with open-ended responses and probes, since the nature of qualitative interviews allows flexibility in questions to obtain in-depth information from the subjects. The interview protocol was designed to elicit information regarding the following research questions:

1. What factors influence the decision to use drugs?

2. What factors influence the settings where drugs are used?

3. What factors contribute to negative or potentially harmful effects of those substances?

4. How can those factors associated with drug use assist in the development of more accurate theories and effective criminal justice and public health prevention policies?

Table 1.2: The Club Kids

Name	Age	Degree	Occupation	Housing	Family	Class
Angelina	26	BA	pharmaceutical sales	with mom	single	middle
Ariel	25	BS	investment banker	on own	dual	upper
Betty Cool	33	Assoc. Deg.	registered nurse	on own	single	middle
David	30	PhD	post-doc fellow	on own	dual	upper
George	22	High school	data analyst	with dad	single	lower
Isaac	34	High school drop-out	club lights operator	on own	single	lower
Jack	29	MD	chief resident hospital	with partner	dual	upper
J. Masters (J.)	30	MBA	owns investment co.	on own	dual	upper
Lucille	25	BA	clothing chain district mgr.	on own	dual	middle
MaryJane (Mary)	25	BA, pursuing MA	special ed. teacher	with parents	dual	middle
Michelle	28	MS	occupational therapist	with partner	dual	middle
Mike	26	BA	paralegal	with parents	dual	upper
Monica	28	MA	marketing rep.	with parents	dual	middle
Osiris (Gary)	28	High school	graphic designer	on own	single	middle
Ralph	25	BA	graphic designer	with parents	dual	upper

Table 1.2: *(continued)*

Name	Age	Degree	Occupation	Housing	Family	Class
SickKid (Sam)	27	High school drop-out	p/t-messenger	with mom	single	lower
Tina	22	finishing BA	student	on own	dual	upper
Tyler	28	MD	surgical resident	with partner	dual	upper
	AVG 27					

In designing the protocol, I ensured that the interviewees would recognize that I was interested in what they had to say, and that I sought to learn what they knew and their experiences about drug use in dance club settings. The interview question guide was structured using Spradley's principles, which include treating the subjects under study as the most knowledgeable sources about the topic, and avoiding judgmental language and why questions. For example, both my open-ended questions and probes asked what and how questions.[43] Questions that ask participants "why," often are interpreted to be judging the participants' ideas, thoughts or behaviors. Most of the questions were descriptive, to allow the interviewee to tell his/her story in his/her "own" language. Furthermore, the questions encompassed "grand-tour" type questions in which I asked for descriptions of significant features of the club culture, such as people, events, activities and objects.[44] I also included probing questions that resemble Spradley's "mini-tour" questions, in which I asked the interviewee to comment and/or describe a particular event or object. At the first interview, Mike reviewed the interview protocol to ensure that all relevant questions were included and that the interviewees could comprehend the language of the questions. He did not foresee a problem.

The Internet Forums

My key informant instructed me to read threads [comments (posts) provided by users often organized by topic] on an Internet forum website.

Internet forums are "virtual networks of connectedness" which are not bound by geographical borders or by restrictions of space and time.[45] For the most part, these forums provide a low level of individual contact as members do not engage via webcams and may or may not post actual photos. On these websites, members post messages and photos, and engage in conversations with readers regarding a host of various topics. On these forums, the club kids discussed which venue they would attend on the upcoming evening or weekend, their thoughts on a party they recently attended, what shoes or CDs they recommended, and future travel plans. Such data provided contextual information and themes within the scene that were important to the group. Furthermore, the Internet forum was a great source for learning about possible venues and events for future participant observation. Ralph and Tina discussed the kind of conversations that occur on the forum:

> Ralph: I'm busy throughout the course of my day at work. So I'll go on [the forum] maybe at lunch for an hour, and I'm not even talkin' like straight, like I'll go while I'm workin' and I'll take a break from what I'm doing and go to the [forum] and see who's doin' what and who's talkin' about what, and then . . . I'll be on for like an hour, and then I'll click, and if I post something whatever, great. Then I'll go back on again at the end of the day, and then . . . if there's something I was interested about that I wanted to see like where it went, I'll go on again at night, but that's very, very rare. So I mean I go on maybe three times a week during work, that's it. Like, I don't go on everyday . . . some people are on everyday, all day. And like a lot of it's just like random babblings about nothing, but there's like different sections. There's a chemistry section, a sex section. I mean for you, I mean what you might find interesting is the chemistry section, ya know . . . but it's more– more interesting when you know like a lot of the parties involved, like you know who's who, what they're talkin' about, it's kind of funny. But like with the chemistry thing, like somebody'll post something, like some like stupid belief that they have about like . . . overdosing and then . . . you'll get like ten responses from this guy, this guy and this guy sayin', "you know what? You're wrong. I disagree," whatever. And a lot of it is actual like, ya know, we'll call them, we could call them I guess, you could call them debates. But yeah it's kind of what happens on that website, so it's pretty interesting. You should check it out.

> Tina: . . . like people really get involved, or like they put every piece of their life on the message board . . . these people get into arguments on those message boards and they sit there in front of them all day.

The forum was an excellent source of information for newspaper stories on the clubs they frequented. Often, many club kids posted links to articles in local newspapers, and they engaged in a discussion regarding the story.

The Internet forums are publicly accessible.[46] While one needs to become a member of the site to write postings, you do not need to be a member to "lurk." Members have the option of sending private messages to one another, keeping out of the public's view. All threads are kept in an archive, which could be accessed by searching a particular term.

Although the Internet forum is considered a public space,[47] I took measures to ensure the anonymity of the participants. All data collected via the Internet forum do not indicate the authors' names, avatars,[48] or usernames. Internet forum data were only collected for contextual information and themes, while also providing possible participant observation venues. No posts or threads are quoted directly, no pages were printed, and no interviews were sought through the forums.

Exiting the Field

I physically exited the field in May 2005. At that point, I discontinued participant observations, but still remained in contact via phone and e-mail with four of the club kids, Michelle, Jack, J. Masters, and Osiris. By June 2005, my contact with them had dwindled. I occasionally hear from J. Masters, and I had recent contact with Osiris. Every few weeks, I lurk on the Internet forum. But, for the most part, I am no longer part of the club kids' scene.

THE CLUB KIDS

The "club kids" are not really kids (see Table 1.2). Rather, the 18 people (8 females and 10 males) I interviewed are well-educated, affluent adults.[49] Their average age at the time of the interview was 27 years. The oldest club kid was 33 years old, while the youngest was 22. While many engaged in same-sex sex, they all identified as heterosexual. Most of the club kids grew up in middle to upper-middle class families.[50] Six grew up in single-parent homes, and seven resided with their parent(s) at the time of the interview. All but one of the participants was either employed or enrolled in post-graduate programs. As can been seen in Table 1.2, the majority of the club kids had high-paying occupations. Five of the participants were in the medical sciences, including: David, who obtained his Ph.D. in neuroscience; Betty Cool, a registered nurse; Tyler, a surgical resident; Jack, a chief resident at a hospital; and Jack's wife, Michelle, an occupational therapist. Other participants worked in the business field, such as J. Masters, who owned an investment banking company and Ariel who was an investment banker.

Some men in the study had higher disposable incomes than other men. In many cases, George borrowed money from Mike and paid him back without interest. Additionally, all the men had higher incomes than the women. It was very common for the men to purchase plane tickets, pay for hotels, and cover the bar tab at the club without expecting the women to pay their share. For example, Paula and her fellow female bartenders had their employer Tom pay for their trip in Las Vegas, including hotel rooms, meals and tickets to a show. The women only had to purchase their plane tickets. The following field notes demonstrate how some of the men supported the women:

> While in the car leaving the Planet, Jodi rhetorically asked, "why does he pay for us all the time?" Paula responded, "why does he buy me clothes? Whatever." (September 4, 2004; field note)

> Over dinner at the Mexican Grill, a few people were complaining that while they ordered food, they were "too fucked-up" to eat. They mostly wrapped the food to go. J. paid the bill, which was $500, and left the waiter a $100 tip. I got up to use the restroom. Near the doors, Pez was talking to Amy, telling her how great she looks. He said, "I can't believe I bought you a sexy dress, and I haven't seen you in it." (September 4, 2004; field note)

Strengths and Limitations of the Research

With ethnographic research methods, it is inappropriate to discuss the validity, reliability and generalizability of the research. Instead, ethnographers refer to validity as credibility, reliability as dependability, and generalizability as transferability.[51] To strengthen the credibility, dependability and transferability of my research, I took the following measures:

1. engaged in frequent observations;

2. recorded field notes in a timely fashion;

3. tape-recorded the interviews;

4. triangulated the data;

5. ensured a key informant reviewed the finding;

6. discussed the data in context; and,

7. compared the data to other studies of drug users in venues where dancing takes place.

Credibility

I engaged in frequent participant observations, which allowed lengthy engagement with drug users, to increase the credibility of my research and of my interviews. By investing an extensive period of time at clubs and other venues with the club kids, I was open to multiple influences, learned the culture, tested misinformation, and built trust. Moreover, spending almost every weekend for over one year with the club kids allowed me to observe each interaction in detail. To ensure data accuracy, I recorded the observations in a timely fashion and tape-recorded the interviews.[52]

Through triangulation (using multiple data sources), I was able to increase both the richness of the research and the accuracy of the data. Regular contact with my informants provided assistance with explanations, clarity, and insight regarding certain events and situations, and offered an insider to review my conclusions. These informants engaged in "member-check" to confirm my work. For example, I obtained comments from Mike when he read the dissertation proposal at the beginning of the research, and Osiris gave his approval to the many sections he read of the doctoral dissertation on which this book is based.

Dependability

For the data to be considered dependable, other researchers should hypothetically be able to collect similar data when they conduct the same study at the same venues during the same time period with the same research goals. Most of the limitations on the dependability of the data result from three inter-related problems endemic to ethnographic research. First, the data rely primarily on self-reported information. Second, the embodied ethnographer influences the data collected. And, third, the individual characteristics of the ethnographer shape the data collection process.

The nature of the type of data collected during my interviews – self-reported information – is a limitation. Self-reports have various problems with recall and honesty, which are the most serious threats to the accuracy of the data.[53] When discussing illegal behaviors such as drug use, individuals tend to conceal or exaggerate information. When drug use is frequent and varied, they may not remember the drugs used. Since the participants were aware that this research addresses the culture surrounding drug use, they may have answered questions in ways that they believed would satisfy my needs instead of being honest. Furthermore, participants may have been reluctant to answer questions honestly because they did not think their responses would be treated confidentially. Still, self-report data collection is the most practical and accurate way of gaining information on behaviors that are not observable or detectable, such as individuals' feelings about the meanings of their drug-using behaviors. This method has been widely accepted as a valid and reliable means of measuring criminal behavior. Furthermore, the time spent in the field with the club kids, and the level of both rapport and trust established with them, minimizes such limitations. The use of lengthy interviews, follow-up questions, and the request for stories about their experiences using drugs and clubbing, also reduced the interviewees' forgetfulness and dishonesty.

My physical experiences collecting the data influenced the fieldwork.[54] I experienced bodily exhaustion and I was often uncomfortable in the hot, crowded dance clubs. My dislike for hot, sweaty places provoked me to leave those areas in search of a more comfortable area of the club. When I was not feeling well, such as sick or too exhausted, I decided to refrain from completing another participant observation. As a consequence, I did not observe everything. Other researchers who may not have similar experiences, or can better tolerate such situations, may, as a result, gather different data.

A researcher with different individual characteristics, such as gender or personality, might also have obtained data dissimilar to mine.[55] For example, my inability to connect with Julia contributed to the lack of interviews among her group of female friends. To address this issue, when in the field I consistently negotiated my personality to avoid confrontation and arguments. I made great efforts to act natural, be engaged, and look comfortable. Still, while at Danceteria I could not hide my discomfort. Since I felt "out of place," I left the club:

> I was standing under the DJ booth watching the dance floor. I began to feel uncomfortable. I was not talking to anyone, and the conversations I attempted to have with the attendees, and even some of the club kids I knew, were both uneventful and short. I started to feel out of place. I decided to leave. (April 15, 2004; field note)

Despite such limitations on the dependability of my research, my informants' reviews of my findings and my use of triangulation enhanced data dependability. As Lincoln and Guba state: "[since] there can be no validity without reliability (and thus no credibility without dependability), a demonstration of the former is sufficient to establish the latter."[56] Since I took steps to ensure the credibility of the data, these steps also certify that the data are dependable.

Transferability

In ethnographic research, generalizability is referred to as transferability, and is defined as obtaining similar findings in a different context. To enhance the transferability of my research, in this book I discuss my findings as embedded in context. In other words, all of my conclusions and analyses are based on a particular place at a particular time. When I witnessed similar interactions at different times in different contexts, I was able to draw more comprehensive conclusions. Moreover, throughout the book, I compare and contrast this research project to other studies of club culture conducted both within[57] and outside of the U.S., particularly in Western Europe.[58] From those comparisons, it is clear that my sample of clubbers (people who attend dance clubs) is similar to clubbers in other contexts. The clubbing experience and drug use patterns also mirror those of clubbers from other studies.[59]

While ethnographies have some inherent limitations, interviews and participant observations were appropriate for this project. Moreover, one of the significant elements of qualitative research methods is its ability to capture and highlight the importance of structural, political and economic factors that have been found to be crucial in shaping the development of drug-using subcultures. In essence, qualitative methods supply "rich data," which "are detailed and complete enough that they provide a full and revealing picture of what is going on."[60]

The flexibility of ethnographic research is an additional asset. I consistently reevaluated my methodology to ensure the highest level of credibility, dependability, and transferability of the data. Coding methods, sampling, observational techniques and the interview guide evolved with the research. For example, I changed my recruitment patterns to solicit more interviews, and I did not limit myself to my initial plan of 20 participant observations. "Research design in ethnography, both as it relates to a selection of cases for study and in other respects too, is a continuous process. The match between research problems and cases selected must be continually monitored."[61] Therefore, by not placing restrictive limits, and not relying on a structural framework for the research, I effectively captured the context of drug use in dance club settings.

Data Analysis

I transcribed all interviews verbatim, and to best reflect the thoughts of the participants, all interview excerpts provided in this book are exact words of the respondents, including use of argot, dialects and hesitations. I managed all interview transcriptions, field notes and journal entries using the Atlas.ti qualitative software program. Both interview and field note analyses were crucial to the development of themes. Field note analysis provided a contextual understanding of the interviewees' experiences, while also providing evidence of the club kids' behaviors. I employed the constant comparative method, in which the data are continually compared with previously collected data. This method of data analysis allowed me to construct categories that captured both common elements and relevant characteristics.[62] In particular, I identified patterns related to the decision-making process around drug use – including where, what and how to use drugs, and patterns and elements that influence the effects of drugs. I investigated similarities and differences among the experiences of the participants. I used the categories that emerged to group, organize, code and analyze the data. Using inductive reasoning, I then derived common themes and overarching frameworks, which are discussed in detail throughout this book.

The process of coding and creating themes began with coding the data using narrow categories. For example, the following interview excerpt was coded with [Harm], [How Use], [MaryJane], [Meth] and [Pattern of Use]:

> MaryJane: Last summer, I was in the Hamptons every weekend sniffing crystal – all weekend 'til Sunday night. And then going, "why, why, why?"

Within this code, MaryJane describes her regrets of frequently using [Harm] crystal methamphetamine [Meth]. In this account, MaryJane also alludes to one of her patterns of drug use (all weekend), and indicates how she used the crystal methamphetamine (snorted). Hence, multiple categories emerge from a single quote.

Likewise, many categories can be linked to a field note. The below field note (March 14, 2004) was coded as [CJ involve/present], [Concealing Drugs] and [Venue Security]:

Two undercovers came to the VIP section to conduct a random search. They only searched three people in the entire VIP section, Todd, his cousin and Julius. Julius tried to explain to them that he is an employee of the club. They stressed their lack of concern. As they were searching the cousin, the cousin was shaking his legs, inserting his hands into his pockets, and yelling, "I don't have nuttin'." He was moving very fast. They told him to stop moving, so they could search him. He did. As with the rest of their searches, the bouncers did not locate any drugs.

This field note describes the security methods venue owners use to locate drugs in their clubs, and how police officers are part of the efforts.

Each code was then linked with other codes to create an overarching category called a family. For example, those codes associated with venue security are considered characteristics of the family Security::Venue. Those codes within the family Drug::Use describe the factors linked to how the club kids use drugs. Codes in the code families can and often are linked to one or more families (i.e., the code families are not mutually exclusive categories). For example, the code [Style] is linked to both the family Culture::Subculture, and the family Participants::Characteristics. The inductive process to code and organize the data generated theories that best represent the culture and drug use of the club kids, and are thoroughly explained in this book.

NOTES

1. Some of the material in this chapter also appears in Perrone, 2006, and Perrone, in press.
2. Hebdige, 1979/2002, pg. 76.
3. 1994.
4. see also Maxwell, 1996.
5. Patton, 1990, p. 24.
6. Ibid.
7. e.g., Adler, 1993.
8. Rutgers University's institutional review board approved these procedures.
9. see Spradley, 1979.
10. 1995, p. 48.
11. In a previous publication, the editor requested that the pseudonyms of some of the club kids be changed (Perrone, 2006). Osiris is also known as Gary in Perrone, 2006.
12. see also Hammersley and Atkinson, 1995; Williams, Dunlap, Johnson, and Hamid, 1992; Williams, 1996.

13. Spradley, 1979, p. 33.
14. Hammersley and Atkinson, 1995, p. 48.
15. see Coffey, 1999, 2002; Davies, 1999; Roberts and Sanders, 2005; Perrone, in press.
16. 1995, p. 94.
17. Bell, 1999; Markowitz, 1999.
18. 1995; see also Goffman, 1959.
19. Coffey, 1999, p. 60; see also Perrone, in press.
20. see Baudrillard, 1975.
21. Hammersley and Atkinson, 1995, p. 83.
22. see Coffey, 1999; Perrone, in press.
23. Liman, 1999.
24. Bailey and Barbato, 2003.
25. Winterbottom, 2002.
26. Greenwald, 2004.
27. Noujaim, 2004.
28. e.g., Douglas, 1973; Polsky, 1967/1998.
29. For a detailed discussion of this see Perrone, in press.
30. see Perrone, in press.
31. e.g., Coffey, 2002; Howell, 1990; Lee, 1997; Williams et al., 1992.
32. e.g., Gearing, 1995; Moreno, 1995; see also Perrone, in press.
33. Adler, 1985; Inciardi, 1993; Jacobs, 1998.
34. Hammersley and Atkinson, 1995; Spradley, 1979.
35. Hammersley and Atkinson, 1995, p. 48.
36. cf., Chatterton and Hollands, 2003.
37. see Lewis and Ross, 1995; Moore, 1991; Sifaneck and Neaigus, 2001; Whyte, 1993.
38. see Johnson, Goldstein, Preble, Schmeidler, Lipton, Spunt, and Miller, 1985; Wright and Decker, 1994.
39. To best reflect the thoughts of the participants, all interview excerpts provided are exact words of the respondents, including use of argot, dialects and hesitations.
40. Greer, 2004.
41. In a previous publication, the editor requested that the pseudonyms of some of the club kids be changed (Perrone, 2006). MaryJane is also known as Mary in Perrone, 2006.
42. In a previous publication, the editor requested that the pseudonyms of some of the club kids be changed (Perrone, 2006). SickKid is also known as Sam in Perrone, 2006.
43. Becker, 1998.
44. Spradley, 1979.

45. Greer, 2004.
46. see Eysenbach and Till, 2001; Pittenger, 2003.
47. Frankel and Siang, 1999.
48. An avatar is an image, which represents the user on a forum or other online community. This image often is placed below the screen name, and it can be changed when the user deems necessary.
49. Forsyth, 1996; Hammersley, Khan, and Ditton, 2002; Hansen et al., 2001; Kelly, 2006; Measham, Parker, and Aldridge, 2001; Ter Bogt et al., 2002; van de Wijngaart et al., 1999. Because most research of club drug users has focused on rave or dance club populations, it may have missed other populations of drug users (i.e., street users) (cf., Novoa et al., 2005). Recent studies have shown that club drug use is increasingly prevalent among other populations (e.g., Fendrich et al., 2003; Krebs and Steffey, 2005; Martins et al., 2005; Maxwell and Spence, 2005; Novoa et al., 2005; Ompad et al., 2005), and among those outside of dance club culture (e.g., Community Epidemiology Working Group, 2003; Fendrich et al., 2003; Krebs and Steffey, 2005; Lankenau and Clatts, 2005; Maxwell and Spence, 2005; Novoa et al., 2005; Ompad et al., 2005).
50. Class status is a subjective conclusion that was based on individual income and family income.
51. Lincoln and Guba, 1985.
52. see Maxwell, 1996.
53. see Graham and Bowling, 1995.
54. see Perrone, in press.
55. Coffey, 1999, 2002; Perrone, in press.
56. 1985, p.316.
57. e.g., Kelly, 2006.
58. e.g., Measham et al., 2001; Topp, Hando, Dillon, Roche, and Solowij, 1999.
59. e.g., Hammersley et al., 2002; Malbon, 1999; Measham et al., 2001.
60. Maxwell, 1996, p. 95.
61. Hammersley and Atkinson, 1995, p. 45.
62. Strauss, 1987.

Part I

THE CLUB KIDS' DANCE CULTURE

2. THE NEW YORK CITY[1] CLUB KIDS AND THE SUBCULTURE LITERATURE

To situate the club kids in a historical context, it is important to understand more generally the development of youth subculture groups and how they compare to the club kids. Specifically, numerous studies on subcultural groups throughout the U.K. and the U.S., including research on the mods,[2] the hippies[3] and the punks,[4] have been analyzed and explained using Hebdige's[5] subculture framework. Although Hebdige's theory has not been the only attempt to explain subcultures, his theory has dominated the discourse on subculture groups.

Hebdige and other subculture theorists[6] have shown that subcultures form as a response to changes in macro-level factors in which these individuals experienced alienation from, and contempt for, the dominant class. While this literature has adequately explained past subcultures, it cannot be applied to the club culture phenomenon. Unlike past subcultures, but similar to other club cultures,[7] the club kids emerged neither to contradict the dominant culture, nor create a cohesive ideology with stylistic representations of the frustration they were experiencing. Rather, the club kids benefit from, respect and reify the status quo. The club kids' characteristics do not neatly fit within Hebdige's taxonomy. Instead, the club kids best fit within more general theories of subcultures,[8] and taste culture theory.[9] In particular, the club kids are a heterogeneous group comprising multiple subsets of clubbers who use club drugs. These club kids come together based on similar lifestyles and taste preferences.

After a historical overview of subculture theory and a brief description of subculture groups following World War II, in this chapter I describe the inability of Hebdige's subculture principles to explain club cultures. I conclude this chapter with a discussion of the implications such a finding has for subcultural theory. In particular, I explain that Hebdige's principles, while narrow, are vital to a comprehensive understanding of subcultures in general, but are too narrow to be applied to club cultures. Club cultures could best be explained using Bourdieu's[10] conceptualization of taste cultures.

A SUBCULTURE

Subculture theory first arose in the 1930s and 1940s when sociologists Sellin,[11] Merton[12] and Shaw and McKay[13] set out to explain crime rate differences among particular groups within lower class communities. Since then, subculture theory has gone through many alterations on its developmental path. During its peak acceptance period in the 1970s and 1980s, when the Center for Contemporary Cultural Studies (CCCS) at the University of Birmingham emerged, subculture theory met strong criticism.[14] Yet, the CCCS successfully overcame the critiques, and Hebdige's theory moved to the forefront of the theoretical discussion on subcultures. However, this overreliance on Hebdige's theoretical premises subsequently impeded the evolution of subculture theory and essentially undermined its ability to explain other subcultures, especially club culture.

Fischer[15] was one of the first to explain subculture theory's defining elements and its development process. Fischer states that, "a 'subculture' is a set of morals, beliefs, values, norms, and customs associated with a relatively distinct social subsystem (a set of interpersonal networks and institutions) existing within a larger social system and culture."[16] Subcultures "diverge from the dominant norms of society," and their members engage in unconventional behaviors, including preferences in style.[17]

While most subcultural theorists would probably agree with that definition,[18] some theorists further elaborated its elements.[19] In particular, Hebdige had the greatest impact on the definition, thereby shaping the understanding of the emergence of youth deviant groups. According to Hebdige and his colleagues,[20] a subculture encompasses a tradition, language and style that together provide power to those alienated from the dominant culture. The dominant group controls the discourse surrounding meanings and ideas about life objects and concepts, as well as intellectual mediums and material forces.[21] Common thoughts and perceptions represent the dominant group's ideas and understandings (i.e., they are hegemonic constructions).[22] The subculture forms as an attempt to both take control of that discourse and alter the construction of individual perceptions, beliefs and thoughts.

According to Hebdige and the CCCS, subcultures take ordinary objects and transform both their traditional uses and their meanings. These objects then become unique identifiers that distinguish subculture members from non-members. Hebdige explains that these objects, such as fashions in clothing, represent the subcultural group's ideology, and are evidence of the subculture's struggle for control over meaning of the objects. The subculture emerges as a reaction to macro-level changes in society, and it develops a unique style symbolizing the social strains that its members experience.

As Hebdige developed his ideas and the Birmingham School emerged, previous subcultural theories were left in its shadow. Researchers began to study the development of various youth subcultures in the United States and the United Kingdom since the end of World War II applying Hebdige's subculture principles,[23] while overlooking other possible interpretations of subcultures. Since the decades after World War II were a period of economic growth – which brought employment, increased production of goods and services, and higher disposable incomes for young people – a strong youth market developed, with young people at "the forefront of conspicuous, fast-paced, leisure-oriented consumption."[24] As Hayward[25] notes, young people are exposed "to the most aggressive forms of 'lifestyle advertising.' " These rapid changes largely influenced social scientists, particularly Becker[26] and Hebdige, to analyze the situational and structural factors affecting young people. They found that changes in economic and social structures, coupled with the rigidity of the values of the dominant culture, tended to motivate individuals with similar experiences to form a subculture. The subculture provided the individuals with a group identity separate from the conventional, dominant class.

For example, the Chicago Dance Musicians of the late 1940s feared that the intellectual properties of their music would fall into the hands of the dominant business and political classes.[27] While most Dance Musicians came from wealthy, privileged families, they rejected the conventional lifestyle, specifically the commercialization of music. Through their use of "occupational slang," as Becker[28] describes it, the Dance Musicians represented their separation from the conventional class. For example, the word "square" described the outsider to this subculture. Additionally, the word "loot" was commonly used instead of "money," "gage" substituted for "marijuana," and "gigs" was used in place of "jobs." This argot allowed Dance Musicians to segregate and isolate themselves from the squares, while "quickly" revealing the outsider.[29]

Since Hebdige's theory was applicable to various youth groups in the post-World War II era, Fischer's[30] more general theory of subcultures was left in the dust. In the rest of this chapter, I highlight seven youth subcultures that arose since the 1950s to demonstrate how their characteristics neatly fit into Hebdige's taxonomy, and to demonstrate the wide acceptance of Hebdige's subcultural theory. Specifically, I review the macro-level forces that provoked both the emergence, and the styles, of the following subcultures: the early 1950s' Cats who originated in Chicago, IL,[31] the 1950s' mods and rockers of the U.K.,[32] the San Francisco Haight-Ashbury hippies of the 1960s,[33] the late 70s'-80s' punks and skinheads in the U.K.,[34] and the mid-1980s' Burnouts of suburban New Jersey.[35]

1950s-1990s DRUG USING SUBCULTURES

The Cats

In the early 1950s, people of color in the U.S. experienced particular macro-level factors such as social segregation and discrimination, which reduced their opportunities to advance up the socioeconomic ladder. During that same time period, the experience of the White majority was much different, as they were progressing economically, financially and socially to a higher stratum.[36] The economic and social constraints that people of color experienced, coinciding with other racial groups' apparent lack of similar restraints, fostered strong feelings of isolation among the former, as well as tension between the racial groups. Largely to escape these social conditions, the Cats developed an alternate world, rejecting "square" (White) class values and creating other means of achievement. Through impeccable taste in clothes and music, and by engaging in "hustles" (e.g., connning) and "kicks" (i.e., fun activities), the Cats attained prestige and respect from their peers.[37]

The 1940s Cats' style of dress represented their escape from the inferior class. They placed value on clothing that emphasized a "highly developed sense of taste."[38] A common clothing ensemble included an expensive hat, along with a well-tailored, non-flashy, conservative colored suit, which covered a "non-functional tie-clip" attached to a sport shirt.[39] Because most Cats came from "the drabbest, most overcrowded and physically deteriorating parts of the city," their fancy clothes were purchased with money from pimp operations (e.g., a Cat received proceeds from "his" prostitutes and from "chick" shoplifters) or from "hustling," (i.e., conning in a game of billiards, petty thievery or begging).[40]

Through their appreciation of and involvement in music, the Cats achieved a valuable experience. Finestone[41] states: "An essential part of [the Cats] social orientation" was the progressive genre of music created by such musicians as Charlie Parker (a.k.a. the Yardbird) and Al Benson. The Cats perceived their knowledge and respect for the music as superior to that of the squares. Those Cats who used heroin were further separated from the squares. Using heroin challenged dominant values since it provided immediate self-gratification. This was contrary to the squares' long-term planning and delayed gratification ideals.

The Mods and Rockers

The U.K.'s mods and rockers emerged as a result of changes in the economic and life structures of adolescents.[42] Specifically, Cohen[43] explains that such groups emerged in response to the economic boom of the late 1950s, which differentially affected middle and working class youths. Among the middle class, the economic boom fostered a large unmarried youth population (between 15 and 21) whose average real earning wage had increased at twice the rate of adults. While their salaries increased, middle-class youth experienced "an absence of a ritualized transition to full adult status,"[44] alienating many adolescents from the culture of their parents. Working class youth, however, were restricted to unskilled, lower-paid repetitive labor. These distinct experiences among working- and middle-class youth triggered the emergence of two subcultural groups, the mods and the rockers.

Since the mods came mainly from middle-class families, the economic boom provided them with the spending power to purchase goods the market offered. Consequently the mods upheld middle-class values, and chose a style that exaggerated middle-class culture. Most mods wore sharp, conservative suits in "respectable colors."[45] Many were excessively tidy and neat, with plain but smart trousers and pullovers. Gender-blurring also occurred within mod style as the mod male wore pastel-shaded trousers and face make-up. Most mod females tended to have an androgynous style, with short-cropped hair and a sexless appearance. Ultimately, the mods were competing with other members of the middle class for the highest level of sophistication and snobbish attitude.

The rockers, on the other hand, emerged as a reaction to their contempt for their unskilled, routinized, manual occupations.[46] Many felt controlled by, and alienated from, the dominant class. Most had few opportunities for excitement and autonomy. In response to their alienation and the constraints of work, these young people found solidarity in the rocker subculture. Many upheld patriarchical norms and masculine prestige, and attempted to assert a "butch image" by riding motorcycles and wearing black leather with metal studs.[47] The rockers preferred listening to the Rolling Stones and The Who, as these groups "stirred up a whole new mood of teen arrogance," with such songs as "I Can't Get No Satisfaction."[48]

The Hippies

Unlike the mods and the rockers, who were mainly associated with one specific social class, the hippies appealed to individuals from all classes. Most hippies living around Haight-Ashbury in San Francisco during the 1960s rejected the rigidity of the dominant class (e.g., traditional sex values, and gender and racial stereotypes). Many actively participated in social change through Vietnam War demonstrations, the Lesbian and Gay Movements, and the Feminist and Civil Rights Movements. Most hippies distrusted the political establishment, conveyed a critical awareness of inequality, and opposed the Protestant ethic.[49] Through their style of dress, musical preferences and drug use, many hippies attempted to alter the dominant class's restrictive social norms.

For example, to express their freedom and rejection of the social norms, both genders grew long hair, and females refused to wear brassieres.[50] Most hippies held strong views against uncontrolled technological advancements and the destruction of the environment.[51] They rejected 1950s materialism and traditional American norms. Their clothing styles reflected a return to "the earth," designed with bright colors.[52]

The hippies' musical preference and drugs of choice also "undercut the straight world."[53] Most hippies tended to listen to political musicians, as well as aggressive rock music, such as Janis Joplin, which "reflected the complexity and rhythmical asymmetry of the hippie lifestyle."[54] Through the use of drugs, many hippies attacked the normal state of consciousness and sought altered states of reality. They consumed drugs to escape the materialistic dominant culture and achieve a higher level of self-awareness.

Most hippies professed that, "the materialistic game was not even real – it is illusory compared to the mystical experience induced by drugs."[55]

The Punks and Skinheads

During the late 1970s and into the early 80s, the British economy was in a "deep recession," and by August of 1981, half of all high school dropouts were unemployed.[56] Many working class youth blamed the lack of job opportunities on the rise in immigration. They tended to feel alienated from middle-class culture and sought an alternative lifestyle. One punk complained: "[l]ook at us, that is what we are bloody reduced to, what bloody future have we got? It is the Government's fault, they should come down here and fucking see what is really going on, what our lives are really like."[57] The punk and skinhead subculture offered a channel for self-expression and an escape from the mundane. Through their musical preferences, drug of choice and style of dress these youth challenged the dominant order.

The punk and skinhead music genres included songs that expressed strong hatred and anger for the employment structure. For example, one lyric from a popular punk song stated: " 'no fucking bosses . . . get off our bleedin' backs.' "[58] As an additional expression of anger and contempt, the punks and skinheads tended to consume barbiturates. Burr[59] stated that the skinhead and punk "nihilistic and disturbed" ideology paralleled the "negative and self-destructive nature of illicit barbiturate use." Barbiturates allowed punks to escape their social conditions through entering a state of oblivion. For many of the skinheads, barbiturate use provided "Dutch courage" to enhance their fighting capabilities. Because skinheads expected all members to be brave and have the ability and willingness to engage in physical confrontations, barbiturate use was valuable. Under the influence of barbiturates, the skinheads achieved a higher tolerance for pain as well as blurred vision, and as result, were less afraid of their opponents.

The punks' and skinheads' clearly defined styles further represented their disdain for the changes in the economy and the rigidity of gender roles. For example, many punks fashioned "freaky" multi-colored hairstyles, and wore torn t-shirts and highland kilts or bondage trousers for a leather look. For accessories, some punks wore swastikas, bondage tape and safety pins. Many engaged in "cockney speech and vulgarity," as well as various sexually deviant activities. In contrast, the skinheads had close-cropped hair, wore "model worker clothes" and Doctor Marten boots.[60] Skinhead clothing represented their subculture's support of the working class and their backlash against immigration.

The Burnouts

The Burnouts of the mid-1980s in U.S. suburbia emerged as a result of changes in the middle-class nuclear family and the employment structure. In particular, Gaines[61] indicated that many White suburban families were divorcing at a higher rate than in the past, and many were employed in service occupations whose salaries fell into lower pay-brackets. That, coupled with an increase in the cost of living and a rise in unemployment, amplified economic pressures on many families. Ronald Reagan's presidency (1981-1989) further exacerbated these tensions as his policies gave low priority to social welfare programs. Consequently, Gaines explains, both parents were forced to work, leaving many youth home to care for themselves and siblings, thereby partly inducing the latchkey kid phenomenon.

As a result of these economic and cultural conditions, the children of these White suburban families, for the most part, had inflated expectations of a prosperous future, while actually experiencing diminishing economic prospects. Obtaining a college education for many suburban youth was largely out of reach, as it became increasingly expensive. Many youth felt "cheated . . . complete alienation and powerlessness."[62] By connecting as the Burnouts, these youths gained a new life philosophy. They valued living in the moment and having "enough fun to kill themselves before everything else does."[63]

The Burnouts' style of dress and preferred genre of music were also evidence of their strong adherence to the Burnout philosophy, as these objects were "a means of expressing profound anxiety and the frustrations of living."[64] In particular, through their style of dress and musical preferences, the Burnouts sought to create an identity and community they "could call [their] own," separating themselves from the dominant "jock" group.[65] The Burnouts created objects of identification to separate themselves from the jocks, much in the same manner as the hippies, punks and skinheads had sought to demarcate themselves. Most Burnouts wore leather or jean jackets and pants, souvenir t-shirts from heavy metal music concerts, and high-top sneakers.

Heavy metal music by artists such as Metallica, Iron Maiden and Ozzy Osbourne provided Burnouts with knowledge about the meaning of life and death. Many Burnouts described their music as a religion, as it gave them faith, courage and advice. Furthermore, most Burnouts indicated the songs "articulated their sense of loss."[66] For example, Metallica's 1983 album *Kill Em All* exposed, "how society ate people up alive,"[67] and Metallica's *Fade to Black* discussed "the dying of a human soul." These songs were particularly significant to Burnouts as many were contemplating, attempting and even committing suicide.

Similar to the hippies, the mods, and the punks, gender-blurring was also common among the Burnouts, as males and females wore similar clothing styles, rode skateboards, and had pierced ears, tattoos and long hair. Substance use among many Burnouts was a means of further separating themselves from the dominant group. For example, "smoking cigarettes became a label, a mark of the uncooperative teen, the rebel, the troublemaker," a label many Burnouts sought.[68] In many high schools, cigarette smoking was enough to categorize an individual as a Burnout. Burnouts particularly enjoyed smoking marijuana joints and drinking beer and liquor. Many claimed that on a "good night" substances consumed also included cocaine, PCP or crack-cocaine.[69] Through consuming these various substances many Burnouts indicated that they could reach a level of obliteration, escape the boredom of suburbia, and experience a higher level of self-respect.

Summary

Clearly, subcultures develop in all socioeconomic backgrounds, and are not endemic to any particular social class or ethnic group. Regardless of the social or economic class from which subcultures emerge, for the most part their development is evidence that the group is experiencing some sort of strain, conflict and/or alienation from the dominant culture. These case studies demonstrate that while subcultures develop during different time periods and with a different style, they have many common factors. Subcultures create an ideology and style, with specific musical preferences and drug-using behaviors to stimulate an identity separate from the dominant culture. Many of the subcultures' styles of dress are shaped by their ideologies and socioeconomic statuses. For example, the mods were able to exaggerate the middle class style of dress because they had the economic means to do so, while the rockers were constrained to maintain a separate style. The selection of a drug of choice for each subculture further exemplifies their ideology and provides a coping mechanism for the difficulties each group was experiencing.

SUBCULTURES AND THE CLUB KIDS

When this project commenced, Hebdige's subculture principles provided the theoretical framework for the research.[70] However, this study's population of club kids does not comprise a subculture in the traditional sense, as Hebdige uses the term. Unlike the subcultures discussed above, that formed as a reaction to the dominant class, the club kids adhere to the values and norms of the dominant class. The club kids have emerged in a highly commercialized, globalized and commodified society, which has altered both the components and the study of youth cultures. Specifically, in a society of excessive consumption and commercialism, people amplify the value of consumerism, and the use and ownership of goods become "markers of self-identity."[71] This rise in consumption, commercialization and commodification of life resources and culture has greatly affected the development and expression of youth cultures. Young people have been primary targets of the expansive consumer market.

Thomas[72] explains that youth cultures in general, and club culture in particular, have been "manufactured and dictated by consumer society and/or the media." The club kids emerged in a commodity culture, which, as theorists predicted,[73] has caused individual identities and styles to be determined by conspicuous consumption. Consumeristic ideals and consumption practices have shaped club culture style. Similar to the U.K.'s Acid house music scene,[74] the club kids both abandoned and offered themselves to the consumer "market." Their style was neither an expressive response to what Hebdige classified as the dominant group, nor necessarily distinct from that "dominant" group (as other subculture theorists such as Anderson,[75] Cloward and Ohlin,[76] Cohen,[77] Miller,[78] Shaw and McKay,[79] and Wolfgang and Ferracuti[80] would have expected). The clubbing scene is a commodified, commercialized, and consumed self-style in which it is important to wear "the latest clothes and be seen getting the right buzz from whatever designer drinks or drugs are your pleasure."[81]

Club Kids and Consumerism

Consumerism denotes that "the self cannot be complete without a wealth of consumer goods and that goals can be achieved and problems solved through proper consumption."[82] Such messages are rampant among social institutions such as the media, the medical industry and the education system. Advertisements, specifically, suggest that "products can correct, enhance, or even create personalities."[83] As Conrad and Jacobson[84] state:

"biology may appear to set limits on bodily development . . . , but individuals can work to improve body size and shape by working out and/or taking supplements, or through other methods of enhancement." Such body modifications as losing weight, tanning, dying hair, consuming drugs and getting cosmetic surgery can effectively change both the self and the outside perceptions of the self.

Consumer culture has fostered the development of identities based on consumption. As Gottdiener[85] states: "consumption remains a major way people seek to realize aspects of their identity." Essentially, "we create ourselves through things, and we change ourselves through changing our things."[86] In modernity, the body and the self have become commodities conveying social meanings, as health, beauty, fashion and personalities could be purchased for a price.[87] When each product is consumed – health, fashion, or food – the individual is simultaneously consuming the sign that the product represents.[88] Dressing a particular way, ingesting a type of drug, and purchasing a type of body modification signify an identity. Within a consumer culture, how individuals present themselves – in how they look, dress and act – are vital parts of their identity. Fundamentally, "Consumer culture has encouraged the development of . . . a performing self, in which appearance, display and impression management become essential resources . . . "[89]

Appearance

All cultures are involved in appearance management.[90] As Ferrell[91] describes this process: "To wear particular clothes drive certain cars, or listen to distinctive types of music is to make oneself *stylistically visible* to those both inside and outside the subculture." Within social interactions, individual bodies become objects, which can be improved and transformed to fit the needs of the interaction.[92] In societies with particularly high levels of consumption, the body becomes a commodity to be sold to the market. An attractive physical appearance is "a more marketable self."[93] Among the club kids, most men and women, are body conscious. Men have been co-opted by the market in a consumer culture in which they are increasingly concerned with "the appearing body . . . through the promotion of exercise, fashion and cosmetics."[94] Men have become just as susceptible to concerns over body image as women have been for a long time, and many men are equally obsessed with diet and exercise as are women. Drummond[95] states:

> Increasingly, men's bodies are being portrayed in ways that commercialize and objectify the male body similar to ways in which the female body has been and remains commodified.

Men are increasingly expected to be muscular and athletic, while changes in sexual politics opened have the door for new male gender identities (e.g., the metrosexual). In the current era, "Young men are more willing to dance [and] to dress up."[96]

Unlike the subcultures of the past, the club kids (both men and women) value and adhere to this consumeristic ethos. The commercialized and globalized market shape club cultures, in particular, and young people, more generally. As a consequence, club culture style has been characterized as style without content,[97] since it emulates mainstream images and definitions of beauty and trendiness. Most club kids conform to consumeristic ideals and to media depictions of masculinity and femininity. As club kid Ralph explains:

> . . . The majority of like the New York house club scene is based on looking good, goin' to the gym, gettin' in shape, bein' fit, ya know, get dolled up, fuckin' showin' off and what not; bein' half naked.

In particular, the club kids purchase high-priced designer clothing, consume body altering substances, obtain body modification procedures and engage in a variety of beautification techniques to enhance their appearance.

Designer Clothing

The club kids favor expensive designer clothing, most of which can be purchased in local department stores, such as Bloomingdales®. Many men tend to wear T-shirts or tank-tops with jeans and sneakers from such brands as Diesel® (average T-shirt price is $60 and jeans are $150), Seven for All Man Kind® (the average jean price is $150) and Coach® (average accessory price $200). As George explains:

> [Seven jeans are] a hundred seventy, a hundred ninety, two hundred dollars. I have a pair of Diesel jeans that were two hundred and thirty-five dollars.

Wearing designer jeans signifies sophistication and affluence; it is an "act of distinction" and a form of self-expression.[98] In a consumerist culture, "identity and self-worth are reduced to simple symbolic codes," such as the visible logos on clothing and accessories.[99] Other designers popular among the club kids are Armani®, French Connection®, Gucci®, Lacoste®, Ralph Lauren® and Louis Vuitton®, as the following excerpts from field notes in March 2004 describe:

> It was very common for guys to be wearing wired sunglasses, and name brand shirts including Diesel®, Armani®, French Connection®. (March 9, 2004; field note)

> Christine was wearing a pair of jeans, with a Louis Vuitton® fanny-pack belt. She wore a Polo® snap-up button t-shirt with a few buttons remaining open to expose her cleavage. (March 5, 2004; field note)

The high cost and brand names worn by many club kids demonstrate the level of disposable income these clubbers have, and the value of "looking good" and "showing-off." For example, Angelina indicates that each weekend, she would purchase a $50 shirt for her night out. Furthermore, she describes how staying afloat with the rest of the clubbers has affected her financially:

> Yo, this scene has completely destroyed . . . my bank account. 'Cause of it I spent . . . enormous amounts of money on clothing, on vacations that I'm still paying for from '99; on drugs, on tanning, on hair, on nails . . . on everything.

Similarly, Betty Cool explains that she "used to buy a new outfit every time" she went out. She adds, "I used to spend like two-three-four hundred dollars on an outfit." Shopping prior to the weekend was necessary since many, like Lucille, MaryJane and Angelina, would not repeat an outfit:

> Lucille: I would never wear the same thing like twice within uh same amount of time, same place, same people, or –

> Angelina: And if I do wear the same shirt, like I did last weekend, which was a rare for me –

> Lucille: She tells everyone.

> Angelina: I'll announce it. I'll be like, "I'm wearing the same shirt." 'Cause then if you say it then it's like you know. You're makin' them aware. So it's not like a big deal.

> (Lucille laughing)

> MaryJane: Or, you'll go out and you didn't see anybody, so you're like, "I didn't wear this outfit this weekend, 'cause I'm gonna wear it next weekend."

> Angelina: No but, I rather play [mock] myself then have people like, "yo, Angelina's wearing the same fuckin' shirt."

Since style and fashion are ephemeral – each weekend the clothing requirements change[100] – it was important for the club kids to stay abreast of the latest trends.

Body Modifications

In addition to purchasing high-end designer brand clothing to enhance their appearance, many of the club kids also engage in body modifications.[101] Langman[102] argues that over the past decades, due to globalization, body modifications have become fashion statements radically transforming the body into art and a marker of identity. Much like clothing and logos, body modification creates identities and can be emotionally satisfying.[103] Through body modifications club kids have reclaimed ownership over their bodies, taking control over their existences. Individuals can purchase the body characteristic they desire and reshape their bodies' form. Since "[e]nhancements that modify biology and the body are a reflection of what is socially valued in a society,"[104] obtaining such modifications is additional evidence of the club kids' belief in dominant views of beauty. The decisions to modify the body are shaped and perpetuated through body objectification and commodification.[105]

Simply by viewing the variety of basic and cable television programs, it becomes evident how consumerism plays a large role in defining a person. For example, such television series as What Not to Wear,[106] Queer Eye for the Straight Guy,[107] and Extreme Makeover[108] demonstrate "through consumption you or your life experience can be fixed or improved."[109] Surgery and cosmetic services are heavily advertised. The body has become something that can be purchased; therefore, identity and self can also be purchased.[110] Accordingly, the club kids have sought to buy a better body and a better self. Such practices are evidence that the club kids uphold, reinforce, and succumb to cultural norms regarding male and female beauty. Among the club kids, appetite suppressants, plastic surgery, steroid use and beautification procedures are common methods of body transformation.

Appetite Suppressants and Weight Management

Certain club drugs, such as GHB, crystal methamphetamine and MDMA, have been commonly consumed among drug users for their weight-managing properties.[111] GHB promotes the release of the human growth hormone, which increases muscle tissue growth, and both MDMA and crystal methamphetamine are appetite suppressants. For many club kids dancing all-night on drugs is a form of exercise.[112] Many female club kids perceive using drugs and clubbing as an effective method of weight loss and control, and a positive and useful side effect. Thinness is an acceptable and desirable goal within the scene among both males and females.[113] For instance, while relaxing at a hotel pool in South Beach, Miami, four women discussed the benefits of ecstasy and crystal methamphetamine consumption on weight loss as follows:

> The girls explained their new South Beach Diet.[114] They basically consume drugs and refrain from eating. Occasionally they'll eat some fruit and have some drinks. (March 5, 2004; field note)

MaryJane also characterized her excessive use of crystal methamphetamine and dramatic weight loss as positive experiences:

> I was doing crystal. I was doing everything. It was like one of those Hamptons fucking weekends, it was horrible. That's when people we're like, "what made you lose so much weight? I'm like this great diet; diet called crystal. Best diet ever in the world."

In contrast to women, men tend to dislike the appetite suppressant effects of drugs, as they tend to be more concerned with building muscle. Ralph explained the importance of ordering protein shakes from club bartenders:

> specifically, guys like me or my friends, we go out, we work out in the gym 4, 5 days a week, okay. When you're up for 24 hours straight, you can't eat solid food, it's impossible. It's not possible to do. So in order to make sure your body has the calories, the carbohydrates, and the protein it needs to function normally, you try to drink– drink shakes – so you get a shake in wherever you can. I mean it's like a meal replacement in a way. So instead of your body running off nothing but the drugs as fuel, it runs off the protein and the carb – the calories that you're putting into it through a shake.

Because eating is perceived to be impossible while under the influence of these substances, George forced himself to eat throughout the drug-using episode to maintain his physique:

> even when I party I eat. A lotta people don't eat for days. I eat. I eat whatever I could get my hands on, I eat. I don't care if it's cookies, cake, donuts. I just eat it.

Unlike George, Osiris tended to forget to eat, and would later gripe about his weight loss:

> Osiris complained that while in Miami he lost a lot of weight. Because of the effects of methamphetamine, he went without sleep and food for about two or three days. (April 23, 2005; field note)

Clearly, drug use and weight maintenance has an antagonistic relationship with the men in the sample and a positive relationship with the women. Ralph explained it best:

> most girls, they go out and they party. They say, "okay, ya know what, I'm not gonna eat for a day and a half so that's gonna be good, 'cause it's gonna help me lose weight . . . " But with guys, it's the exact opposite. We wanna make sure we don't lose weight, and keep on whatever we have. So we have to try to drink the shakes.

Plastic Surgery and Steroid Use

In 2004,[115] 62% of all plastic surgeries in the U.S. were cosmetic procedures.[116] According to the American Society of Plastic Surgeons,[117] the top three cosmetic surgical procedures are liposuction (19%), nose reshaping (18%), and breast augmentation (15%). Breast augmentation was the second largest surgical procedure among female patients, and nose reshaping was ranked fourth. In 2004, 264,041 women had breast implant surgery, which had increased 24% since 2000.

In keeping with this national trend, some of the club kids also had breast implant surgery, nose jobs and lip augmentations to enhance their physique. For example, during an observation in a hotel room, a few of the club kids were sitting around the table awaiting room service. They were discussing a variety of topics. I was wondering about their perception of the prevalence of breast implants in the clubbing and drug-using scene:

> I sat down on the counter in the Castle Hotel penthouse. I asked Ralph, "what percentage of females in the club scene have fake breasts?" He said it is very prevalent, "about 50%." The guy sitting next to Ralph at the table said, "no, not that many." Ralph retracted his statement and said, "fine; 33%." (March 6, 2004; field note)

On Creda's first trip to Miami after her breast implant surgery she exclaimed:

> Tomorrow I want to go to the beach first and then spend the afternoon at the pool. This is my tits' first time in Miami and I want to expose them. (March 5, 2004; field note)

While many women physically augment their appearance through breast implants, men use illicit anabolic steroids to enhance their appearance. Since physical strength and muscularity are signifiers of masculinity, steroid use is common among male club kids to enhance feelings of self-confidence.[118] George describes how his use of steroids is partly influenced by the clubbing scene:[119]

> okay, yeah I will say it [the scene] had an influence because you see so many people with nice bodies and shit, ya know? You wanna constantly get bigger.

Beautification Techniques

A large majority of the club kids' appearance enhancements are less permanent and occur immediately prior to the clubbing events, such as weekly grooming practices and tanning. Betty Cool's account describes this:

> If I'm goin' out that night, I'm gonna get my nails done. If I'm wearin' open toe shoes, I'm gonna get my feet done . . . If I go tanning let's say, I know that I'm gonna go out and I'm gonna sweat and my face is gonna get flushed 'cause I have that light skin, so I'll tan that day for that night, but I'll cover my face, ya know, in particular for that night.

Like Betty Cool, many men also groom prior to clubbing, as the following excerpt from a field note indicates:

> While at the Planet, a guy commented, "you know you have to get all ready for the weekend. I got my nails and hands manicured and eyebrows waxed." (May 29, 2004; field note)

To further contextualize the process in which men engage to prepare for their night out, a field note excerpt from George, Mike, and Ralph's hotel room in Miami sheds light:

> The guys were in the process of getting ready. Mike was removing hair off a male friend's back with a buzzer. Ralph explained that he only buzzes his body hair. Most of his friends shave their entire bodies including their backs, chests, arms, legs, and private areas. (March 5, 2004; field note)

Summary

For the most part, the club kids' cultural style is highly commercialized. The club kids' adhere to the consumeristic ideals of the American capitalist society, placing high value on designer clothing and commodified images of male or female physiques. The club kids are not a resistant group, who are reacting and separating themselves from the dominant class. Rather, the club kids and club cultural style embrace the consumeristic ethos of the dominant class. Moreover, the club kids perceive conventional successful adulthood as a key life goal (Table 1.2). Five of the participants are in the medical sciences, and other participants work in the business field. The majority of the club kids are in positions of relative economic power, well connected both socially and financially, making them members of the mainstream/dominant culture that Hebdige describes.

Subcultures of Taste

Within a culture and within a subculture, a variety of subcultures exist, some based on a common ideology opposing the dominant culture, and others structured around occupation or a common interest. Gottdiener[120] appropriately states: "people belong to many subcultures, many lifestyles, because their social roles are increasingly complex." The opportunities to interact with groups define the subculture's boundaries.[121] Individual common interests, leisure activities and work, as Bourdieu[122] and Fine and Kleinman[123] explain, are shaped by prior interests. While the club kids possess a common consumeristic and commercialized style, how each club kid chooses to use that style varies, and it does not represent a cohesive club kid ideology in opposition to the dominant group. For the most part, the club kids are a heterogeneous group with taste differences in drugs and music. They prefer to listen to electronic music, go clubbing and use drugs (each has used the drug known as ecstasy at least once), but within those categories their preferences differ. Thornton,[124] a sociologist who studied clubbers in the U.K., also found it difficult to locate a "typical, average, ordinary, majority or mainstream" group of clubbers. Any attempt to demarcate groups within the scene always led to a negative case. In other words, at least one individual did not fit within the group, and even between the groups their preferences tended to overlap.

The differences in the defining characteristics of the club kids' culture further demonstrate the limits of Hebdige's subculture theory in accounting for this youth culture. Rather, these data suggest that the club kids are best understood as a group comprised of multiple subcultures – as Fine and Kleinman,[125] Fischer,[126] and Sullivan[127] would explain – based on taste.[128] Each subculture has specific music, drug and club preferences. These preferences, according to sociologist Bourdieu,[129] are based on the individual members' "habitus," which has been shaped by socioeconomic status, age, gender, social position and location. These habiti shape nightlife as well. Since the club kids include individuals with a variety of interests, the scene encompasses very different subsets of youth cultural styles, expressions and meanings.

Bourdieu explains that living under certain social conditions and the aid of particular types of economic, social and cultural capital – such as family upbringing, economic status, and education – produce different experiences, which shape individual opportunities and individual tastes. Throughout the course of an individual's life, that individual develops "internalized categories" of taste, liking some things and disliking others; these tastes feel "natural."[130] Through such experiences, a person develops a habitus, which both encourages and discourages certain practices. The habitus enables an individual to "assert one's position on social space," and opens opportunities of experiences with others who have similar tastes.[131] The habitus is arranged around taste and consumption practices, ultimately constructing a "distinctive set of consumption patterns, a lifestyle ('manifested preferences') that both expresses and serves to reproduce the habitus."[132] Age, gender, class and ethnicity are key features of the habitus. Those within a particular social class form particular tastes in music and style. Factions within and among cultural groups and socioeconomic classes correspond to different lifestyles. Each lifestyle has a market, which shapes that group's consumption practices.[133]

For example, the differences in the club kids' styles, drugs of choice, and music shape shopping locations and practices as well as the clubs they choose to attend. Some club kids, like Jack, prefer to listen to Euro House music. George prefers New York House, and others, like Ralph, enjoy Tribal music. Some club kids dress in tight-fitting clothing, while others wear their clothes in a baggy fashion. A description of club kid SickKid's outfit from a field note and a quote from club kid George illustrate this:

> At club Wax, SickKid was wearing baggy pants, timberlands, a long sleeve t-shirt, a grandpa hat, and between 6 and 9 fake gold and silver chains. (April 25, 2004; field note)

> George: I tend to wear tighter jeans. Well, tight jeans . . . like a snug fit jean. I don't wear baggy jeans . . . For the most part, tigh-tighter clothes that fit me tighter, ya know.

Occasionally the club kids vary their style, shifting from casual and form-fitting to work-out/gym attire. For example, a woman observed at club Danceteria the previous week was wearing a contrasting style at club NRG:

One of the girls I recall wearing sweatpants and a sports bra at Danceteria, was now wearing jeans and a dressy tank-top. (May 15, 2004; field note)

As the club kids' music and clothing style preferences differ, their drugs of choice vary as well. While all club kids are polydrug users and have used ecstasy at least once, each club kid had a particular drug preference, which is unrelated to their style and musical tastes. In many cases, individual drug preferences are different from their friends' drug of choice. For example, some club kids prefer to consume GHB, ketamine or crystal methamphetamine, while others intend to avoid the effects of those substances. Jack and Michelle explain:

> Jack: . . . I can't imagine doing GHB and K, like to me that's just not – it doesn't sound like a good time to go dancing. Because it's such a depressing–
>
> Michelle: Yeah. K, only if I did little bumps with ecstasy. Otherwise, it's like, "what's the point?"
>
> Jack: To me, that's like being really, really drunk. I mean it's slightly different, but it's in the same family.
>
> Michelle: Yeah, it's hard to move.
>
> Jack: Like I just don't understand how people enjoy that, like to go partying with –
>
> Michelle: It's also hard. It's a fine line of just doing K, a fine line of being really okay and then being in a stupor . . .

Similarly, Angelina does not understand how people use crystal methamphetamine while in a club:

> You see like, when I'm doing a drug, I'm not gonna put a drug in my body – that's why I don't understand crystal. Like I do like it but . . . I don't wanna be in a club and be that alert. I don't wanna be alert and see what's goin' on. I wanna be distorted and weird.

In contrast, some, like Betty Cool, desire the stimulant effects of crystal methamphetamine. She explains:

> I like crystal because it uh, makes me hyper, and I like to be hyper. I like to be like, hyper and happy, and running around. I'm like, not one to really – usually stand in one spot. Like I'll separate from everybody, and run around by myself and ya know, do my own thing, talk to people and stuff like that. So I like that 'cause it gives me that, that kick. It makes me hyper.

Among these subcultures of taste within club culture, the club kids separate themselves from those club kids they dislike. As Fischer explains, the greater variety and size of a subculture provoke an intensity of commitment to that subculture, in which members reaffirm their identity and seek separation from others. Malbon[134] describes this in relation to clubbers:

> The clubbers distinguish themselves from others through their tastes in clothing, music, dancing techniques, clubbing genre and so on. These tastes are trained and refined, and constantly monitored not only in order to distinguish oneself from another, but also in identifying with those that share one's distinctive styles and preferences.

Each friendship group among the club kids has designated areas, which they consider "a space of [their] own . . . which is more or less colonized throughout the night," and each night they attend that venue.[135] These spaces are meeting areas and comfort zones, which provide immediate security in case someone were to get lost. If a club kid arrives late, it is very easy to find friends, as they are in the same spot each week.[136] Often, when the club kids leave their colonized area, they tend to feel uncomfortable. A field note excerpt from the club Plant II describes this segregation:

> Osiris also brought me to the area of the club that Asian clubbers tended to occupy. In this section I heard oriental languages spoken, and all appeared to be of Asian decent. Being in the far left corner, this group was very separated and segregated from the rest of the clubbers. Osiris indicated people call it the "Asian Invasion." (April 3, 2004; field note)

This is expected in a strong climate of individualism, where individuals are suspicious of and mistrust others. Individuals are stigmatized based on style, look and demeanor,[137] and the club kids upheld strong notions of inclusion and exclusion. Quotes from Jack and George exemplify this tendency:

> Jack: Ya see, my group of friends and like the heads that we would meet at clubs, we would consider them the white trash of like the New York club scene that do GHB and crystal meth and listen to garbage salsa house or whatever. We're snobs . . .

> George: I mean things are so diverse now . . . 'Cause it's more about attitude than anything else, ya know whatta mean? I hate goin' into a club and seein' little fuckin' tacky little kids around . . . But I guess maybe it's just people who don't look like they belong, ya know whatta mean? Like people just look like they don't fit in there . . .

The club kids define themselves as those whom they are not. Specifically, the club kids state that they are not crack users, they are not excessive methamphetamine users, and they are not posers. The dance venues are a meeting place for like-minded individuals – such as the club kids – and it is common to see the same people at each DJ's spinning night.

The separation among, and between, youth cultures occurs prior to club entry. The urban economy is marked by social and spatial inequality, and segmentation of consumer markets.[138] Nightlife, in general, is segregated, as the social inequalities and divisions that exist around class, gender, ethnicity and sexual orientation persist in nightlife.[139] Within dance venues, such as NRG and Birdland, club owners use club design to separate different kinds of people. They offer VIP areas for those willing to spend the added financial costs, and on one night, they provide different music genres in separate areas of the club (see Chapter 4).

The night the club kid chooses to go to a club, the club to which the club kid chooses to a ar attend, and the music scheduled at the club that night, determine the type of clubbing group of which that club kid is a member. The club kids engage in a self-identification process when deciding which venue to attend. They choose to attend spaces where the club patrons will be similar in taste to them and likely to be on the same coolness level.[140] The club kid waiting outside a venue to enter has "already decided that they are 'right' for that club and think that they could belong."[141] Essentially, the door becomes "a test of identity."[142] Still, the clubs are often mixed, attracting individuals with different sexual preferences and from a variety of cultures.

In addition to physical segregation to "structure, envelop, protect, and foster its subculture," each subcultural lifestyle creates a "social subsystem."[143] For example, in club culture, each subculture has an Internet community, magazine and peer social network through which they transmit music, DJ, and style preferences.[144] (This finding is further discussed in Chapter 4) The use of social institutions or "social units"[145] to diffuse the subculture causes variations within club culture. Fine and Kleinman[146] explain that a subculture communicates its knowledge and behaviors within interlocking groups of a social network. That social network is never totally bound or infinite; it is interactional.[147]

In the 21st century, globalization and communication technologies have expanded diffusion boundaries and intensified the transmission process of knowledge and behavior.[148] As Hunt, Evans, Wu, and Reyes[149] explain, increasing globalization and diffusion, especially through print and electronic media, have allowed different elements of club culture to reach a variety of cities. Those places create a subculture of club culture with distinctive localizing characteristics.[150] As subculture members travel to visit DJs in particular cities, or merely migrate from one place to the next, the subculture relocates. This causes overlapping memberships, intergroup contact and transmission, adaptation and alteration of the subcultural elements. Essentially, a greater variety within the club culture scene develops. Holt[151] states that, "with interactional groups multiplying and in constant flux, it becomes exceedingly difficult to develop stable consensus goods that represent the group." A variety of taste cultures exist in the scene as Angelina describes:

> Angelina: I don't know, I just, you know what people? . . . Within the scene, there's different scenes.
>
> Lucille: Right.
>
> Angelina: 'Cause the scene for me is drugs.
>
> Lucille: It's going out.

While club cultures, and subcultures more generally, are spreading across the world, access to the subculture is not equal. Rather, subcultures tend to be illustrative of class boundaries. As Bourdieu explains, the structure of the field (network relations within individual lives) influences the practices available to the individual. Certain characteristics of the individual, such as his or her capital and habitus, affect the available leisure choices, while also structuring taste. Specifically, involvement in the club scene is mediated by both social position and social location. For example, the club kids are more able than other young people to engage in the clubbing lifestyle. Many young people during the transition period from college to family experience an increase in disposable income with a corresponding decrease in financial commitments. The club kids have both the time and finances to spend in a commodified, commercialized, consumed, and costly leisure lifestyle;[152] they have relatively equal access to the same cultural and material resources.[153] Those involved in the club scene, for the most part, are in some ways socially positioned in a similar manner. Most of those club kids of the lower socio-economic classes, such as George and Isaac, tend to first work in the scene as dancers or drug dealers prior to becoming a club kid.

IMPLICATIONS FOR SUBCULTURE THEORY

Subculture theory first arose in the 1930s and 1940s when Sellin,[154] Merton[155] and Shaw and McKay[156] set out to explain crime differences among particular groups within particular places. Since then, subculture theory has experienced many alterations on its developmental path, and has been the subject of criticism.[157] However, Hebdige's premise that a subculture's morals, values, norms, beliefs and customs are antithetical to the dominant culture in which it emerged, has received the widest application and acceptance. A review of the subculture literature indicates that 8 of 14 subculture theories agree with Hebdige (see Table 2.1). Consequently, throughout the 1980s researchers of subcultures applied Hebdige's subculture theory while overlooking Fischer's, Sullivan's and Fine and Kleinman's premises. Moreover, the postmodern literature dissecting subcultural theory has, for the most part, ignored the definition of a subculture. Instead, it has focused its attention on questioning Hebdige's principles, while lending support to Bourdieu's theory of distinction. However, as briefly explained above, Bourdieu seemed to further clarify Fine and Kleinman's explanation of the process of transmitting culture, while maintaining Fischer's and Sullivan's premise that subcultures can encompass a group of individuals who have a common interest, such as clubbing, without being antithetical to dominant class values.

Some of the U.K. club culture literature[158] has been equally to blame for the excessive attention given to discrediting Hebdige. These researchers have argued the inadequacy of Hebdige's theory and the failure of the Birmingham School to explain the variations within club culture. In so doing, they have failed to recognize that, as Fischer explained and Tittle's[159] research has empirically supported, within a particular culture, variations will exist. Thus, club culture is a subculture, and the groups within the subculture of club culture, are also subcultures. Fine and Kleinman[160] add that "subcultures are conceived as emanating from group cultures."

While Hebdige has significantly narrowed the definition of the subculture, ultimately creating its demise, his work is of vital importance. Hebdige, along with other subculture theorists from that period,[161] appropriately drew researchers' attention to the social structure in which those subcultures develop, thereby allowing a better understanding of how subcultures emerge.[162] Hebdige's subculture principles provide researchers with three useful tools to dissect youth subcultural groups. First, Hebdige[163] explains that subcultures are not independent of "the larger social, political and economic contexts." Therefore, researchers must understand the macro-level factors from which these groups emerge. Second, it is important to understand the roles that style, music preference and drug of choice play as markers of group identity. Finally, Hebdige[164] stressed the importance

Table 2.1: Subculture Theory Comparison

Theory	Not Middle/ Dominant Class	Alienated	Reject Dom. Values	Values Against Norm	Values Related to Structure	Own Ideology	Non-Utilitarian	Impulsivity/ Short Term Goals	Aggressive/ Toughness	Drugs	Excitement Hedonistic	Risk-taking
Anderson (1994)	1	1	1	1	1	1	0	1	1	1	1	1
Cloward & Ohlin (1960)	1	1	1	1	1	1	1	1	1	1	1	1
Cohen (1955)	1	1	1	1	1	1	1	1	1	1	1	1
Fine & Kleinman (1979)	0	0	0	0	1	0	0	0	0	0	0	0
Fischer (1975)	0	0	0	0	0	0	0	0	0	0	0	0
Hebdige (1979/2002)	1	1	1	1	1	1	0	0	0	1	0	0
Kornhauser (1978)	0	0	0	0	0	0	0	0	0	0	0	0

Table 2.1: (continued)

Theory	Not Middle/ Dominant Class	Alienated	Reject Dom. Values	Values Against Norm	Values Related to Structure	Own Ideology	Non- Utilitarian	Impulsivity/ Short Term Goals	Aggressive/ Toughness	Drugs	Excitement Hedonistic	Risk- taking
Matza & Sykes (1961)	0	0	0	0	0	0	0	1	1	1	1	1
Merton (1938)	1	0	0	1	1	0	0	0	1	1	0	0
Miller (1958)	1	1	1	1	0	1	1	1	1	1	1	1
Sellin (1938)	0	0	1	0	1	1	1	0	0	1	0	1
Shaw & McKay (1942)	1	0	1	1	1	1	1	1	1	1	0	0
Sullivan (1989)	0	0	0	0	1	1	0	0	0	0	0	0
Wolfgang & Ferracuti (1982)	1	1	1	1	1	1	1	1	1	1	1	1
	8	6	8	8	10	9	6	7	8	10	6	7

of understanding the subcultures, their clothing styles, and music preferences within "the contexts in which they are produced and worn." Using these principles, the next chapter explains the emergence of the club kids and the clubbing experience.

NOTES

1. Some of the material in this chapter has previously appeared in Perrone, 2006.
2. Cohen, 1972/2002.
3. Davis and Munoz, 1970.
4. Burr, 1984.
5. 1979/2002.
6. Brake, 1980; Cohen, 1972/2002.
7. e.g., Malbon, 1999; Redhead, 1997; Thornton, 1996.
8. Fischer, 1975; Fine and Kleinman, 1979; Sullivan, 1989.
9. Bourdieu, 1984; see also Muggleton, 2000.
10. 1984.
11. 1938.
12. 1938.
13. 1942.
14. Kornhauser, 1978.
15. 1975.
16. Fischer, 1975, p. 1321.
17. Fischer, 1975, p. 1322.
18. e.g., Sullivan, 1989.
19. Anderson, 1994; Hebdige 1979/2002; Wolfgang and Ferracuti, 1982.
20. Brake, 1980; Cohen, 1972/2002.
21. Hebdige, 1979/2002.
22. Ibid.
23. Brake, 1980; Cohen, 1972/2002; Hebdige, 1979/2002.
24. Chatterton and Hollands, 2003.
25. 2004, p. 175.
26. 1963.
27. Becker, 1963.
28. 1963.
29. Becker, 1963, p. 100.
30. 1975.
31. Finestone, 1964.
32. Cohen, 1972/2002; Hebdige, 1979/2002.
33. Brake, 1980; Davis and Munoz, 1970; Douglas, 1973.
34. Burr, 1984.
35. Gaines, 1990.

36. Finestone, 1964.
37. Finestone, 1964, p. 286.
38. Finestone, 1964, p.282.
39. Ibid.
40. Finestone, 1964, p. 283.
41. 1964, p. 293.
42. Cohen, 1972/2002; Hebdige, 1979/2002.
43. 1972/2002.
44. Cohen, 1972/2002, p. 150.
45. Hebdige, 1979/2002, p. 52; see also Cohen, 1972/2002.
46. Ibid.
47. Cohen, 1972/2002, p. 160.
48. Cohen, 1972/2002, p. 159.
49. Davis and Munoz, 1970.
50. Brake, 1980.
51. Ibid.
52. Davis and Munoz, 1970.
53. Brake, 1980, p. 96.
54. Brake, 1980, p. 97.
55. Douglas, 1973, p. 166.
56. Burr, 1984, p. 933.
57. Ibid.
58. Burr, 1984, p. 932.
59. 1984, p. 935.
60. Burr, 1984, p. 936.
61. 1990.
62. Gaines, 1990, p. 101.
63. Gaines, 1990, p. 103.
64. Gaines, 1990, p. 188.
65. Gaines, 1990, p. 196.
66. Gaines, 1990, p. 154.
67. Gaines, 1990, p. 203.
68. Gaines, 1990, p. 96.
69. Ibid.
70. Since criminological theories tend to focus on lower class deviance neglecting that social structure is a significant factor in the creation of subcultural values, those theories were only reviewed for historical context. As a whole, they were not applicable to the study.
71. Thomas, 2003, p. 23.
72. 2003, p. 199.
73. e.g., Baudrillard, 1995; Veblen, 1899/1994.

74. Redhead, 1997.
75. 1994.
76. 1960.
77. 1955.
78. 1958.
79. 1942.
80. 1982.
81. Parker, Aldridge, and Measham, 1998, p. 27.
82. Murphy, 2000, p. 636; see also Fiske, 2004; Gottdiener, 2000b.
83. Murphy, 2000, p. 637; Davis, 1995; Fiske, 2004; Gottdiener, 2000b.
84. 2003, p. 223.
85. 2000b, p. 16.
86. Twitchell, 1999, p. 16; Appadurai, 1996; Harvey, 1990.
87. Featherstone, 1982; Gimlin, 2000; Langman, 2003.
88. Baudrillard, 1989; Harvey 1990.
89. Featherstone, 1982, p. 18.
90. Goffman, 1959.
91. 1995, p. 176; emphasis in original.
92. Appadurai, 1996; Conrad and Jacobson, 2003; Davis, 1995; Langman, 2003.
93. Thomas, 2003, p. 52.
94. Thomas, 2003, p. 55.
95. 2005, p. 270.
96. Hunt and Evans, 2003, p. 798.
97. Rietveld, 1993; Redhead, 1997.
98. Fiske, 2004, p. 7; see also Gottdiener, 2000b; Harvey, 1990.
99. Hayward, 2004, p. 182; see also Baudrillard, 1989; Gottdiener, 2000b; Harvey, 1990.
100. Appadurai, 1996; Castells, 2000, 2004; Harvey, 1990; Hayward, 2004.
101. cf., Malbon, 1999.
102. 2003.
103. Appadurai, 1996; Fiske, 2004; Langman, 2003.
104. Conrad and Jacobson, 2003, p. 223; see also Bourdieu, 1984.
105. Conrad and Jacobson, 2003; see also Davis, 1995.
106. Slotar, 2007.
107. Holmes, 2007.
108. Biewend, 2005.
109. Deery, 2004; see also Conrad and Jacobson, 2003.
110. Deery, 2004.
111. Crank, Dugdill, Peiser, and Guppy, 1999; Hammersley et al., 2002; Henderson, 1993; Joe-Laidler, 2005; Measham et al., 2001.
112. see Crank et al., 1999; Measham et al., 2001.

113. see also Hargreaves and Tiggemann, 2003.
114. Since this observation occurred while in South Beach Miami, these participants thought it appropriate to use the popular South Beach Diet (Agatston, 2003) name to describe their drug-induced diet.
115. This study was conducted between 2004 and 2005.
116. American Society of Plastic Surgeons, 2005.
117. 2005.
118. see also Drummond, 2005; Monaghan, 2003.
119. see also Drummond, 2005; Wright, Grogan, and Hunter, 2001.
120. 2000b, p. 24.
121. Fine and Kleinman, 1979; Sullivan, 1989.
122. 1984.
123. 1979.
124. 1996, p. 106.
125. 1979.
126. 1975.
127. 1989.
128. Bourdieu, 1984.
129. 1984.
130. Bourdieu, 1984.
131. Bourdieu, 1984, p. 57.
132. Holt, 1998, p. 4.
133. Bourdieu, 1984; Gottdiener, 2000b; Ritzer and Ovadia, 2000.
134. 1999, p. 55.
135. Malbon, 1999, p. 96.
136. see also Malbon, 1999. Spaces of their own were essential to the data collection process. It was always easy to find previously interviewed club kids, or those whom I have previously met.
137. Greer, 2004.
138. Chatterton and Hollands, 2003.
139. Chatterton and Hollands, 2003.
140. see also Malbon, 1999.
141. Malbon, 1999, p. 68.
142. Ibid.
143. Fischer, 1975, p. 1326.
144. Kornhauser (1978) overlooks this reality.
145. See Kornhauser, 1978, p. 130.
146. 1979.
147. Castells, 2000, 2004; Sullivan, 1989.
148. Appadurai, 1996; Castells, 2000; 2004; and Harvey, 1990.
149. 2005.
150. This effect of globalization was also evident in the localization of McDonald's in Israel (Ram, 2004).

151. 1998, p. 3.
152. Chatterton and Hollands, 2003; Measham et al., 2001.
153. MacRae, 2004.
154. 1938.
155. 1938.
156. 1942.
157. Kornhauser, 1978.
158. e.g., Redhead, 1997.
159. 1989.
160. 1979, p. 9.
161. Cohen, 1972/2002; Becker, 1973.
162. Kornhauser's (1978) critique overlooks this reality.
163. 1979/2002, p. 76.
164. 1979/2002, p. 130.

3. ESCAPE THROUGH THE CARNIVAL OF CLUBBING[1]

Unlike the subcultures of the past that formed as a reaction to the dominant class, the club kids represent a different form of youth culture that adheres to the values and norms of the dominant class. The club kids emerged in a highly commercialized, globalized and commodified society. The very nature of late capitalism,[2] coupled with the rise of the commercialized U.S. society, increasingly creates the desire to escape and enter a fantastical carnivalesque reality. The club kids frequent clubs with a carnivalesque atmosphere – full of loud music, lighting effects, dance and drugs – as a means of having fun and escaping the unsatisfying daily life such a commercialized and consumed society creates.

Carnival spaces become increasingly necessary within commercialized, consumed and commodified societies. Such societies create daily lives that are empty of deep, fulfilling content. Carnival spaces provide individuals with controlled hedonistic experiences without threatening or attempting to overthrow the society. In fact, such spaces facilitate the growth of com-modified societies since participants can easily escape during carnival to another consumed and commercialized culture,[3] and return to their work or school life once it is over. Thus, carnival, while creating a diversion from everyday life, helps maintain the ideological foundation and the customary operation of that lifestyle. Socoiologist Lauren Langman[4] states: "the move from an industrial society to a consumer society has required the relaxation of restraints in order to allow consumerism to flourish." Through such collective rituals, elite power and, therefore, the status quo are maintained.[5]

The dance club is a carnival space where people can enter a fantasyland that is wholly consumed with sensation. The elements of the clubbing experience – Friday and Saturday nights spent at transgressively themed parties and featuring corresponding performances, pulsating music, color-fully artistic light displays, individualized, androgynous and de-sexualized dancing, and sensory manipulating substances – create a carnivalesque reality that allows the pursuit of a type of pleasure that is perceived to be fulfilling. These inherent components of the carnival of clubbing provide participants with: (1) an escape from normativity and the control of everyday life, (2) gratifying and stimulating experiences, and (3) a sanctioned space for blissful consumption. Maintaining the historical role of carnival, clubbing allows patrons to engage in excess and to transgress from normality, after which they return to daily life once the club closes. Essentially, through clubbing, attendees can act out their frustrations with the conventional world while remaining tied to that world. Clubbing is very much a part of the mass-marketed culture industry. The carnival of clubbing functions "exclusively to normalize hegemonic ideologies and to provide an escapist realm of leisure in which workers psychically renew their capacity for work."[6] By going to clubs, dancing and consuming drugs on the weekends, the club kid is able to escape the stressful work-week and become rejuvenated to start up the new week come Monday.

THE NECESSITY OF CARNIVAL

Capitalism, Consumerism and Carnival

Commercialization and consumption-oriented societies provoke a "less and less bearable" daily life that is rid of "deeper content."[7] Baudrillard[8] explains that in modern globalized, commercialized and consumed societies, culture becomes flat, depthless and hyper-real. Essentially, in modernity, social relations are disembedded – "lifted out" of their "local context of interaction" – across space and time, and spanning far beyond local communities.[9] Social relations and meanings of objects are influenced by both the local and the global. The interaction in the local can easily occur and be defined elsewhere – it is a mass produced reproduction. As a result, social relations lose distinction; they lose their meaning. Best[10] summarizes Baudrillard's argument as follows:

> the commodity form has developed to such an extent as to constitute a new postmodern society where . . . previous distinctions between illusion and reality, signifier and signified, subject and object, collapse, and there is no longer any social or real world of which to speak.

Essentially, experience and culture have become commodities leaving society devoid of social relations and social meaning. Through print and electronic media, such as video games, film, television etc., culture is commodified, as it is "produced and reproduced."[11] Through commodifying culture, an illusion of satisfaction is created; that satisfaction will never be reached. Adorno and Horkheimer[12] state: "the culture industry perpetually cheats its consumers of what it perpetually promises." The culture industry essentially creates a hyper-reality fraught with illusions, impersonality, and depthlessness and an overwhelming drive for instantaneous and excessive stimulation.[13]

In a powerful capitalist system, a constant search for "new exhilarating 'peak' experiences,"[14] and an "insatiable appetite . . . for fresh sensation" exist.[15] Under a late capitalist system, stimulating experiences have been co-opted by the market, thereby amplifying values of capitalism, individualism and materialism. Consumption has become the key means of obtaining life resources and pleasures, and solving life's problems.[16] People consume such products as music, media, fashion, food and drugs for the instantly gratifying pleasures they provide. Through capitalism, the consumer is shown that all his/her needs are capable of fulfillment. Consumers are told that happiness can be achieved by purchasing and consuming a variety of products, including drugs.

Increasingly both goods and services have become commodified, commercialized, and globalized, and consumption has skyrocketed.[17] Twitchell[18] states: "[t]he average American consumes twice as many goods and services as in 1950; in fact, the poorest fifth of the current population buys more than the average fifth did in 1955." Today, an inadequate consumer is a "socially degraded" and "internally exiled" person.[19] The result is that the individual and the consumer are linked to such an extent that an individual's self-concept is determined by what s/he owns.[20]

To thrive under these social conditions, young people have been spending a significant portion of their lives obtaining advanced degrees, hoping to receive greater-than-average salaries so as to compete with their peers and purchase the necessary products for survival. Currently, 67% percent of Americans are entering college after graduating high school.[21] However, as Langman[22] explains: "large numbers of youth complete school, yet their job prospects are dim." Most face fewer opportunities for social mobility, while the standards and costs of living are increasing.[23]

Giddens[24] describes how a changing economy through globalization has left many individuals "fraught with anxieties." Specifically, as globalization has transported manufacturing jobs overseas, the result has been a growing emphasis on the service economy in the U.S., which, as Gottdiener[25] explains, has made consumption practices grow in "importance." Moreover, as occupations have become more flexible, wages have declined and on average a worker's tenure in a particular job is shortening.[26] The intensification of globalization and commodification causes an increase in market instability, unpredictability and complexity.[27] Because both employment prospects and pensions rely on this insecure market, economic security is uncertain, and long-term planning is much more difficult.[28] It is always possible that a company designed to produce, market or sell a particular product will fail, resulting in downsizing or the termination of all employees. As Carnoy[29] states: "downsizing is becoming a regular part of work life." Thus, rampant situations of excessive economic risk characterize daily life, which Giddens[30] argues, "seem in large part outside of our control."

While many young people are seeking to obtain higher degrees, cuts in grants and financial aid, coupled with the rise in tuition fees, have made post-graduation independence difficult to achieve. The means for independence (from both family and state) are less available,[31] forcing many young people to remain living with their parents for longer periods of time. Dependence on family for financial support extends beyond college graduation, as only 50% of 24 and 25-year-olds have "achieved economic autonomy."[32] The experience of the 18 club kids interviewed in this study has been typical. Six still lived at home with a parent and two did not move out of their parent's home until their late 20s (see Table 1.2 in). Throughout their 20s, many of the club kids, with the exception of J. Masters, Michelle and Osiris, continued to rely on their families for financial support (see Chapter 6).

Such conditions have further altered marriage and family commitments. Among the club kids, only one couple was married, and another was engaged. This was much different from 1970, when the average age for marriage was 21 for women, and 23 for men.[33] By 2000, the typical age for marriage had risen by 4 years to 25 for women and 27 for men. Many young adults have been putting off "settling down" until their mid-to-late 20s to early 30s.[34]

Cohort studies document the rising differences between generations. In 1946, 34% of men and 19% of women graduated high school. In 1958, the percentages had increased to 53% of men and 39% of women. While the percentage of men who had graduated high school stayed relatively stable (54%) as of 1970, the proportion of female high school graduates rose to 46%. By 2004, the US Census reports that the percentage of men who had a high school diploma was 78.7%, compared to 80.3% of women.[35]

Similarly, a large gap exists between the ages at which the cohorts had their first child. In the 1946 cohort, 92% of men and 84% of women had had their first child by the time they were 30. In contrast, only 33% of men and slightly more than 50% of women in the 1970 cohort had had their first child by that time.[36] By 2004, the proportion of births to women prior to age 30 had continued to decline[37] (see also Chapter 6). The average age at which a woman first bore a child rose to 25 years in 2004,[38] and about 25% of American and European women between the ages of 18 and 35 "do not intend to have children."[39]

Because changes in spending, market forces and educational attainment partly forced most young people to delay both family responsibilities and economic independence, a greater than traditional time lapse between the stages of adolescence and adulthood developed, thereby forming a new transition period in the life-course termed "emerging adulthood"[40]. These shifts have greatly affected how the younger generations use their time. Childless individuals and those with fewer family responsibilities spend more time in leisure activities and more time obtaining an education.[41] Within this transition, young people are confronting "personal futures that are much more open than in the past," bringing both opportunities and hazards.[42] Individual social roles within the workplace, home and community are left unstable. Self-identity is often unclear and tends to be "created and re-created on a more active basis."[43]

Despite young people's economic constraints and anxieties, they have not escaped the consumeristic ethos. In the U.S., full-time undergraduates enrolled in four-year colleges spend on average, not including college costs, some $21 billion per year.[44] Many continue to engage in conspicuous consumption, both to escape and to address their problems, pushing them further into debt.[45] Students often become trapped in a buying cycle that leads them to spend well beyond their means in an effort to establish their self-worth and acceptance among their peers. Twitchell[46] explains that consumption is based on debt, as the credit card culture has replaced the savings culture.[47] A survey in 2000 indicated that nearly one-third of students had at least four credit cards.[48] The availability of credit cards may be dangerous, as they allow excessive shopping, that may produce debt and anxiety. Hoover[49] states that: "largely because of credit-card use and higher student-loan balances, students are graduating from college with nearly twice as much debt as a decade ago – consumers under 25 are filing for bankruptcy in record numbers (est. 120,000 in 2000)."

This highly consumption-oriented and uncertain lifestyle has created an anxiety filled, unsatisfying and empty daily life, with the need for irresponsible, hedonistic escape. Presdee states that: "under the unbearable rationality of modern life, acts of carnival became a daily need for social survival."[50] Langman[51] explains:

> Capitalism fostered impulse gratification as a marketing tactic that eroded constraints to spend money. Promises of forbidden pleasures have become integral aspects of mass marketing. Consumerism now depends on the production and diffusion of carnivalesque dreamworlds, fantastic realms that promise and often provide more pleasurable moments of bodily gratification than does the constraining rationalized quotidian.

Thus, such societies create the need for ritualized carnivals. Carnivals provide excitement hedonism, and a "controlled sense of decontrol."[52] Thus, society authorizes periods of carnival that allow "controlled violations of the cultural order"[53] to facilitate the sustenance of that order.

Components of Carnival

Carnivals have been used throughout history to allow transgression, celebration of the absurd, excessive consumption, indulgence and release.[54] Carnival first occurred among peasant folk in feudal Europe, providing the peasants with "liminal spaces" for "pleasurable release."[55] Because carnival is sanctioned by society, it provides a time and place to release and escape, without questioning or attempting to alter the status quo. In fact, once carnival concludes, people return to work and everyday life resumes. Carnival allows sanctioned deviance that maintains social moral codes and the standard operation of daily life. Carnival and other forms of relatively controlled deviance offer "a way of overcoming the conventionality and mundanity typically associated with the banal routines and practicalities of everyday 'regular life.' "[56] Examples of carnivals include Mardi Gras,[57] Kalends, the Saturnalia Roman and Ati-atihan[58] Festivals, and the Caribbean[59] and Rio Carnivals.

These social rituals include elaborate themes, dancing, brightly colored and fantastical costumes, and loud music. Another important element of carnival is the blurring boundary between spectator and performer.[60] The patrons not only watch the carnival, they also play a large role in creating and executing the carnivalesque world. As Bakhtin[61] states, "Carnival is not a spectacle seen by the people; they live in it, and everyone participates. . . . "

For example, patrons will dance, dress according to the theme, and interact with the music and lights to facilitate the carnival experience. Essentially, all participants are, "swept up by its music, passion and excitement,"[62] and, most importantly, are able to disregard and abandon the life that exists outside carnival.

Clubbing

As young people experience increasing stress, pressures to achieve success and the anxiety of "keeping up with the Jones's," along with less job security, increasing debt and delayed adult independence, they desire places to release, engage in excess, transgress from normalcy, and, as one club kid, Michelle states, "go nuts" on weekend nights. However, their ties to the conventional world (see Table 1.2) mean that the leisure space they choose cannot turn against "the establishment that regulates school or work"[63] – the conventional world remains intact when the weekend finally ends. Furthermore, as the economy shifts from manufacturing to services, and working time and work schedules diversify – some varying from all night to all day[64] – it is essential for leisure spaces to extend entertainment and operating hours[65] without curtailing worker productivity.[66] Since dance culture is a 24-hour activity that covers all night and, usually, all weekend days, it exists "alongside" social norms as nothing more than a leisure culture.[67] As a result, clubbing is the ideal hedonistic escape activity. Further, the routinization of the clubbing lifestyle – certain DJs perform on certain nights and major parties planned in advance occur on evenings prior to national holidays – makes it easily mapped into the schedules of daily life,[68] and brings certainty to a shifting world.[69] Most clubbers limit clubbing primarily to weekends or other vacations from daily commitments (e.g., work and/or school), such as on holidays, allowing them to become "weekend warriors" who return to their daily lives as employees or students on Mondays.[70]

When the club kids walk through the doors of a dance club, they enter a carnivalesque reality filled with fantasy, fun and freedom "removed from 'normal' time, spaces and social relations of their everyday lives."[71] The club kids seek spaces to escape that work week, release their "pent-up energy" and push against their limits. The weekend and evening become young people's "time and space outside the rigors and rules of the workplace and watchful eye of bosses" or parents and teachers.[72] In these spaces, the club kids release their anxieties of rational, commercialized life,[73] and become "sensation gatherers."[74]

Carnival Inside the Club

Clubs are "play spaces"[75] with an alternative set of orderings based on excess and consumption, and concentrated on fun. Dance clubs legitimize behaviors that would otherwise be considered deviant, and maintain a clear separation from the outside work world. As technology – such as cellular phones, e-mail, and blackberrys – increases employees' availability to seven days a week and 24 hours a day, and employers can thereby demand "*instantaneous action*,"[76] the desire to divide work and leisure time becomes increasingly pressing.[77] Clubs and the pleasures they provide "temporarily obliterate the concerns of life before, beyond and outside the clubbing experience."[78] For example, one club kid, George, forgets about his daily concerns and enters carnival:

> I just enjoy it [clubbing], ya know whatta mean? . . . I always say that the point of drugs and the point of partying is-is you leave all your drama and your bullshit in your daily life at home, ya know? Check that shit at the door, come in and enjoy yourself. That's what I do every time I go out. I don't carry my drama out wit me . . . I'm out here gettin' fucked up, I don't give a fuck what's goin' on, ya know whatta mean? I'll deal with that when I'm sober and I'm back home and it's Monday or Tuesday and I have to deal wit' it.

A quote from Ariel additionally exemplifies this point:

> A lot of people have really stressful jobs who need to blow off steam, and that actually drives a lot of this [clubbing scene], actually the need for this.

Similarly, Lucille explains that her daily routine is stressful and dull, and she uses clubbing and drugs for excitement and relief:

> It's like I go out to relieve the stress of like working all week . . . You know, it's like alright I'm gonna go have fun now because everything else sucks . . . Like I go to work, I eat, and I watch TV for an hour and I go to sleep.

George describes his daily life to be equally as dull as Lucille's:

> The gym is the most I do after work during the week. The gym and come home, cook, cook dinner and also lunch for the next day and go to sleep.

The particular components of clubbing and clubbing spaces create carnival worlds. Clubs are adorned with themed parties, elaborate performances, loud music, eye-catching lights and dancing and drugs, all of which allow an escape into carnival to celebrate indulgence, transgress from normalcy and consume fun. While the club kids (and I, in this chapter) discuss each element of the clubbing experience as separate exclusive parts, they interact to heighten each other and to create a hyper-sensory experience.

Party Themes

The club owners, DJs and party promoters often decide on a theme for upcoming clubbing events. The themes tend to reflect personal interests in the lives of frequent clubbers, allowing them to enter those places where they are most relaxed and have the most fun (i.e., their "happy place"). The club owners, promoters, and DJs are attentive to all aspects of the clubbing environment to ensure that through the club doors, the theme comes to life. For each theme the club is decorated appropriately and staged performances correspond to that theme. The clubbers also take part in the creation of the fantasy, as most dress in costumes reflecting that party's theme. For example, at the Lingerie Party women wear lacey lingerie and men wear pajamas or robes and boxer shorts. Clubs with beach parties line the surrounding floor areas with sand, and the clubbers wear bathing suits. Often, at the control of the DJ and during intense moments of the music, inflated beach balls fall onto the crowd.

Most of the themes for clubbing parties involve transgression of norms. Aspects of androgyny and questioning of the dominance of heterosexuality, are evident in these carnivalesque club spaces. Celebrations of alternative sexual lifestyles and the adornment of nudity, especially of the buttock, are common themes, as my field note excerpt exemplifies:[79]

> The announcer for club Live started to introduce some of the male and female dancers. He was only wearing a half corset, exposing his chest and buttock. His penis was carefully hidden, as one patron explained, "tucked away." The dancers entered the stage shaking their buttocks. After the announcer slapped both his and the dancers' buttocks, the dancers gathered on the top left steps of the stage. All the dancers were dressed in black leather-like, glossy attire, which both accentuated and exposed their butts. When one female dancer entered the stage, she repeatedly shook and slapped her butt to a cheering audience. (August 30, 2004; field note)

The theme-decorated club and the orchestrated performances intersect with the clubbers' activities to further enhance the carnival experience. An excerpt from my field note on the Sadomasochist party at club Heart describes this interrelationship:

> Most clubbers were appropriately dressed for tonight's party theme: S and M. They were wearing black leather, faux leather or plastic pants, shorts, shirts or bras. Many women were wearing fishnets, while men were topless. For example, one man with dark eye make-up wearing black fitted-leather-like pants and a collar around his neck was handcuffed to two women. Both women were wearing leather-like boy shorts, fishnets, boots and a leather-like bra. They were pulling and leading each other through the club. Most passer-bys were heading to the crowded dance floor to view the performance upon the stage. Three women dressed in skirts and corsets, which exposed their breasts with pasties covering their nipples, were performing, what is best described as, human corset tying. One woman was acting as the dominatrix inserting thick needle-like metal hooks down each side of the spines of the other two women. The dominatrix slid a string through each of the hooks creating the shape of a corset-tie, and placed a bow at the bottom. (April 23, 2005; field note)

The party theme, staged show and costumed clubbers interact to allow the club kids to enter an alternative reality celebrating the offensive and deviant. The fantasy worlds created by the club owners, the party promoters, the dancers, and ultimately the patrons mesmerize and excite the club kids. In many instances, it becomes difficult to distinguish between the real and the illusion.[80] For example, club kid Monica describes how one club is transformed into a winter wonderland when it snows on the crowd:

> When the club Plant II had the snow coming down, that was really cool. It's just like . . . the whole thing; the lights, the dancers, the, the shows . . . It comes together all one big picture that makes it more exciting.

The changing themes allow novel stimulation where each night out the club kids enter an event filled with – to quote Isaac – "adventure."

The Music

As the club kids seek spaces to escape from their work reality, venues attempt to maintain a separation from the outside work world. For the club kids, the music, electronica – a particular genre of music, which has evolved over the past 30 years – is the most essential element. The music provides the club kids with a new experience of exploration focused on "creating a pleasurable moment rather than telling a story."[81] The music tends to be wordless, lacking a clear message, but importantly providing a complete bodily experience.[82] The high speeds of electronic music intensify experiences, evoke emotional responses and prevent verbal interaction.[83] Once the club kids enter the club, the music takes control.

Table 3.1: Music and Beats per Minute (BPM)

Genre	Origin	BPM	Period of Highest Popularity	Associated with Dance Club Culture?
Acid House	Chicago	120-130	1980s–1990s	yes
Breakbeat	Hip-Hop	135-170	late 80s–1990s	yes
Drum & Bass	UK	160-180	1990s	yes
Gabber	Netherlands	220	1990s	yes
Happy Hardcore	Netherlands	160-180	1990s	yes
Hardcore Techno	UK & New York	200+	1994–1997	yes
Hip-Hop	New York	80-110	1980s–today	no
House	Chicago & Detroit	110-140	1990s–today	yes
Jungle	UK	160	early 90s	yes
Pop	US	80-110	always	no
Techno	Detroit	120-140	1980s–1990s	yes
Trance	New York	130-160	1980s–today	yes
Tribal	Unknown	120-130	1990s–today	yes

Source: Data compiled by the author.

Club culture is associated with a variety of styles of electronic music, some more popular at particular times than others (see Table 3.1). Club kid Ralph lists some of these styles of music within the club scene:

I mean, there's techno, there's tech house, there's trance, there's euro-trance, there's goa trance.

During the 1980s in the U.K. and in the 1990s in the U.S., club culture was largely associated with Acid House music, which consists of "a simple, repetitive melodic structure and some samples."[84] Techno from Detroit and Garage and Trance from New York City, which usually have no lyrics, are other styles of music associated with club culture.[85] Techno music functions at 120-140 beats per minute (bpm),[86] and "vocal pieces are used as pieces of sound rather than meaningful phrases."[87] For comparison, hip-hop and pop music functions between 80 and 110 bpm. Hardcore techno, happy hardcore or gabber occasionally exceed 200 bpm and "rarely possesses anything discernible in the way of melody or rhythmic variation."[88] House music, on the other hand, comprises methodic beats and singing.[89] House music "retains disco's emphasis on rhythmic repetition, and the centrality of the bass-line, while decentering more 'conventional' melodic, vocal or song elements."[90] This is evident when New York House music DJs spin popular 1970s hits such as Donna Summer's "I Feel Love"[91] during their sets. While these are some of the common elements of House music, a variety of styles of House music exist. Club kid Jack explains his preference:

> We like Eurohouse. There's very few New York House DJs that I really like. Italian Stallion is the best one I think. He's like considered one of the best house DJs all over the world.

In contrast to Techno and House music, which are beat focused, Drum and Bass, Jungle and Tribal music are bass focused. Jungle is best described as a collision of breakbeat techno and Jamaican reggae. It has "twice the speed of reggae," with "multiple-fissured breakbeats" and an "intense sub-bass."[92] Club kid Ralph attempts to describe Tribal music:

> More drum driven, no words, just fuckin' like, think like, think African tribal drums, like dum, dddum, ddddum.

This constant pulse of the bass, as Thornton[93] explains, "blocks thoughts, affects emotions and enters the body." The precision and monotony of the rhythm of electronic music, especially when played at a high volume – which is often done at these venues – is hypnotizing.

Music plays a significant part of the experience. It effectively separates the patrons from their work world, and allows them to enter carnival. For most club kids, as with other clubbers, "music comes before all other aspects of the night."[94] Club kid George explains:

> The music's gonna be the like . . . the underlying definition to me whether I'm havin' a good night or a bad night. If the music sucks there's just no energy in the club, ya know whatta mean?

The music evokes memories of the lost past and unifies the dance floor. The DJ has to demonstrate his/her skill through reading and reacting to the crowd on the dance floor. Excitement is especially expressed on the dance floor when the DJ spins particular songs. Successful songs tend to canonize "as end of the night anthems,"[95] which the clubbers greet ecstatically. Club kid George provides an example:

> That song, "Going through It"[96] . . . was like the New York City anthem and everyone loved that song.

Music, as sound, has the benefit of being felt throughout the body, in many cases propelling the clubbers to move. In particular, the bass, the slowest vibrating sound wave, delivers a corporeal experience. The sound shifts between both the inner and outer self, resonating throughout the body. Unlike vision, sound "is the only major medium of communication that actively vibrates inside the body."[97] Three field note excerpts capture this:

> At club Waves, the bass was so strong, the floor was shaking. I could feel the energy in the room, as the bass got stronger and repetitive. (May 2, 2004; field note)

> When we walked passed the speakers at the hotel pool party at the Hacienda, we could actually feel the bass. It felt like strong gusts of wind. (March 7, 2004; field note)

> As the music got faster, and the bass got deeper, more of the crowd danced. I was then influenced to dance as I moved with the crowd. (March 7, 2004; field note)

Many responded to the music, and practically conducted the music. Their arms and hands shifted to the beats and the tunes, slowly moving upwards, awaiting the "kick-off" to the loud thumps and faster bpms, when the arm would drop to the ground with the music.[98] The club kids timed their moves "precisely so that they fit in with the musical rhythms":[99]

> Tyler: It's the fuckin', it's the meltdown comin' into the build-up, goin' for the drop. And I turn around and this kid, he's got his fist all the way up in the air, and he's just tryin' to time the fuckin' drop of the bass line when it's gonna go "dooooooszdddddooosz." So he could just pile drive the fuckin' floor.

> David: That's when the beats slows down, and there's usually no beats, there's no kick drum.

> Tyler: Percussion's gone.

> David: And you basically sort of slowly, continuously, smoothly, more soul music, which is sort of landscape of melodies and sounds; more like synthesizers and uh, uh, it can be acoustic style, dude. It could even be a guitar.

> Tyler: Yeah there's a bunch of–

> David: And everything slows down, and then suddenly it starts building up again, and you start getting kind of a beat and . . . it's just like, "doosz doosz doosz" ya know? It just starts building up and then drops, and that's a drop – the drop is when it finally the beat goes back to "duum, duum."

> Tyler: And everyone goes nuts and just starts jumping into walls.

While most dancers seek to time their moves to the rhythm of the music, the high bpms of the club kids' musical genre makes this a special and arguably, a difficult, endeavor.

"What authenticates contemporary dance cultures is not so much a unique DJ performance, as the buzz, vibe, mood or atmosphere created in the interaction of DJ and crowd."[100] The DJs absorb the excitement generated from the dance floor, and channel "it back by choosing tracks to intensify or alter the mood."[101] The audience and the DJ engage in conversations eventually developing a relationship. Reighley[102] indicates the importance of the DJ's connection with the patrons, "Developing a rapport with the audience is essential for a successful gig." An excerpt from a field note describes the strong relationship of a DJ and his devoted clubbers:

> Again, we walked through the crowded dance floor of club Wax to the smoking area. On our walk, Italian Stallion (I. S.) got on the microphone and began to discuss what would happen to him once this placed closed. He said that the people here are his "family," and despite what the rumors say, he would and could never leave New York City. This is his home. He continued that he's very upset, and emotional about this place closing down, as it was home to him. He had a few venues lined up, although there will be a 24-hour party starting at 6pm Sunday. He told the crowd that next Friday he will be spinning at Heart. The crowd screamed we love you "I. S." (April 25, 2004; field note)

In essence, both the DJ and the patrons "share the spotlight."[103] The club kids participate in both the production and the consumption of the night. A dancing crowd is the best indication of a good night. One DJ explained: "Somebody who's conscientious of what's going on with the dance floor make a great DJ."[104] Since music is an essential element of clubbing and entering carnival, the club kids feel uncomfortable when the music stops, as that indicates playtime is over.

> George: If music is not on, everyone's like, "yo, somebody throw on the fuckin' music," ya know whatta mean? It's always needed, but, it's a necessity. But it-it's not always on, ya know whatta mean? Usually you think no music, "the party's over. No party," ya know whatta mean?

The Lights

Lighting further acts to "both sensuously disorientate and physically insulate the clubbers."[105] Light productions create "an illusion . . . of being in an-other place at another time, of momentarily inhabiting a dream-world, of being beyond or outside "normal" time and space."[106] When it is dark and crowded, eye contact is problematic, and it is easy to withdraw from reality and escape daily life. The darkness in the club is broken with streams and flashes of colorful lights, which disorient the clubbers' perceptions of those around them and alter their own appearances. Like music, once the production lights are off, and the bright fluorescent lights overhead are turned on, they "indicate that 'time' is back, that the experience is effectively over, [and] that this space only exists within the wider city waiting beyond the door."[107] My field note from the club the Plant II highlights this:

> The music stopped and the lights went on. At first I thought something was wrong with the sound, but the lights were remaining brightly lit. The DJ announced on the microphone that the police were closing down the party. Mike explained that when the music is off and the lights are turned on, these are indicators to quickly rush to the coat check and exit before these areas get "crazy." (March 14, 2004; field note)

Throughout a clubbing event, the club kids often complain when daylight shines into the dark club, thereby disrupting their transgression. For example, at club Tavern:

> J. pointed to the open doors on both sides of the club allowing the sunlight inside the dark club. He thought the bouncers should keep the doors closed to keep reality out. Some clubbers close to the doors screamed "close the doors!" (September 5, 2004; field note)

In various instances during the clubbing night, light guys (the technical name for those employed to control the light effects) flick on the bright white lights, giving the DJ the opportunity to see the faces of the crowd. This also gives the crowd the opportunity to see the real faces of those with whom they have been dancing or talking. As Malbon[108] explains, this light guy tactic often reveals "the usually less than beautiful bodies." One field note from Birdland describes my reaction to the bright lights:

> The lights turned on real bright, where I could see everyone's true face. I did not realize how darkness and flashing lights can mask the faces nearby. The believed to be clear skinned man actually had very large pimples on his face, which the darkness hid. (May 22, 2004; field note)

The lights ultimately provide the visual effects to the bodily experience. Light guys often program the lights to shine and move in accordance with the beat of the music. At club Danceteria:

> The light guy, Isaac, had certain buttons on the light console which had pre-programmed light sequences moving in synchronization with

the beat of the music. Isaac explained that because most of the tracks
have the same bpms, this is an easy task. (October 25, 2004; field note)

The lights can alter the clubbers' moods and perceptions. As club kid
George describes it:

Whenever you really start seeing things like between the strobe lights
and all the lights and all the people around you-when you start
seeing weird shit ... and ... really start like tweakin' out [crystal
methamphetamine high], ya know?

The light guy develops a relationship with the patrons and the DJ,
much like the DJ develops a relationship with the clubbers. The light guy
is required to pay attention to the dance floor and to the stage. For example,
a field note describes how Isaac's lights at club Danceteria interact with
the crowd:

When Ibi was mixing, Isaac would turn off all the lights and shine
the lasers, which illuminated to the back wall of the club. Most clubbers jumped to place their hands, arms or bodies through the lasers
deflecting the light. This made Isaac smile, as he liked it when he
made the patrons happy. (October 25, 2004; field note)

Dancing

"Dancing for long periods at a time [is] central to contemporary clubbing,"[109] as the typical categorization of the music signifies Dance. Clubbing
is primarily about dancing, as club kid Betty Cool explains:

Um, it's just, ya know, now with, going out now, not as often as I do
working all week long and then going out on the weekend is kinda
like a release of stress ... I see myself in the middle of the dance
floor dancing with a smile from ear to ear, just happy and free, and
that's it ... If it's a good night, ya know, I was on the dance floor
like, ninety percent of the night, ya know?

The club scene is less centered on one-on-one dancing and more focused
on dancing alone or within a crowd. Dance styles allow the club kids
to escape their sexuality and gender, and to experience the lights and
the music.

The club kids' dance appear as a "celebration of sexual equality,"[110] as
men dance in groups with other men, and women dance alone. For this
reason, some women, such as club kid Michelle, find clubbing particularly attractive:

It's not like a major pick-up scene ..., you can dance without fear
of some guy grinding up beside you.

Dance is pleasurably experienced without "the expression of sexuality [as] its primary aim."[111] Certain styles of dance like "gyrating hips" and bodily contact are frowned upon:

> A guy got in the center of the circle at club NRG. The two of them started "battling." The goal seemed to be to not touch one other. Their bodies were leaning back and forth, while the legs were moving in the dance sequence. When a new guy entered the circle to battle her, it did not look like he knew the norms of the dance. She tried giving him cues, but his hands often grazed her body. Appearing annoyed, she stepped out of the circle. (May 15, 2004; field note)

The dance techniques to electronic music are also ungendered, as both males and females have similar dance styles. For the most part, aside from styles of dress, gender cannot be discerned by viewing dancing club kids. SickKid explains how most people at the clubs dance similarly:

> To be honest right now, almost everybody, they dance the same. Like when I used to go to the [club] Plant, all got the same style and all that shit.

A field note from club NRG attempts to describe the common dance move:

> Males and females on the dance floor seemed to have a similar dance move: left leg forward, right leg crosses in the front, left leg crosses behind right leg and moves back. The body shifts forward and back as well. It is then repeated. (May 15, 2004; field note)

For the most part, the clubbers' movements are asexualized, fluid and robotic:

> At club NRG, one girl danced in the circle. Her moves seemed choreographed and practiced, or perhaps frequently repeated. She often swung her arms, pounding the air to the bass of the music. She interlocked her hands and moved her arms in unison to the beat of the music. When the beat slowed, she repeated the motion starting over her head moving down to the floor. Throughout this arm sequence, her legs were kicking out towards the side. She appeared to move like a robot, but with more fluidity. (May 2, 2004; field note)

Through dancing, the club kids engage in a predominantly individual experience, orchestrated by the clubbing atmosphere of the lights, music and decorations. Malbon[112] explains that clubbers are "picked up by the music and commanded . . . in their dancing, unable to stop, not wanting to stop, unable to even conceive of stopping." Club kid MaryJane, for example, lost her toenails when she danced for "maybe 10 hours":

I danced my ass off. I was so fucked up. That-that was the night I lost my toenails. Because my toe nails were long and they grow up and I was wearing sneakers that were too small for me, but I was so fucked up that I guess I didn't realize that they were pulling against the thing from dancing so much . . . We would start dancing, we would go crazy, we would be on the street dancing, blah, bblah, bblah . . . - dance in the showers, it was so much fun.

Drug Use

While many clubbers, such as club kid Paula, enjoy clubbing and its music without the use of drugs, usually drugs are a central part of the clubbing experience.[113] Drugs have been critical to most dance-oriented cultures since the 1960s.[114] As the music, lights, themes and shows are visual and auditory elements of the hedonistic experience in the club, the drugs are the chemical mechanisms of physical pleasure, allowing both the mind and the body to become the ultimate leisure machine.

The 2001 executive director of Dance Safe, a non-profit organization promoting harm reduction policies at electronic music events, Sferios,[115] explains that the use of psychoactive drugs in bars, clubs and parties around the globe is a natural behavior, especially "among novelty-seeking youth in a consumer culture that promotes instant gratification." Drugs and clubbing serve as both an escape from consumer-oriented society and an extension of that society. The names of songs, artists and records, as well as the samples and vocals within the music, often allude to drug use.[116] For example, a common track heard in clubs is DJ Thick Dick's[117] Tweakin', in which the chorus states: "We be tweakin/ Like every weekend – we be tweakin'." Tweaking is the argot used to describe the pleasurable effects of crystal methamphetamine.

The patrons' use of drugs in these themed spaces enhances the club experience and promotes a fantastical reality. Through the use of drugs, the club kids say they can escape into a happy and pleasurable space. Club kid Betty Cool expresses her experience from taking one-half of an ecstasy pill:

I just remember it from like, just going up my whole–my body, from my toes to my legs, through my ya know, stomach to my chest. I just remember that feeling to this day. It was just like, I don't know, I can't even describe it. It was like a rush of just feeling good, like all of sudden I just felt like, like a relief that I just felt so good. Like I just felt so good, and I just remember dancing my ass off.

As Betty Cool indicates, drug use also facilitates the clubbers' ability to dance. A quote from club kid Tyler describes this:

> When you take the E and you're rollin' [high from ecstasy] hard even if you're like me and you don't like to dance, you can dance up a storm because every fuckin' movement comes completely naturally and without thought and without volition. Ya know, you could just – before you can hear and process the music you're already moving to the music and you're moving with the music when you're high on the E.

Club kids, like Osiris, Angelina, Lucille, MaryJane, Ariel and Tyler, further explain that drugs enhance the music, and the music and the setting cannot be separated from the drugs' properties:

> While at Club Wax Osiris complained that he was sober . . . 'without G (GHB), you can't feel the music, and with G you can feel the music, and the music is incredible. You just feel incredible. It's a feeling you never want to go away.' (April 25, 2004; field note)

> Osiris: When you're on G, you don't just hear the music; you feel it. It enhances all your senses and dulls your inhibitions, which makes the club experience much more enjoyable. Shit, I can't imagine going clubbing without it.

Similarly, Angelina describes the relationship between the drugs and the music:

> Yeah but you know what I feel like music and drugs go hand and hand because when I was in junior high school and I smoked all that pot [marijuana], I would have to listen to hip-hop. It was like hip-hop and smoking [marijuana] all the time. And then you would go into the city and it was like ecstasy, K [ketamine], and house music. You know . . . it's like peanut butter and jelly . . . Why are you going to listen to music if you're not mangled [high on drugs]?

Club kids, like Tyler, explain the use of drugs allows them to connect to the music:

> you are connected in ways that you were never connected when you were sober, with the music, with your friends that are standing around you, with everything. It feels like the entire fuckin' universe is moving to that one goddamn rhythm from the song.

Essentially, through the interaction of the elements of carnival – the themes, the music, the lights, dancing and the drugs – the carnival experience is heightened. As club kid Ralph describes it:

well, with K in the club-it's like, the K fucks you up because of the lights and everything like that. That's what has the most effect when you're on K, 'cause the lights and the music and everything, you feel like, you're like literally in your own like . . . video game. Everything's just fuckin' fucked up. Everything's just weird and abnormal.

CONCLUSION

Clubbing is a carnival space where themed-style spaces, music, lights, drug use and dance allow clubbers to escape from their work week and to experience carnival every weekend. Clubs are hedonistic environments allowing an escape from the stressful life that commercialized and consumed societies create. Through clubbing, the club kids can fulfill the need for weekend sensation, and return to their less satisfying daily life once the party ends. Rojek[118] explains the appeal:

> Out of the bleak noir settings of the cosmopolis created by industrialization emerged an urge to travel away from the confined existence of the rat race into a more gorgeous, anomalous world in which cultural simulations defied geographical space and historical time evaporated. Artificiality and supersimulation are key attributes of this expanded world . . . [And] [t]hese attractions obviously give pleasure.

Dance clubs offer "complete sensory experiences – ones often intensified by the use of alcohol and/or drugs."[119] The club themes, the shows performed, the music, the lights and the drugs legitimize participants' behavior that would otherwise be considered outside of the norm. By entering a club, the patron could act deviant by, for example, becoming a powerful, uninhibited, drug-using dominatrix.[120] Here, the club kids can become apart of something much larger and more reliable than daily life. The clubbing elements pinch each of the sensory mechanisms of the body, allowing a festive and fantastical getaway:

> Monica: When you go to a club it's a way to not think about anything. Ya know, lights start flashin', music's loud, you can't think about anything, but having a good time. So, it's a way to unwind from your week at work, or whatever stresses, or not even necessarily to make up for a bad week, to celebrate a good week, or celebrate a birthday . . . just a way for everybody to get together.

As Giddens[121] argues and Castells[122] demonstrates, "[m]uch that goes on in the world is outside anyone's control," so temporary and instantaneous nourishments of pleasure are necessary.[123] Thus, contrary to Hebdige's[124] notions of resistance, clubbing is not a reaction to dominant group norms, but an escape from daily responsibilities, identities, and insecurities. Club kid Tyler explains:

> This [clubbing] was one of things when the good doctor [friend] first introduced me to it that was, it was wholly consuming. It was so new and so fresh and so invigorating and so powerful that uh it was consuming. Ya know, between the whole new genre or several genres of music, sounds and things that I've never known, experienced, or even known were possible . . .

The carnival of clubbing is an indication of the desire for something "wholly consuming" in a depthless world.

NOTES

1. Some of the material in this chapter also appears in Perrone, 2006, and Perrone, in press.
2. Late capitalism is the period when the society's economy is more service-oriented than production-oriented, and the economy is structured around "flexible accumulation" (Harvey, 1990).
3. (see Kates and Belk 2001; Kozinets 2002). Carnival spaces outside of the U.S. are also becoming commercialized and commodified (e.g., Green, 2007; Zavitz and Allaher, 2002).
4. 2003, p. 244.
5. Gramsci, 1992.
6. Seiler, 2000, p. 203; see Adorno and Horkheimer, 2000.
7. Presdee 2000, p. 62; see also Baudrillard, 1995; Malbon, 1999; Thornton, 1996.
8. 1995; see also Giddens, 1990.
9. Giddens, 1990, p 21; Appadurai, 1996; Castells, 2000, 2004; Harvey, 1990.
10. 1989, p. 24.
11. Gottdiener, 2000b, p. 19.
12. 2000, p. 130.
13. see Castells, 2000; 2004.
14. Chatterton and Hollands, 2003, p. 83.
15. Gilbert and Pearson, 1999, p. 32; Baudrillard, 1998; Hayward, 2004.
16. Fiske, 2004; Gottdiener, 2000b.
17. Appadurai, 1996; Castells, 2000, 2004; Harvey, 1990; Measham et al., 2001; Ter Bogt et al., 2002.
18. 1999, p. 16.
19. Bauman, 1998, p. 38; Chatterton and Hollands, 2003; Viser, 1994.
20. Hayward, 2004; Murphy, 2000; Veblen, 1899/1994; Viser, 1994.
21. Bureau of Labor Statistics, 2006.
22. 2003, p. 238.

23. Langman, 2003; see also Castells, 2000, 2004.
24. 2003, p. 19.
25. 2000c, p. 282.
26. Castells, 2000, 2004; Harvey, 1990.
27. Appadurai, 1996; Castells, 2000; 2004; Harvey, 1990.
28. Castells, 2000, 2004; Harvey, 1990.
29. 2000, p. 48.
30. 1990, p. 3; see also Castells, 2000, 2004.
31. Redhead, 1997.
32. Parker et al., 1998, p. 24.
33. Arnett, 2005.
34. Castells, 2004; Measham et al., 2001; Parker et al., 1998.
35. U.S. Census Bureau, 2005.
36. Bynner, 2005.
37. Martin, Hamilton, Sutton, Ventura, Menacker, Kirmeyer, Munson, 2007.
38. Martin, Hamilton, Sutton, Ventura, Menacker, Kirmeyer, 2006.
39. Giddens, 2003, p. 58.
40. Arnett, 2005.
41. Gauthier and Furstenberg, 2005.
42. Giddens, 2003, p. 28; see also Harvey, 1990.
43. Giddens, 2003, p. 47; see also Harvey, 1990; Hayward, 2004.
44. Chatteron and Hollands, 2003; Student Monitor, 2008.
45. Appadurai, 1996; Hoover, 2001; Manning, 2000.
46. 1999.
47. see also Appadurai, 1996; Bauman, 1997; Draut and Silva, 2004; Manning, 2000.
48. Hoover, 2001.
49. 2001, p. A35.
50. 2000, p. 33.
51. 2003, p. 244-245.
52. Hayward, 2004, p. 191; Measham, 2004.
53. Langman, 2003, p. 224; see also Measham, 2004.
54. Bakhtin, 1968; Langman, 2003; Presdee, 2000; Redman, 2003; e.g., Alcedo, 2007.
55. Langman, 2003, p. 226.
56. Hayward, 2004, p. 149; see also Rea, 1998.
57. e.g., Gotham, 2002; Redman, 2003.
58. Alcedo, 2007.
59. e.g., Green, 2007; Hill, 1985; Ho, 2000; van Koningsbruggen, 1997.
60. Fiske, 2004; Langman, 2003.
61. 1968, p. 7.
62. Langman, 2003, p. 228.
63. Ter Bogt et al., 2002, p. 175.
64. see Castells, 2000, 2004.

65. This is similar to the historical legislation of the nighttime drinking economy (Chatterton and Hollands, 2003).
66. Chatterton and Hollands, 2003; Hayward, 2004.
67. Ter Bogt et al., 2002.
68. Fiske, 2004.
69. Giddens (1990) explains that "the predictability of the (apparently) minor routines of day-to-day life is deeply involved with a sense of psychological security" (p. 98). It provides familiarity, comfort, security and ease.
70. Allaste and Lagerspetz, 2002; Chatterton and Hollands, 2003.
71. Malbon, 1999, p. 83; Langman, 2003.
72. Chatterton and Hollands, 2003, p. 114; see also Appadurai, 1996; Langman, 2003.
73. Presdee, 2000.
74. Bauman, 1997; Chatterton and Hollands, 2003.
75. Malbon, 1999; Measham, 2004.
76. Hayward, 2004, p. 54; emphasis in original.
77. Castells, 2000, 2004; Harvey, 1990.
78. Malbon, 1999, p. 102.
79. Modernity is fraught with intersections of intimate and impersonal themes (Giddens, 1990).
80. see Baudrillard, 1995.
81. Gilbert and Pearson, 1999, p. 167.
82. Fiske, 2004.
83. Malbon, 1999.
84. Ter Bogt et al., 2002, p. 159; Hammersley et al., 2002; Lyttle and Montagne, 1992; Measham et al., 2001; Redhead, 1993a; Thornton, 1996.
85. Reighley, 2000; Ter Bogt et al., 2002.
86. Gilbert and Pearson, 1999.
87. Gilbert and Pearson, 1999, p. 38.
88. Gilbert and Pearson, 1999, p. 95; Ter Bogt et al., 2002.
89. Measham et al., 2001.
90. Gilbert and Pearson, 1999, p. 73.
91. Summer, Moroder, Bellotte, 1977.
92. Gilbert and Pearson, 1999, p. 79.
93. 1996, p. 60.
94. Malbon, 1999, p. 80; see also MacRae, 2004.
95. Gilbert and Pearson, 1999, p. 74.
96. Peters, 2002.
97. Gilbert and Pearson, 1999, p. 86-87.
98. see Malbon, 1999, p. 93.
99. Malbon, 1999, p. 94.
100. Thornton, 1996, p. 65.
101. Reighley, 2000, p. 24; Presdee, 2000.

102. 2000, p. 147; see also Thornton, 1996.
103. Thornton, 1996, p. 29.
104. Reighley, 2000, p. 127.
105. Malbon, 1999, p. 97.
106. Ibid.
107. 1999, p. 102.
108. 1999, p. 102.
109. Thomas, 2003, p. 193.
110. Thomas, 2003, p. 183.
111. Gilbert and Pearson, 1999, p. 67.
112. Malbon, 1999, p. 105.
113. Gilbert and Pearson, 1999; Hunt and Evans, 2003.
114. Thomas, 2003.
115. 2001, p. 10.
116. see also Gilbert and Pearson, 1999.
117. 2004.
118. 2000, p. 67.
119. Thornton, 1996, p. 57; see also Melechi, 1993.
120. This is very similar to the use of the masks at carnivals (e.g., Rea, 1998), or the alternative identities expressed in both carnivals and festivals (e.g., Alcedo, 2007).
121. 1990.
122. 2000.
123. Giddens, 1990, p. 135.
124. 1979/2002.

4. THE COMMODIFICATION, COMMERCIALIZATION AND GLOBALIZATION OF CLUB CULTURE[1]

Many club kids sought to escape a commercialized and consumed society by entering carnival. Paradoxically, the milieu in which they engaged was as commodified and commercialized as the everyday life from which they were escaping. Within the social and economic settings in which club culture emerged, clubs quickly became spaces of consumption. In these clubbing spaces adorned with décor organized around a particular theme, clubbers consumed ambiance, drinks, drugs, music, and ultimately, the clubbing space. Themed environments equipped with decorations and shows created, "a spatial experience that was an attraction by itself, that is, they promote the consumption of space."[2] Dance clubs had become "cathedrals of consumption,"[3] and their components, including the clubbers, had become commodities.

In a late capitalist, commodified and commercialized society, all resources are commodities that are assessed by their use and exchange values[4] (see Chapter 3). Harvey [5] states:

> Entrepreneurialism now characterizes not only business action but realms of life as diverse as urban governance, the growth of the informal sector production, labour market organization, research and development, and it has even reached into the nether corners of academic literary and artistic life.

Culture and cultural forms are commodified and are under the control of the market. In other words, the type of culture produced is based on supply and demand. In most cases, commercial enterprises turn emerging cultures into commodities. Major entertainment corporations seek and attempt to market new trends and fashions globally.[6]

Promoters, dance venue owners and the club kids play large parts in the commercialization, commodification and globalization (CCG) of dance club culture. Together they market and expand the reaches of clubbing, and turn dance venues into commercial nightlife consumption spaces providing pleasure, overindulgence, hedonism, stylization and exclusivity. Rather than escaping the capitalist and consumed life, the club kids enter a culture that is hyper-commodified and ultimately, supportive of late capitalism. Consequently, the club kids find their cultural objects – music and style – in mainstream media, pay extremely high prices for their leisure activity, and seek exclusivity and demarcation from the homogenizing elements of CCG. Moreover, the club kids perpetuate the establishment, which they seek to escape, embrace the commercial, consumed, and hyper-real culture, and become commodities within the clubbing industry.

COMMERCIALIZING CLUBBING

Most novel music-based cultures, such as hip-hop, disco, and punk, begin as an underground, youth culture outside of the mainstream and, hence, desirable. In a highly capitalist system, however, these desired cultures eventually become consumable. While these cultures originally emerge outside of commercial influences, in a late capitalist system cultural materials are reproduced and marketed for commercial gain "in the vision of western interests and consumer tastes."[7] For example, in reference to rap music, Hayward[8] states that, "it has become very difficult to tell whether 'gangster rap' imagery and styling is shaping street gang culture in the US or vice versa." Likewise, dance club culture, which was a largely underground phenomenon, has come under the control of various entertainment companies who market the clubbing lifestyle, including its fashion and music, to global audiences. The ephemeral clubbing fashions interact with the clubbers' desires for distinctiveness, creating a circular pattern that promotes and continues the commodification and commercialization of clubbing styles and expands the market to new, interested consumers.

The current electronic music club culture is rooted primarily in hidden, unlicensed (illegal) and secretive parties known as raves.[9] Raves were popular in the U.K. during the late 1980s and in the U.S. in the early 1990s. Raves' characteristics – underground, low cost ($5-entry fee), and a non-branded clothing style – are evidence of their non-commercialized origins. In fact, research indicates that the rave culture emerged as a reaction to the "Designer Decade" of the 1980s.[10] Ravers (individuals who attend raves) sought to separate themselves from mainstream materialism through creating an underground recreational activity that both opposes and escapes the "co-opting media."[11]

The Rave scene, however, could not avoid commercialization when electronic dance music events eventually moved into legal and licensed venues open to the general public in the 1990s.[12] At that time, the music and leisure industries commercially exploited dance culture by organizing – with the police, professional security, and legitimate promoters – dance parties in large, fashionably-designed nightclubs.[13] As a consequence, clubbing, much like other leisure activities, became a part of the mainstream and globalized market. Clothing designers and their advertisements (i.e., billboards) began to portray the dance club style as a novel and fashionable social norm (see Chapter 2),[14] and club music began appearing in advertising jingles, such as commercials for high-end cars.[15] For example, trance music,, which usually functions between 130-160 bpms without lyrics, was used in a commercial for the sports car Audi A3.[16]

To successfully compete in this already saturated market, the clubbing industry adopted marketing strategies, promoted events and obtained sponsorships to broaden its clientele and ensure a profit. Once dance club culture was co-opted by the market, the dance club culture industry – including party promoters, Internet entrepreneurs, club owners, electronics innovators, and fashion designers (see Chapter 2) – and the clubbers, strengthened and expanded the commercialization of the dance club culture.

Club Promoters

Many ravers who later became club goers express their disdain for club and party promoters, as they play a large role in commercializing and commodifying club culture. For example, one survey from Perth, Australia found that 40% of electronic music party attendees felt they "were being exploited by promoters who were not part of the rave community themselves, but had come in to make money out of the events."[17] Promoters unaffiliated with the club scene are also common in New York City. The following field note describes Ice, who wears a large poster-board advertising the club NRG:

> Ice works part-time for a company that promotes the clubs, rather than a particular party at the club. Party-promoters, on the other hand, advertise for a particular party or DJ at a venue. Ice earns about

$15 an hour, and works for about 8 hours. He is not permitted to promote for more than one club since that is considered a conflict of interest. His boss organizes the street promotions (distributing fliers and wearing signs) for a variety of clubs in New York City. In the early-mid 90s, Ice's boss promoted parties, but complained that "it was too much." He quit that business, and currently runs street promotions. He explained that while he does not like the music, "it's really good money," to which Ice agreed. (October 2, 2004; field note)

The task of the promoter is to advertise upcoming clubbing events to a wide audience in hopes of attracting them to the club. In doing so, promoters receive a percentage of their solicited clubbers' entry fees. Club and party promoters advertise particular events through five primary methods: (1) distributing fliers at various club-related locations throughout the night/day, (2) mailing party fliers to frequent attendees' home addresses, (3) e-mailing party information to listservs, (4) text messaging cell phone numbers regarding upcoming events and parties, and (5) advertising on clubbing Internet sites and in magazines. While the effectiveness of such measures is not assessed here, the sheer volume of text messages, e-mails, and fliers is difficult to escape. For example, upon leaving a club, the club kids are "bombarded with over a dozen fliers." One field note provides an example:

> I walked out the exit, where a girl strategically stood distributing passes for upcoming summer beach parties. A crowd of four promoters also stood by the door handing-out fliers for other parties. As I walked down the street, two other guys distributed fliers for additional parties. (May 22, 2004; field note)

Although a large part of the motivation for clubbing is to escape the stressful and depthless commercial and commodified daily life (see Chapter 3), members of the clubbing community also assist in increasing the accessibility of the clubbing industry. These individuals seek to gain a portion of the clubbing industry's profits. In particular, some club kids, such as Mike, created party promotion companies through which they sell advance tickets to parties, and sponsor various clubbing events in New York and Miami. These club kids receive both monetary and social profits, as they and their closest friends receive free entry to parties and special treatment from club owners and DJs. George describes how he receives "free" nights:

> I really don't pay for much when we go out. I made enough friends, enough promoters to get in for free, enough places I know bartenders to get drinks for free, uh-ya know, and-and drugs for free-at least cheap, ya know whatta mean? So, I refuse to really go all out and

spend on everything I wanna do. And if I have to, then most likely I won't do it. I-I refuse to, I don't give a fuck.

Angelina's experience is similar:

It's like, and you know what it's like all those years of like me fucking going to Asia and like doing all that shit, all those years of me paying $20 and waiting on the lines – like now – I know Antwon, I know Mike, I know everybody . . . all those years of going out was like leading up to finally like reaching an area where you could just go out freely and like not be worried about lines or anything . . .

THE GLOBALIZATION OF CLUBBING

The expansion of late capitalism has demanded additional consumer markets to ensure profits and manage competition.[18] Castells[19] explains: "the real challenge for individual firms and for capitalism as a whole . . . [is] to find new markets able to absorb a growing productive capacity of goods and services." Technological advances in communication and travel, and the expansion of globalization policies have facilitated the growth and success of most industries, including the dance club culture industry. Specifically, such innovations and international free-trade agreements have opened the borders around the globe to trade, largely erasing markets' geographical boundaries.[20] This has transformed dance club culture into a global industry with an expansive and diverse consumer market.

Pedersen and Skrondal[21] note that with globalization:

[Y]outh cultural patterns and the accompanying industry are international. Everything diffuses at lightning speed, unhindered by international frontiers, and spreads to larger groups than previously.

Not unlike the introduction of McDonald's franchises around the globe, such as in Israel,[22] or Starbucks and Gap franchises in Turkey, electronic dance clubs have emerged in multiple cities outside of their home regions in the U.S. and Western Europe. For example, research on club drug use in Estonia explains that with the collapse of the Soviet Union and the proliferation of globalization, Estonia became apart of a new world system that has provided a wider scope of media influences in addition to new economic policies.[23] In particular, the commercialization of club drugs and its culture successfully made its way to Estonian media outlets.

The demand for profits compels many club owners to expand their franchises, reach out to additional markets, and cross-merchandise their products. For example, one venue owner has additional dance clubs in

New York, Brazil and Spain. Others have franchises in Miami, New York and London. Increased profits can also be gained through selling a variety of merchandise at dance venues, such as insignia T-shirts, CDs and venue-branded bottled water to clubbers. Such merchandise commemorates events, and provides evidence of the clubbers' attendance.[24] By purchasing and holding on to memorabilia – like photos, balloons and fliers – the club kids can relive the experience. The following field note describes the significance of Osiris' collection of souvenirs:

> While at Birdland for its beach party, a few of the beach balls dropped on the clubbing crowd after the sound of a loud horn. Most volleyed them around the crowd; others let them fall to the floor, while some hid from them. Osiris grabbed one for a souvenir and was trying to deflate it. I helped him. He told me that one party at the Plant club was decorated with penis shaped balloons. When Osiris got a hold of one, he walked around the entire night pointing it at people. He eventually deflated the balloon and still has it at home. Osiris then took a picture of us with the deflated beach ball. Osiris enjoyed taking pictures of his time clubbing. He takes many pictures that he will eventually show his children. When he is old, he wants to show them how he used to party. (June 12, 2004; field note)

Furthermore, many dance clubs' hours of operation are now much longer (closing much later) than in the 1990s, which also helps to increase profits. For example, while most New York City venues close around 4 am, when bartenders can no longer sell alcohol, some dance clubs remain open into the late morning hours. During these morning hours bartenders in the dance clubs continue to serve water, juice, and sports and energy drinks. As George states, "Clubs didn't stay open as long as they do now, ya know?"

The commercialization and commodification of the dance club culture has increased the desire and need to gain profits among the industry's players. Tyler nicely sums up the current effects of CCG on the dance club culture and industry:

> The clubs are concerned now – not with bringing DJs or like lettin' people have a good time – it's all about, ya know, crowdin' in as many people in there as you can. It's like a big, premium cover charge. So it's about money; clubs makin' money . . .

Technology and Music

Communication innovations, new marketing strategies, and technological advances in the creation of music have commodified, globalized and commercialized the electronic music industry. As dance club culture increasingly develops commercially and globally, instrument and equipment manufacturers took advantage of the needs of electronic music DJs by creating virtual analogue synthesizers and sound generators to emulate DJ desired sounds.[25] With the innovation of computers and other digital equipment, DJs are able to create and sell ample amounts of records, air their music on radio stations and appear on pop countdown lists without the backing of major record labels or recording advances.[26] Young people no longer need to rely on "record corporations or music publications for their information."[27] Local and satellite radio stations often air DJs performing live from a dance club, allowing dance culture developments in one country to quickly reach clubbers in others. This has translated into both greater demand of, and higher salaries for, the DJs. J. Masters explains:

> They're [the DJs] more like popular now. I think that the whole business, the whole thing's gotten a whole lot more popular. For instance with DJ Basho, DJ Basho gets like 40-50 thousand dollar a pop now. Ya know, when he was at, what's it called, him and DJ Carl they got like 22 thousand dollars to spin at club Moon and they made the place. I mean, they were club Moon or whatever they may be. And then he made a fortune from there and then he was all over the place. So, it's like they make a lot more money now.

Often on clubbing Internet forums, promoters and DJs advertise when a popular artist is performing on a radio station, or supply an Internet link for newly recorded music. Technological advances in music files – from the creation of records to cassettes, CDs, MP3s, and downloadable music formats – further allow music and culture to spread easily to diverse populations.[28] For example, Osiris routinely downloads music, uses his computer to create new electronic music, and shares CDs with his friends. After a night of clubbing at Birdland, Osiris played a track he created, in which he inputted the following lines from the film *The Matrix*[29]: "what's the reason?" and "the only thing that matters is the feeling" (February 11, 2005; field note).

The Internet

The rise and expansion of the Internet has played a role in increasing the popularity of the dance club culture.[30] Gottdiener[31] explains that, "social interaction today plays out increasingly, not in any material realm staging communion, but in a virtual space through a computer connection to other virtual selves." For example, Ralph remains connected with his clubbing friends throughout the workday,

> 'cause I know with me, like all of us work full-time, so we stay in contact through e-mail . . . you can e-mail somebody ten times in an hour and not have anybody know about it, as opposed to the telephone with everybody in your office sees you on a telephone.

Via e-mail, Internet chat rooms, instant messaging, Internet forums, and web-blogs, individuals can connect with those around the world who have similar interests (see Chapter 2).

Internet forums dedicated to club culture are very common. In the same manner that members of the clubbing community become promoters, the clubbers also create Internet forums focused on clubbing. These forums provide opportunities and links to purchase advance tickets for upcoming events, as well as purchase airline tickets and hotel reservations for the next trip. Most club kids are active members of at least one Internet forum, spending ample amounts of their week discussing a variety of topics and utilizing its services. One club kid, Ralph, explains that when he arrives at work, he immediately logs on to his Internet community and participates in the latest discussion on the forum. On forums, the club kids discuss which venues to attend, clothing styles, DJs, travel suggestions and personal concerns, such as problems at work or requests for relationship advice. For example, in one thread (a discussion or conversation in a series of written posts by commenting individuals), a female posted a photo of herself and asked the fellow clubbers' opinions on receiving cosmetic nose surgery. Another thread discussed the fire department's early closing of a party at a dance club.

Since the Internet allows both the formation and sustenance of intimate relationships outside the boundaries of geographical distances,[32] the clubbing culture continues to expand within these commercialized and commodified realms. Predictably, the relationships created on these forums as well as the threads are also commodified, as each member can accumulate fake dollars for gifts, discounts, and forum purchases. Dollars are accumulated based on member ratings, such as friendliness, and the ability to begin a thread in which many members post comments. Members often attempt to increase their revenue by beginning threads that have a history of successfully soliciting responses from members, such as asking members to post pictures and beginning the roll call for an upcoming music event.

Global Club Drug Market and Localized Use

Commodification and globalized trading and consumption patterns have fostered the growth of illicit drug trade routes and drug markets. Parker et al.[33] explain: "global markets, the ascendancy of consumption and the transportability and transnationalization of youth culture" have transferred the interconnectedness of drugs, music, fashion, dancing and partying across the world. The illicit drug market, in which dance culture plays a part, is also "one of the largest commodity markets in the world."[34] In the U.S., it is estimated that ecstasy is a $9.8 billion wholesale market and $23.38 billion retail market.[35] The use of ecstasy has spread "increasingly to Eastern Europe as well as developing countries, notably to the Americas, Southern Africa, and the Near and Middle East as well as South East Asia."[36] The United Nations Office on Drugs and Crime estimated in 2004 that the annual production of ecstasy is approximately 1.4 billon tablets or 50-200 tons of ecstasy.

The club kids are knowledgeable about the ecstasy market. Many keep track of the supply, paying close attention to those pills arriving from the Netherlands, which are known for higher quality. "The UN reported that, *three-quarters of the countries reported that their imported ecstasy originated in the Netherlands . . . The next most frequently mentioned country of origin was Belgium*" (italics in original).[37] Between 32% and 42% of the world's supply of ecstasy comes from the Netherlands. Betty Cool explains the perception of pure MDMA ecstasy pills from Europe:

> We just bought a couple of pills from a friend of mine, who is a good friend, and got that from somebody who just came back from Europe and brought them back from there. And they're supposed to be, from what this person says, supposed be really like pure. Yeah, supposed to be like really pure MDMA.

Similarly, some countries are known for their poor quality of certain drugs. For example, Tyler explains how he refuses to consume ketamine (K) from Mexico:

> Mexican K is no good. Send it back to Mexico! It was like a D-dimer, instead of the fuckin'– it's the wrong isomer dude. All it did was make me sneeze and snot. I never got fuckin' high.

The international nature of dance club culture facilitates the global club drug market, and the commercialization of dance culture influences

Armani®   Mitsubishi®   Audi®   Chanel®   Nike®   Dolce & Gabbana®.

the marketing and design of ecstasy pills. Most pills have distinct, commercial and culturally identifying names, and are branded with symbols (see photos above).[38] One example is the ecstasy pill Mitsubishi, which has the automobile emblem engraved on each pill.

Labeling the ecstasy pills allows users to be smart drug consumers. They can then, "select a particular variety . . . on the basis of both its chemical composition and its commercial identity."[39] The packaging or emblem of the drug denotes a particular experience.

The Annual Music Event

All elements of the dance club culture industry intersect at its annual electronic music conference. Here, workshops and events are held on such topics as how to become a DJ, how to sign with a record label, how to open a successful dance club, and the effects of new drug and cabaret legislations on the industry. Additionally, the club culture industry competes for consumers; record labels scout upcoming DJs; club owners try to book DJs for upcoming events; promoters seek out DJs and clubs for new contracts; and graphic design companies provide examples and discounts for their work on fliers. Most importantly, DJs from around the world attend the event seeking to obtain awards and compete with other DJs in battles (competitions) to dancing fans. For most clubbers, this is the highlight of the event, as they neither register for the conference nor are aware of the various workshops or panels available. The club kids arrive at the annual event to take advantage of the ability to consume more than a thousand DJs and parties over a one-week period. Clubbing events occur continuously from the conference's commencement through to its completion. The club kids review the various events and tend to map out their clubbing schedule leaving few hours for sleep. For example, at the conference in 2004, Ralph printed out the events for the week. He stated: "It was 80 pages long. I spent the plane ride reading through it and planning the weekend."

THE CLUB KIDS' EXPERIENCE

Club promoters, dance venue owners, technological advances, the Internet, and the proliferation of dance club culture into mainstream media and industry practices have changed two major aspects of the clubbing experience: its cost and the need for VIP areas. Clubbing is a very expensive leisure activity; it no longer costs a mere $5 for entry. Moreover, club kids seek both physical and hierarchical demarcation and exclusivity from other club attendees. Club owners have created VIP areas to both satisfy this need and profit from this desire.

The High Cost of Clubbing

Depending on the location, venue, drug of choice and social capital (the network/who the clubber knows), the cost for a night-out clubbing ranges from $100 to $500. On average, the cost of a 24-hour period of clubbing is $350. In England, the average cost for a complete night-out is approximately £50, or about U.S. $90.[40] In Canada, an evening out dancing and taking club drugs is more costly. The price of admission to a venue could range anywhere from C$10 to $50 (US$8 to $45); while the cost of drugs ranges from C$10 to $40 (= US$8 to $35), depending largely on the types and the amount of drugs sought.[41] Clubbing and consuming drugs on the eastern seaboard of the U.S. exceeds those costs. In New York City, bars, lounges, clubs and music venues bring approximately $10 billion to the city.[42] The cover charge for entry to a venue in New York City, the Hamptons, Jersey Shore or Miami is rarely less than $15 and sometimes as much as $60. Additional money is spent on preparation costs (e.g., clothes, beautification: see Chapter 2), drinks and drugs.

The cost per night for drinks depends on the venue, and the price for drugs varies by drug preference and desired drug amounts. For the most part, drinks in New York City dance venues are between $8 and $15. A field note from club NRG describes a typical scene:

> I walked to the bar and there were many people waiting to purchase drinks. Behind the bar, there were 4 bartenders, and one bar back. There were two female bartenders at my end of the bar, and one male and one other bartender, at the other end. The bartenders were making drinks quickly . . . A common drink purchased was alcohol + Red Bull®. Often times, the customer would ask the bartender to add more Red Bull® to the drink. The average cost of a drink was about $9.50. (May 15, 2004; field note)

In comparing her drug use to her friend Angelina's, Lucille explains, "Like for her [Angelina's] she spends $80 on K. I'll spend $80 on drinks." Ralph often shares his purchase of a quarter-gram of crystal methamphetamine for a price between $50 and $60, which he describes as "good for the whole night; for a good 24 hours." The cost of one pill of ecstasy is about $15, and Osiris spends about $190 for 4 ounces (enough for two nights of clubbing) of what he classifies as "good" GHB.

To cover the total sum of their expected costs, most club kids withdraw cash from their bank accounts prior to entering the club. For example, Betty Cool indicated that she needs at least $200 in cash to cover the costs of her night-out:

> How much money do I usually keep on me? I'd say two hundred, cash.
>
> *Dina: Is that how much you spend in a night?*
>
> Betty Cool: More or less. It depends on how the night's going. I could spend less if I'm lucky. I could spend more if I'm having a great time and just don't care. Ya know, I could run back to the ATM, or I've gotten caught by the ATMs in the clubs that cost me ten bucks just to take money out, yeah. Um, so it could be more or less, but I always take uh, I'd say two hundred, ya know? Between the cost of getting in the club and then drinks and then ninety percent of the time we take cabs into the city, back and forth, so money for that.

Club kids like Betty Cool, who reside in the boroughs of New York City, tend to pay for taxicabs to venues. With the exception of two clubs, all venues are in remote areas far from subway stops and main public transportation hubs. Those who live in either Long Island or New Jersey tend to drive to their destinations, and parking in New York City is an additional expense. The parking lots near dance venues charge, as George states, "like thirty-five dollars for like four hours." To avoid these high costs, most club kids seek alternative parking methods. For example, Osiris tends to arrive at a club 20 minutes early to drive around the surrounding residential blocks in search of a legal street parking spot. In contrast, George prefers to park his car further away from the club in a college student parking lot for a total fee of $25. George usually parks in that lot on a Saturday night, cabs or car pools with friends to the clubs, and removes his car from the parking lot on Sunday afternoon.

Aside from parking fees, for most club kids additional traveling fees include costs to DJ events outside of the New York City area. The globalization of clubbing has made it both a nationwide and an "international leisure pastime."[43] It is not uncommon for the club kids to spend annual holidays clubbing outside of New York City, including summer weekends in the Hamptons, long holiday weekends such as Labor Day and Memorial Day in Las Vegas and Miami, and trips to major European cities such as London and Amsterdam, or to the island of Ibiza in Spain.

Clubbing vacations dig deeper into club kids' pockets as many require efficiency hotel suites equipped with kitchen refrigerators, microwaves, televisions, radios, couches and tables:

> All of the guys began to complain about not having a radio, and
> stated that they would buy one, since "they don't cost more than 50
> bucks." (March 5, 2004; field note)

These appliances in hotel suites are deemed necessary as many spend ample amounts of time beginning and ending drug experiences in their hotel rooms. Refrigerators and microwaves are also essential appliances for storing and altering substances. Large quantities of ketamine are often purchased and transported to vacation spots in liquid form. The club kids place the liquid ketamine in the microwave to convert it into a snort-able powder form:

> Todd was glad the room was equipped with a microwave [for cooking
> k]. Last year they purchased one and left it in the hotel upon returning
> from their trip. (March 6, 2004; field note)

In addition to hotel suites, appliances and flight costs, the club kids purchase large amounts of drugs for their trip. Angelina's account exemplifies this:

> But if you're talking about a vacation, like we were going down for
> like Miami; I would bring like a thousand dollars worth of drugs.

The approximate bill of an entire night of general clubbing is $350. If typical preparation costs are included (see Chapter 2), then the cost of clubbing increases to about $500. When travel costs for one week are added to the check, then the cost could rise to nearly $2,000 per person. The desire for exclusivity while clubbing further escalates this already high cost.

Individualism, Exclusion, and Hierarchy

Mistrust of strangers has penetrated various leisure spaces, including dance venues. Individualism in dance culture stimulates the need for safe, gentrified entertainment. Competition among groups also fosters the need to maintain one's social status and display distinctions from the other group. The commercializing and globalizing of club culture also encourage such leisure spaces to be inscribed with notions of inclusion and exclusion (see

Chapter 2). As CCG of an industry tend to homogenize markets, many consumers, such as the club kids, seek to create an identity separate from others and distinguish themselves from others. The club kids market themselves both inside and outside the club to sell their own and their friends' insider status and to demonstrate their differences from less worthy groups. Through style and VIP areas, the club kids achieve distinction and exclusion.

Style

As discussed in Chapter 2, clubbing style, drug use and music preferences, and peer identity act as elements of distinction. The club kids engage in a variety of body modification techniques and purchase designer clothing to both identify and market themselves as clubbers. Through these techniques, the clubbers become commodities through which both their worth and their social capital in the clubbing scene are determined. By dressing and acting as clubbers, they demonstrate their authenticity and become desirable to the group; reciprocally, that clubbers' group becomes desirable. George explains the undesirable as follows:

> I hate goin' into a club and seein' little fuckin' tacky little kids around. Like, I know I get fucked up, ya know whatta mean, but like, I see people all fucked up walkin' around . . . I guess maybe it's just people who don't look like they belong, ya know whatta mean. Like people just look like they don't fit in there-yeah . . . So it's like, the thing I don't like seein' . . .

Displaying themselves as a commodity does not only occur inside clubs. The club kids' sell themselves and obtain a value on the Internet forums. Ralph states, "people who frequent that website they like . . . just like with anything else, you wanna be known." Posting photos is one means through which the club kids market their bodies and their sexualities. Additionally, forum members, as described above, are evaluated and given a monetary value based on postings and amiability.

VIP Areas

For spatial exclusion, many club kids spend the extra amounts needed to be physically separate from others clubbers in VIP sections. VIP areas are comparable to gated communities, a form of spatial exclusion representing "sanitized and purified communities."[44] The VIP areas allow their members to distinguish themselves from the mass commercialized nightlife market, maintain separation from those below them – which in many venues is literal – and establish distinction.

VIP tables are placed on separate floors, behind closed doors or in a roped-off section of the venue. The cost of VIP tables varies by venue and by the number of people requesting a table. J. Masters explains:

> If you're with four [people], you have to buy one bottle [of alcohol]. A bottle will cost you around $400. Eight people, that's two bottles, and it goes on from there.

> *Dina: Are the mixers, such as juice, included in the price?*

> J. Masters: Yup. Those are free and waters [bottles of water], but not Red Bulls. They really get you with those. I don't know, but it's like $5 a Red Bull.

The high cost of the VIP table comes with benefits. Each group is provided a table, seats and a server separated from non-VIPs. Depending on the table, many VIP areas have clear views of the DJ and the dance floor below. Each person in the VIP section is given a brightly colored bracelet to demarcate him or her from the non-VIPs. Bracelets also provide access to various areas throughout the venue, including private restrooms. The following field note describes the VIP area in the club NRG:

> A rope and a doorway led to the VIP area, which outlined the club, like a catwalk. Booths and tables, and a separate dance floor were on this level. Since the VIP area only outlined the club, the center was open allowing VIPs to observe the occurrences on the main dance floor. Only those wearing yellow bracelets were permitted to enter this level, and a bouncer wearing a white coat stood at the doorway checking clubbers' wrists for colored plastic bracelets indicating access to the area. (May 15, 2004; field note)

VIPs enter the venue without waiting on extensive queue lines, as J. Masters describes:

> If you were with me, you'd walk right in. It's like the line, ya know, it's crazy, the line's like wrapped around the damn street and we walk right up and walk right in. It's nuts. That's a cool thing too. That's why, ya know, I hate, I would never stand in line to go to a club ever in my entire life; never in a million years.

J. Masters considers himself of a higher status than those who wait on a line to enter a venue. Many club kids had similar opinions to J. Masters's as they sought to remain in VIP areas separate from those below them – both figuratively and literally. Lucille and MaryJane explain:

Lucille: When we went, we went downstairs into the main section I think once. We walked through and right back upstairs we couldn't deal.

MaryJane: Uh, uh it was horrible.

Dina: Oh! You were in the VIP section?

Lucille: Yeah.

The club bouncers and managers reinforce these perceptions, as they give VIPs special treatment. For instance, VIPs are rarely, if ever, searched prior to entry through their private entrance.

Dina: They don't search you?

J. Masters: Very seldomly. They searched me at Birdland once or twice. They searched me at Birdland one time, and actually pulled it [drugs] outta my pocket and handed it back to me. Danceteria, they did the same thing. I had a joint in my ear when I walked into Danceteria. The girl grabbed it outta my ear and put it back in. Isn't that funny? That's actually hilarious.

Two additional field notes describe the VIP experience at two separate clubs:

When we reached the entrance of Birdland, Pez was about to call his connection. Luckily, Martin spotted us and quickly shuffled us in through the ropes. We walked right in, entering through the VIP doors avoiding the security and cashier counter. We walked inside and up the stairs. Martin ran to get us bracelets so we would not have a problem moving in and out of the VIP section. We headed up the stairs and sat at the corner table. Martin brought us the bracelets, some Red Bulls and bottled water. A bottle of Grey Goose vodka was already chilling in a bucket on the table. Unaware at first of where in the club we were, I realized I was in the VIP, VIP section. This is the more exclusive area of the club, in which the cost was a little higher than the regular VIP section, but as Shauna stated, it is "worth it." This section has a huge bar in the center and couches bordering the walls with tables. The doors looking outside to the main floor are frosted so you cannot see inside. (October 2, 2004; field note)

We finally arrived at Ritchie's, exited the cab, which Kevin paid for, and noticed the long length of the queue line. The guy working the door recognized Kevin and said that he'd get us in right away with VIP passes and a table. We walked up a separate staircase, one used by the employees, and we entered a fairly empty and completely white room. They gave us a table in the back with a bed. Everyone immediately took off their coats and J. began to order Level vodka, Grey Goose orange vodka, cranberry juice and Red Bulls. (January 7, 2005; field note)

Some club kids, such as Monica, Jack and Osiris, argue that VIP is an inflated status, and on principle, prefer to save their money. Monica explains:

I'm not a big fan of the tables. I'll tell you why. I think it's such a rip off and I really don't understand. And again, have I gotten tables? Yes. I've gotten them at Park, but um, it's just, I don't see how much more important you feel just because you're one foot away from everybody else. Um, you're paying 300 dollars for a 35-dollar bottle of vodka. Ya know, it's not about being cheap. It's just I think it's insane. It's totally insane. It's wrong. I think they're taking advantage of people. I don't know how kids can afford it. And they do. Ya know, I work. I have a job. I get paid well, and I just almost refuse to like pay into it. If there's a group of us that are doing it, yeah okay. But I'd say I've had a VIP table maybe five times in the last seven years.

Accordingly, those who do not pay for VIP status are denied VIP benefits. For example, when Monica is searched at clubs, she sometimes feels violated:

They're [the security] giving you, uh, ya know, cough and turn your head type check, or I'm expecting dinner after they search me, 'cause it's really quite invasive.

Moreover, Jack was twice "kicked-out" of a club for drug possession:

There were two nights I got kicked out of the club for posses-sion . . . like an hour into like rollin' with the first E . . . they just pulled me away, and like just searched me and kicked me out . . .

Non-bracelet wearing club kids are often quickly approached and appre-hended for utilizing VIP services. A field note from the club NRG describes one such event:

David was sitting on a little round cushiony stool in front of the VIP area. A waitress walked over to him and told him he couldn't sit there. He asked, "why?" She replied, "forget it; I'm going to get the bouncer." He commented, "fine." The bouncer approached David and instructed him to leave the club. David asked, "why?" The bouncer replied, "because you are not permitted to sit in the VIP area and the waitress told you that." David replied with a question, "this is VIP?" The bouncer insisted he leave. David was very annoyed. He did not understand why he was getting kicked out of the club when the VIP area was empty. (May 15, 2004; field note)

CONCLUSION

The effects of the mass commercialization of dance club culture and club drugs are twofold. On the one hand, this trend had enabled the subculture to reach a more diverse consumerist market, expanding well beyond North America and Western Europe.[45] On the other hand, clubbing has become another cultural and leisure pastime that is hypercommodified and successfully exploits its consumers.[46]

Hunt and Evans[47] explain that, "globally the dance scene is connected." Club owners have franchises around the globe, clubbers across oceans interact via Internet forums, and electronic music is heard and sold worldwide. While the club kids frequent dance clubs for escape and avoidance, these spaces further promote the capitalistic and consumeristic culture of conspicuous consumption (consume drugs, music, lights, performances, club merchandise). Specifically, club and party promoters, the Internet, instrument and equipment manufacturers, dance venue owners, and the club kids commercialize, commodify and globalize dance club culture.

Dance venues are intensified spaces of consumption selling experiences, merchandise and clubbers. While the club kids seek to escape their consumed lives, through entering carnival, they continue to support commodification and consumerism. Ultimately, the club kids escape into another culture of "consumeristic narcissism"[48] where they produce and market themselves and club culture as desirable and profitable objects, and engage in their consumption.

NOTES

1. Some of the material in this chapter has previously appeared in Perrone, 2006.
2. Gottdiener, 2000c, p. 284.
3. Hayward, 2004; Presdee, 2000.
4. Baudrillard, 1995.
5. 1990, p. 171.
6. Appadurai, 1996; Castells, 2000, 2004; Connell and Gibson, 2004; Harvey, 1990.
7. Connell and Gibson, 2004, p. 344; see also Harvey, 1990.
8. 2004, p. 170; see also Harvey, 1990.
9. Measham et al., 2001; Redhead, 1993b; Silcott, 1999.
10. Rietveld, 1993; Thornton, 1996.
11. Thornton, 1996, p. 6; see also Rietveld, 1993; Weir, 2000.
12. Ter Bogt et al., 2002.
13. Measham et al., 2001.
14. see Hunt and Evans, 2003.
15. Hayward, 2004; Thornton, 1996.
16. Hayward, 2004.
17. Lenton and Davidson, 1999, p. 155.

18. see Appadurai, 1996; Castells, 2000, 2004; Harvey, 1990.
19. 2000, p. 95.
20. Appadurai, 1996; Castells, 2000, 2004; Giddens, 1990; Harvey, 1990.
21. 1999, p. 1705.
22. Ram, 2004.
23. Allaste and Lagerspetz, 2002.
24. see also Gotham, 2002; Seiler, 2000.
25. Gilbert and Pearson, 1999.
26. Chatterton and Hollands, 2003; Gilbert and Pearson, 1999.
27. Hunt and Evans, 2003, p. 782.
28. Connell and Gibson, 2004.
29. Wachowski and Wachowski, 1999.
30. Allaste and Lagerspetz, 2002; Hunt and Evans, 2003; Pedersen and Skrondal, 1999; Salasuo and Seppälä, 2004; Thornton, 1996.
31. 2000b, p. 25; see also Appadurai, 1996; Castells, 2000; Harvey 1990.
32. Castells, 2000, 2004; Harvey, 1990.
33. 1998, p. 31.
34. Fitzgerald, 2002, p. 202.
35. Blickman, 2004.
36. Blickman, 2004, p. 7.
37. Blickman, 2004, p. 6; emphasis in original.
38. see also Fitzgerald, 2002. Photos were taken from Ecstasydata.org, 2008.
39. Fitzgerald, 2002, p. 202.
40. Measham et al., 2001.
41. Weir, 2000.
42. Newman, Caras, and Dubin, 2006.
43. Malbon, 1999, p. 6; Salasuo and Seppälä, 2004.
44. Chatterton and Hollands, 2003.
45. see Allaste and Lagerspetz, 2002; Hunt and Evans, 2003.
46. Gottdiener, 2000a.
47. 2003, p. 780.
48. Castells, 2004.

Part II

DRUG USE AMONG THE CLUB KIDS

INTRODUCTION TO PART II

Part I of this book describes the use of drugs among the club kids, an affluent group of club attendees who consume illegal substances primarily in expensive, carnivalesque, highly consumption-oriented and commodified leisure spaces. Most of the literature on drug use, however, depicts a different picture of drug users, tending to center on drug users from impoverished communities and the harmful consequences these users experience, including bodily harm. While club kids consume large quantities of drugs, many do not experience the harms, physical or social, typically associated with drug use. Although some immediate physical harm occurs in the club scene, club kids do not engage in crime to purchase their drugs. Moreover, they are nonviolent; they avoid the potential damage that drug use can inflict on their careers; and they evade the stigma of a criminal justice record. Given the club kids' links to the conventional culture, these club kids take various steps to avoid jeopardizing those connections. Most importantly, their adherence to the norms of the conventional culture, and their social and economic privileges, enable the club kids to engage in relatively controlled and safe drug use, and to escape the war on drugs.

In the second half of this book, I will show how the club kids keep their jobs and meet family responsibilities, while using large quantities of hard drugs. Furthermore, I will demonstrate how the club kids avoid criminal justice sanctions and limit experiences of serious physical harm. I apply a theoretical framework to describe how factors (drug, set, setting,[1] timing and capital) in the club kids' lives permit safe and controlled drug use. This theoretical framework is based on the prior work of physician Norman Zinberg. Here, I expand that framework and add additional concepts that I have inductively derived from my data. In addition to Zinberg's three concepts, I add capital and timing, which encompass both resources and stages in the life course.

Zinberg developed the concepts of "drug, set and setting" in a book on his study of LSD users. His work transformed the way in which many researchers sought to understand drug using practices.[2] The most critical finding from his study was that many people can use drugs without (1) using daily, (2) becoming "hooked" on drugs, or (3) experiencing harms associated with their use. Essentially, he demonstrated that controlled drug use is possible.

Zinberg explained that users generate, negotiate, and regulate harms throughout the practice of using drugs. With an understanding of the pharmacological properties of the drug, the mindset of the drug users at the time of use, and the settings in which the drug is used, it becomes clear how drug users control their use. The cultural norms of use that drug users create in the settings where they use drugs shape what to use, when to use, and how to use. These norms of use often allow drug users to consume drugs in a controlled manner and avoid the potential physical and social harms that are typically associated with the use of drugs.

While Zinberg's concepts have been critical to the understanding of drug use, my study of the club kids shows that Zinberg missed two key factors: *timing* and *capital.* The drug user's access to, and utilization of, all forms of capital (human, cultural, social, and economic) affect drug access, the setting options for drug use, and the user's mindset. Moreover, the timing of the usage during the user's life shapes the choices of drug, set and setting. Certain transitions that occur during the life-course, such as finding a new job and ending an unhealthy relationship,[3] and the level of capital (i.e., social and economic) that the user possesses[4] mediate Zinberg's drug, set and setting concepts. In particular, the drug's properties, the settings in which the drug is used, the user's mood (set) and resources (capital), and the stage of the user's life-trajectory (timing) shape drug-using practices and influence the relationship between drugs and harm (see Chapter 6). Drug, set, and setting vary at different stages in the user's life as well as in relation to the user's possession of, and access to, capital (see Chapter 6).

In Part II, I describe five theoretical constructs – drug, set, setting, timing, and capital – in detail. I also show how these concepts resonate throughout the data. In Chapter 5, I focus on Zinberg's theory, and demonstrate how the factors Zinberg outlines influence the club kids' drug use. In Chapter 6, I discuss life-course theory[5] and describe how capital (economic, human, social and cultural) affects both an individual's life- course trajectory and an individual's drug-using practices. Specifically, I show how life-course factors and the club kids' capital influence the club kids' set, setting, drug-using practices, and prevention of drug-related harm. Finally, I conclude this section of the book with a discussion of the interactions among these factors, and how those interactions affect the club kids' drug-using trajectories. The club kids' cultural norms (as discussed in Part I), capital, timing in their life-course, choice of drugs, mindsets, and settings of use in combination influence the participants' ability to prevent harm, engage in controlled drug use, and escape the war on drugs.

NOTES

1. Zinberg, 1984.
2. e.g., Jackson-Jacobs, 2004; McElrath and McEvoy, 2005; Shewan and Dalgarno, 2005; Shewan, Dalgarno, and Reith, 2000.
3. e.g., Sampson and Laub, 1993.
4. e.g., Bourdieu, 1986.
5. e.g., Sampson and Laub, 1993.

5. DRUG, SET, AND SETTING AND CONTROLLED DRUG USE[1]

Drug, Set and Setting

Zinberg[2] and Becker[3] explain that although drugs have particular pharmacological effects, these effects are not solely determined by the chemical properties of the drugs. In fact, drug effects differ greatly depending on variations in the characteristics of the individual and in the situational factors within which the drugs are consumed. What a person knows about a drug influences the way he/she uses it, the way he/she interprets its effects, and the way he/she responds to those effects.[4] According to Zinberg, an individual's attitude, personality and mood encompass that individual's "set." In contrast, the "setting" includes the social and environmental places in which the individuals consume the drugs. And the drug's chemical/pharmacological properties are the final component in this framework. Becker and Zinberg indicate that the interactions among these three factors contribute to the use of particular drugs in particular settings and at particular times, which ultimately create the way the user experiences the substances. As the drug users become knowledgeable of (1) the pharmacological properties of the drug, (2) the appropriate mindsets and (3) the suitable settings for drug taking, these users can engage in controlled drug use. Such drug users can take informed steps to monitor, conceal, and prevent harms associated with their drug use. While most of the club kids' techniques of controlled use were successful, at other instances their attempts failed. Importantly, however, these users consciously adopted the methods to control their use and prevent potential harms.

The importance of drug, set and setting in shaping drug-using behaviors is not new. Over the past 40 or so years, drug researchers have demonstrated the importance of such factors among a variety of users, among diverse drugs of choice (e.g., crack, heroin and ecstasy) and in a variety of settings.[5] While Zinberg was the first to operationalize and measure drug, set, and setting as variables for understanding the possibility of controlled drug use, many drug researchers have described the importance of such factors in experiencing, defining, and consuming drugs.[6] In this chapter, the club kids discuss the importance of drug, set and setting in their decisions to use certain drugs, their ability to prevent drug-related harms, and their attempted methods – both successful and unsuccessful –to engage in controlled drug use.

DRUG

The pharmacological factors consist of the chemical properties of the drug and how those chemicals affect the individual's body. Pharmacologists indicate that a drug's effects vary depending on how it is consumed (smoking, ingesting, injecting), the dosage, and the person consuming it.[7] George's description of the varying effects of crystal methamphetamine supports the pharmacologists' point:

> Crystal affects people in a lotta different ways. Ralph, like he enjoys it as much as I do, if not even more. But he definitely suffers the consequences a lot more. Well, maybe because he's doin' longer, he's older, ya know? . . . It's just the way the chemicals react in your body. Everyone's different. I don't get like all paranoid and like quiet, ya know whatta mean? Like, I just enjoy it, ya know whatta mean?

Throughout their involvement in the club scene, the club kids consumed various drugs, with LSD, psilocybin mushrooms, crystal methamphetamine, cocaine, ecstasy, ketamine and GHB being the most commonly used. Compared to five or ten years ago, LSD, shrooms and ecstasy were less popular, LSD and ketamine were more difficult to obtain, and GHB, cocaine and crystal methamphetamine were growing in popularity. George describes this trend:

> Like crystal and G right now are the E and K combo of the late 90s, ya know . . . People still do pills [of ecstasy] ya know whatta mean, but by far crystal and G have overpowered any kind of pills you do, ya know whatta mean?

Such period effects or secular trends in drug use patterns nationally also indicate comparable shifts in drug consumption.[8] These larger trends in the club scene and within the general population affect drug availability and hence, drug using decisions (see Chapter 6). Not only do the drugs change the drug scene, as George's quotes explain, but the scene also changes the drugs. For example, the need to stay out longer, as the clubs remain open for longer periods of time, makes meth a useful drug. Additionally, the move towards a more body conscious subculture makes GHB and meth more appealing, as they can control and reduce body weight (see Chapter 2).

Because these drugs are illegal and their production is not regulated, users tend to ingest substances that are marketed as a particular drug, even though they may in fact contain different substances. Often times these drugs are adulterated with toxic substances other than the purported drug. Although the club kids may actually consume a different substance than the one they thought they purchased, this section provides information on the substances the club kids believe they are consuming, and on how the pharmacological effects of the drugs influence their drug use decisions.

Stimulants: Cocaine and Crystal Methamphetamine

Cocaine

Cocaine is a stimulant most commonly extracted from the Erythroxlon coca plant, which is native to the Andes.[9] Since at least the 6th century, the coca plant has been a facilitator for people working in high altitudes, especially in South and Central America. The coca plant did not reach Europe and the U.S. until the late 1800s, when chemists began to purify the extract, creating cocaine.[10] Today, the leaves of the coca plant are mixed with various solvents and processed to make either cocaine or crack.

Cocaine, a Schedule II drug (see Appendix A), also known as coke and larry, is a white powder that is commonly snorted, but is also applied to the mouth, rectum or genitalia. Other users dissolve cocaine in water in preparation for injection. When applied to the body or snorted, cocaine is absorbed through mucous membranes and blood vessels. Snorting, the most commonly used method among the club kids, is the slowest method of delivering cocaine to the bloodstream since cocaine constricts the blood vessels it enters. The peak effect of cocaine takes about 30 minutes to achieve.

Crack, a form of cocaine that the club kids refused to ever try, is the pure-base of cocaine. Crack is heated and smoked. This method, along with injecting cocaine, is a much more efficient way to deliver cocaine to the bloodstream. Its peak high is generally reached within 1-2 minutes, and the level of cocaine in the blood vessels is much higher than "ever observed" from snorting.[11] In any form, cocaine is removed from the body within the first hour.

In the brain, cocaine/crack increases simultaneously all monoamine neurotransmitters – serotonin, norepinephrine, dopamine and epinephrine (adrenaline) – in the synapse. It also prevents the re-uptake of these neurotransmitters, keeping them in the synapse for extended periods, which affects the sympathetic nervous system.[12] The increased norepinephrine causes blood pressure and heart rate to rise, blood vessels to constrict, and bronchioles to dilate. The user experiences increased alertness, attentiveness, and energy. Most users physically react with excess movements, such as fidgeting and chattiness. Increasing serotonin levels enhance the users' moods and control appetite. While cocaine can benefit those with asthma, problematic use could harm the cardiovascular system, causing irregular heartbeats. Death from cocaine, however, is rare.[13] J. Masters describes his experience on cocaine:

> I like the feeling of doing coke. I mean, I hate to say it, but I really do. I mean it, it gives me like a rush that I'm just like, I'm comfortable with . . . And coke makes me feel like I'm here and you're on top of the world practically. It's like you could do pretty much whatever you want to.

Methamphetamine

Methamphetamine was first synthesized in Japan in 1919, where it was found to be easier to make than its parent drug, amphetamine. In the early 1900s, amphetamines were used primarily to treat asthma symptoms, but were only available in pill form. Methamphetamine is a more effective asthma treatment because it provides two benefits. First, it is soluble in water, and thus can be injected, and second, it is more potent than amphetamine. While methamphetamine is currently available through prescription only, it is a Schedule II substance[14] (see Appendix A). Like cocaine, methamphetamine is a type of stimulant that acts on monoamine neurotransmitters – norepinephrine, epinephrine, serotonin, and dopamine neurotransmitters.[15] When methamphetamine enters the body, it prevents the re-uptake of these neurotransmitters, which regulate various forms of behavior, including mood, purposeful movement, locomotor abilities, appetite, and attention. As a result, the effects of meth include increased locomotor skills, attention, and heart rate, and accelerated breakdown of fat, while simultaneously reducing appetites. The effects could last up to six to eight hours.[16] Methamphetamine is used commonly to treat such disorders as obesity, attention deficit disorder, and narcolepsy. Many club kids, such as Betty Cool, favor the stimulant effects of crystal methamphetamine:

> I like the crystal because it uh, makes me hyper and I like to be hyper. I like to be like hyper and happy, and running around. I'm like not one to really usually stand in one spot, like I'll separate from everybody and run around by myself and ya know, do my own thing, talk to people and stuff like that, so I like that 'cause it gives me that, that kick. It makes me hyper.

Tina, however, does not enjoy the "jittery" effects stimulants often cause:

> Um, like coke and crystal . . . is just wrong, um, maybe if it didn't give you that jittery feeling I'd probably like it . . .

Methamphetamine is commonly known as tina, meth, ice and crystal, as its appearance in powder form resembles small crystals or pieces of ice. Clandestine laboratories in the western part of the U.S. commonly produce methamphetamine for recreational use.[17] Methamphetamine is typically sold for about $60 per gram. George refuses to spend more than $40. He states: "a quarter bag of meth . . . like in clubs, the street value is like sixty bucks, but I won't pay more than forty bucks. I don't give a fuck, I ain't payin' you more than forty dollars for that bag, ya know.' "

Hallucinogens: LSD and Psilocybin Mushrooms

LSD

Sandoz pharmaceutical company originally synthesized Lysergic acid diethylamide (LSD or acid) in 1938. At that time, the Food and Drug Administration (FDA) controlled the drug and allowed it to be marketed solely to physicians.[18] In 1963, LSD was distributed to researchers for experimentation with its effects. Seven years later, in 1970, LSD was deemed to have high abuse potential and was classified as a Schedule I substance (see Appendix A).

LSD's usual doses are between 10-80 micrograms, which is considerably lower than the 100-200 micrograms of the 1960s.[19] LSD is often diluted and dissolved in liquid and absorbed into a piece of paper, in which it is often sold for about $7 per "tab" (one individual dose of paper). Club kid Tyler and his friends have a connection who can supply them with "single tabs of acid for, uh, what now seems like a ridiculous prices; it was like 7 or 10 bucks a hit. . . . "

The LSD experience begins between 30 and 60 minutes after taking the drug. It can last up to 12 hours because the liver degrades LSD slowly, allowing active LSD to remain in the body for hours. LSD acts on the two serotonin receptors in the cerebral cortex of the brain. It blocks one receptor and stimulates the other, creating hallucinations. LSD also indirectly affects glutamate. Glutamate is the main neurotransmitter for sensation, perception and abstract thought. With LSD, users experience an altered state of perception and reality. At the beginning of the LSD "trip," users tend to experience some nausea, followed by numbness, muscle weakness or trembling. Mild increases in blood pressure, heart rate and breathing may also occur. As the trip continues, users often report "frank hallucinations,"[20] such as a confusion of the senses (i.e., he/she sees sounds and hears colors). The trip also consists of a distortion of time and a sense of oneness with the world. Adverse effects of LSD include anxiety and a fear that the trip will not end. Some users report flashbacks some time after the LSD experience. However, many perceive them "as an acceptable side effect of an otherwise positive experience."[21]

Tyler, the surgical resident, describes his experience on LSD:

> Acid was a completely cerebral, ya know, like uh cortical experience. And it was almost like the somatosensory tingling and nastiness that went on with your other senses was kind of ancillary and at times interfered with the actual thoughts that came about. It was almost like you had two competing processes. Like, you could choose to ignore the thoughts and focus on the fact that your skin was bubbling, or, ya know, you felt like you pissed your pants seven times even though they were fuckin' dry. Or you could sit there and wallow in this, ya know, this architecture of fuckin' meanings goin' on bouncing around in your head. You're like . . . , "my skin's crawlin' off." I don't know if I pissed my pants. I've got like a lobster and seven shrimp that are chewing holes in my intestines, and I just connected faith and god with the p-orbital of protium atom, and this is the, ya know, a fundamental and profound experience for me.

In contrast to other drugs the club kids consume, LSD, psilocybin mushrooms, and ketamine (only when taken in very large doses), cause intense hallucinations.

Psilocybin Mushrooms

Shrooms, to which they are commonly referred, are dried mushrooms from the Psilocybe (the bulk), Panaeolus, and Conocybe family. Throughout South and Central America, psychedelic mushrooms have been used since at least 100 A.D. in healing and religious ceremonies. Numerous mushroom statues can be seen throughout that region, some dating back to 500 B.C., which are reported to be used in worship.[22]

Shrooms contain psilocin (4-hydroxy-N,N-dimethyltryptamine) and psilocybin (4-phosphoryloxy-N,N-dimethyltryptamine).[23] Once the liver removes the phosphate compound, the active ingredient, psilocybin, enters the brain. In its typical dose, 4-10 milligrams of psilocybin or 2-4 mushrooms, the user often experiences perceptual and visual distortions, physical sensations, relaxation and numbness. In high doses, feelings of nausea and anxiety usually occur. Kuhn, Swartzwelder, and Wilson[24] claim, "[t]he psychological effects mirror those of LSD." The following quote from George describes his experience on shrooms:

> Shrooms are the kinda drugs that fuckin', I'll take and like drive to the seaside and walk around. 'Cause that's all I wanna do. I'll walk in the city, ya know whatta mean? I did shrooms like a year and, two years ago. Just walked around. I walked around in the city. All I had was a tank-top on, and this little Armani Exchange® jacket. It was like forty degrees out and windy as hell in the city and I'm like chillin'. I had a tank top on underneath and this little fuckin' thin Armani Exchange® jacket . . . It was like a biker jacket. I didn't give a–but we were in the subway, everyone's like [rolls lips]. Me and these two girls were like chillin', fucked up on shrooms; we're like buggin' out. We walked. We must've walked like thirty or forty blocks. Funniest fuckin' thing, but we didn't know how far it was.

Like George, most of these club kids discuss how the effects of shrooms elicit a desire to be outdoors.

MDMA/Ecstasy

MDMA varies in drug classification: it is sometimes classified as a methamphetamine because of its chemical make-up, and other times it is classified as a hallucinogen because of its perceived effects, which actually differ dramatically from LSD and other psychedelics. While MDMA is sometimes labeled as a designer drug, Kuhn et al. argue that the most fitting classification is as an entactogen. Still, its taxonomy has been debated since Merck patented MDMA in 1914.

Until 1985, MDMA was commonly used in psychiatric settings, both in individual sessions and in couples' counseling. This method of treatment came to a halt after much debate in July of 1985, when MDMA was legally categorized as a Schedule I drug because of its arguably low-to-nonexistent medicinal value, and for its high abuse potential (see Appendix A). Currently, some researchers have obtained grants and legal access to MDMA throughout the U.S. and in Israel to test its effectiveness as a treatment for Post-Traumatic Stress Disorder.[25]

MDMA, also known as E or ecstasy, is most commonly sold in oral tablets containing somewhere between 50 and 150 mg of MDMA. The retail price for each tablet ranges between $15 and $30. However, in 2004, J. Masters was able to purchase a large quantity for $8 a pill, as he explains:

> We were in the Planet on Saturday and the guy had like 200 pills or whatever it was. So we bought 50 of them . . . , it was 400 bucks, 8 dollars a pill. It's cheap right? That's why I said, "I'll take fifty." And then he looked at me like I had nine heads. He said, "how many ya want?" I said, "well how many ya got?" He said, "however many you want." I said, "well give me fifty."

As J. Masters indicates, purchasing drugs in quantities can greatly reduce the price of a single dose.

MDMA chemically increases brain levels of dopamine, norepinephrine and serotonin. The increase of these neurotransmitters in the synapse causes a feeling of empathy, openness and compassion.[26] Physically, people tend to experience increased body temperature, heart rate and blood pressure. Jitteriness, teeth clenching, a loss of appetite, muscle cramping and occasional nausea are also reported. MDMA's euphoric and stimulative effects, which last between four and six hours, make it an attractive drug for dance venue attendees as it facilitates dancing for extended periods of time.[27] Club kids Tyler and David debate and describe the effects both on the brain and behaviorally:

> Tyler: Ecstasy was like, ya know, a dipole – a completely opposite experience [from LSD]. To this day I would say there's nothing at all cerebral. There's nothing at all cortical about ecstasy. At best it gets up to you're fuckin' amygdula and makes you fall in love with everyone around.

> David: That's true, well maybe it gets to your insular as far as the cortex. It's actually meaningful, believe it or not.

> Tyler: Yeah, but, that's like dinosaur, pre-historic cortex, right?

> David: Well it's probably who you really are.

> Tyler: But I thought pre-frontal's who you really are.

David: If you think you're like the thinking person. But the sense of feeling good, insular.

Tyler: Alright. Good. Insular: spirit.

David: Yeah, the emotional self.

Tyler: Fine . . . Ecstasy is the polar opposite, so rather than having these detracting sometimes vile things happening with your other senses, ecstasy kind of unites your whole body in this feeling of wellness and warmth and beauty and at the same time extends beyond that and connects ya to the music and what's great about it, and connects you to everyone around you. When you're at the peak of your ecstasy, when you're rolling [experiencing the high from ecstasy] your balls off, you really feel the true sense of brotherhood, the unity of existence of man, of what connects you to everything that in your normal existence, ya know, you pass by people in the street, and you say, ya know, you hate this person. This is violent and disgusting to me when you're rolling on ecstasy. Ya know, you're all one and you're mired in the same quagmire triangle somehow making the species survive.

Both Tyler and David describe the loving, communal, feeling commonly associated with the effects of ecstasy.

While most club kids enjoy the effects of ecstasy, many report that the pills sold as ecstasy tend to have unpredictable effects. Often, these pills are not pure MDMA: consequently, taking a pill is like, as Angelina states, playing "Russian roulette." As Betty Cool describes:

With E it's different, because the hits are always different. And you don't know what you're gonna get till you try it. Ya know, it could be dopey and make you tired, and sometimes you just feel like you can't dance, and you just wanna sit down and watch everybody and listen to the music. It could make you hyper, ya know? It could make you sexual. Um, that's one of the reasons why I kinda like tina [crystal methamphetamine] now a little bit more often, because I know what I'm to expect.

Ariel has the same reaction to ecstasy pills:

E's very interesting because it varies, the kind of quality that you have. 'Cause they lace it with stuff, right. So MDMA is the actually pure drug that makes-up actually E, and they lace it with ether or speed or other stuff, which is horrible, right. So if we happen to get E with more MDMA, you'll have a better high versus something that's speedy. When something is speedy you wanna like, you're just up and you can't really breathe and it drowns that elation that you get.

With Betty Cool as an exception, the varying effects of the ecstasy pill have not prevented many from taking it.

Depressants: Ketamine and GHB

Ketamine/Special K

In August 1999, ketamine's classification was lowered from a Schedule II to a Schedule III drug[28] (see Appendix A). Since 1970, ketamine, also known as Special K or K, has been used as a method to treat alcohol dependence and as an anesthetic for both humans (including children) and animals. While ketamine was created and continues to be used for its anesthetic properties, it acts more like a stimulant, causing the heart rate and breathing to increase.

Ketamine is sold on the street in jars (also known as licks), in which one gram costs about $80. Angelina also purchases her ketamine for that price: "I would buy a lick which is $80. . . . " In large doses, it can cause such reactions as dream-like states and hallucinations. This effect results primarily from the way ketamine blocks the actions of the neurotransmitter glutamate, which produces a feeling of disconnection from one's body or environment.[29] Ketamine users tend to report "near death experiences" from the drug, in which they see visions, die, and enter other realities.[30] Many users describe achieving a sense of enlightenment from experiencing a separation of their mind from their body.[31] SickKid describes his experiences on ketamine:

> There's been times, like, ya know whatta I'm sayin', I felt like I was gonna die, I felt like I was in a fuckin', ooh, I don't know how to explain it. Like I was in a cartoon; I was in space. I thought I was like, I don't know how to explain it. I thought I was like Freddy Kruger, Incredible Hulk, I thought I was gonna die. I thought I was like 400 lbs, I thought my hands were gonna drop one time I came out. Crazy shit.

In SickKid's account, the visions and near death experiences on ketamine are revealed.

GHB

Gamma-hydroxybutyrate (GHB), commonly known as G, is another drug like ketamine that was originally created for its anesthetic properties. Laborit produced the substance in 1960, and until early 1990, it was sold in health food stores. GHB was marketed to treat insomnia and drug and alcohol abuse, and to assist bodybuilding (GHB increases muscle mass as it promotes the release of growth hormones). In late 1990, the FDA banned all nonprescription sales of GHB, and in 2000, GHB was reclassified as a Schedule I substance[32] (see Appendix A). GHB is sold on the street for $5-$10 in a clear, salty liquid-form.[33] Osiris purchased 16 ounces of "the good sodium stuff" for $120. The dose varies from 500 milligrams to 5 grams and tends to be taken in capfuls or teaspoons. The effects of GHB are usually experienced within 15-30 minutes of ingestion. The process of elimination of GHB from the body is quite rapid, approximately 2-3 hours, and it is virtually undetectable in the urine 12-hours after ingestion. This is because GHB is a naturally occurring fatty acid derivative of the central nervous system (CNS) neurotransmitter y-aminobutyric acid (GABA). Thus, GHB easily crosses from the blood to the brain.[34]

GHB has been known to enhance social activity and well-being, and increase libido, while also depressing the CNS. Slurred speech, lightheadedness and drowsiness are likely experiences.[35] This depressant effect of GHB has reportedly been used to reduce victim resistance during sexual assaults.[36] Club kids who consume GHB explain the importance of learning how the dosage changes its pharmacological effects. As in drinking alcohol, many explain that GHB users have to learn their limit. As George explains:

> G works, it's funny, it works in two ways. It could either make you really up, ya know? Mad [a lot] energy, ya know? Or it could put you to sleep. It's funny how it works. You do a little too much, you'll be dyin' out.
>
> *Dina: How do you know how much is enough?*
>
> George: Yo, it takes time. Anyone who starts doin' G for the first time is gonna go down a few times the first time. You gotta learn your limits, ya know whatta mean? You gotta learn, ya know whatta mean? You gotta learn.

While many club kids enjoy the effects of the depressants GHB and ketamine, others, like Michelle and Jack, cannot grasp the appeal of only consuming depressants while clubbing:

> Jack: I can't imagine doing GHB and K. Like, to me, that's just not – it doesn't sound like a good time to go dancing. Because it's such a depressing, I don't know … to me that's like being really, really drunk, I mean it's slightly different but it's in the same family.
>
> Michelle: Yeah, it's hard to move.

Jack: Like I just don't understand how people enjoy that; like to go partying with.

Pharmacological Properties and Decision to Use a Drug

Understanding the pharmacological effects of the drugs allows the club kids to identify the appropriate dosage and methods of use to heighten the positive, and reduce the negative, effects of drugs. Essentially, these club kids are able to become fairly "scientific," acting as doctors or pharmacists, and medicating themselves and their friends in an attempt to regulate and heighten the drug effects. While not without potential harmful effects, many users prescribe themselves and one another various substances depending on how they are feeling. Jack explains:

> Yeah, we tried to like not drop [take ecstasy] till we got inside the club, so better we can maximize our ecstasy time . . . We were all really scientific about it . . . We tried to take it at the right moments, that way we'd start rolling [experiencing the high from ecstasy] as soon as the DJ was gonna start spinning . . . We'd smoke joints [marijuana] and do bumps [single snorted dose] of K once the E started dying down . . . We called it giving ourselves turbo boosters; it makes you feel the E more.

Heightening the Positive

As Jack describes, club drug users tend to snort ketamine in "bumps" while on ecstasy. With this low dose, the effects usually do not last longer than an hour. Taking ketamine in combination with MDMA actually reduces the effects of ketamine, making the dissociation from reality less likely, while increasing both the positive effects of MDMA and the duration of those effects.[37] SickKid describes his experience:

> Ecstasy and K, that's the best, like paradise. It just goes with it; ya know what I'm sayin'? The mix, the high, I was gone. I thought I was in another world, and all that stuff, ya know?

Michelle and Jack's description is illuminating:

> Michelle: We do a bump [of ketamine] throughout the night; like we carry the vial and just do little hits . . . It gives you like a rush . . .
>
> *Dina: Can you describe the feeling?*
>
> Jack: I don't know, I thought it just sort of numbed you. It just made you feel like, um you were floating on air. And . . . in a club, with the lights it was pretty hallucinogenic for me.

Angelina also enjoys the combination:

> E and K is like god's gift . . . Well you know what it is? I used to be able to take E like a champ. Like, I would be able to take like 7 hits of E in a night, no problem. Now I will not take ecstasy if I don't have K. It just, it won't happen, because I feel like I get so antsy, you're edgy and you're just like racing, and you fiend for K. And then you do a bump of K and it kind of like takes the edge off . . . and just mushes everything together and it like makes sense.

Other common combinations are GHB and crystal methamphetamine, and acid and ecstasy. Ralph describes the effects of combining GHB and crystal methamphetamine:

> The crystal keeps you up and keeps you goin', but the G gets you stimulated, both like, both like emotionally, sexually, everything. It kind of like enhances your mood and everything like that. So . . . the combination of the two, gives me like an insurmountable amount of energy. Like unbelievable amount of energy. I'll be like nonstop, go, go, go, go. Like you could keep, if you think about, you could keep doin' it and doin' it and doin' it and the longer you go, the longer you go, you just feel better and better. If you could believe that, you could feel better, and better, and better, and better as the day goes by.

Users define the acid and ecstasy combination as "candy-flipping." Tyler describes it as follows:

> So when you candyflip it's literally like you've got these two completely opposing forces just yankin' you in opposite directions and if one of them starts to win you hope it's this ecstasy, 'cause you could fuckin' dance around like a maniac. You know, you could, one moment be like rollin' your balls off, and be like, "whoo, hoo hoo," and then the next moment the acid kicks in and you're like, "whoo, hoo, hoo, was that my ass talking to me? What the fuck? Goddamn! Ahhh!" And then you have to find a table. And then it gets, it could get overwhelming. Like you have to, you definitely have to get used to the feeling of just ya know, goin' in two completely different directions at the same time. But once—once you do get used to it, then, uh, ya know, it's, it's another just completely different phenomenal experience.

David has a similar description:

> Uh, this is the best situation. You have the acid world and you have the ecstasy world, and those two worlds are very different and they just suddenly crash. And uh, so they're not really too compatible, because in one of them you're more like lovey, like ya know, I feel the greatest feeling and you're just very like emotional and somatosen-

sory and good; positive. But then in the other, in the acid side, you have like uh, insane thoughts, and like serious hallucinations, even auditory, like, ya know? And your experiences overall gets really altered. So you're like thinking in terms of new concepts, ya know? You're not concerned about what you're usually concerned when you're sober. You're concerned about completely different things. You're still thinking, but you're focusing on little things, little details. So the two worlds just crash, and so now you're in a super-position of those two worlds.

David's quote, like the others above, provides an excellent description of the ease of escape into a fantastical reality via the combination of drugs such as LSD and ecstasy (see also Chapter 3).

Counteracting the Negative

The club kids often add substances to their already ingested drug cocktail to counteract the effects of another drug. For example, Tina consumes a depressant, ketamine, to offset the "edgy" effect of cocaine:

I definitely done the mix. I used to like to do the, ya know? . . . back and forth, do K and coke, K, coke. 'Cause like, I didn't like that edge with coke.

Consuming additional drugs is much more common when the club kids want to ease the "coming down" process.[38] For example, many club kids, like J. Masters, smoke marijuana to relax and induce sleep after using ecstasy and cocaine:

Um, one night I remember droppin' a pill [ecstasy], remember doin' a lotta coke, I remember doin' K to wake myself up, and smokin' pot to put myself to sleep.

Likewise, Ralph deems it necessary to have CNS depressants such as Xanax (alprazolam) or Valium (diazepam) to counteract the lengthy effects of crystal methamphetamine:

That's what sucks about it [crystal methamphetamine]. With this shit, if you don't have something to knock you out when you–when you don't wanna be high, you get fucked. You just sit there and stare at the ceilings. Like literally, you stare at the ceilings, you can't go to sleep. This is what sucks about it. So we counteract that with prescription medications, such as Xanax or Valium . . . without those you'd be miserable . . . For instance, this past weekend I was doin' it [crystal methamphetamine], I was hangin' out like all night Saturday night, Sunday whatever, fine. Sunday night I took half a Xanax and I went to sleep at around 11 o'clock. My last bump [single snorted dose of crystal methamphetamine] was at 6 [pm], went to sleep at 11 o'clock [pm], woke up at 6 in the morning, slept like a good 7 hours, went to work, no problem. So you see the necessity?

Acting as doctors or pharmacists also tends to become essential when counteracting negative reactions to drugs. For example, upon returning from a night out of clubbing, Angelina and MaryJane swiftly address Lucille's cocaine induced panic attack:

> Angelina: You [to Lucille] only get panic attacks when you do like uppers, like coke and crystal . . . it makes them like very antsy . . . you just actually gotta wait it out, ya know? Talk them through it and just like –

> MaryJane: Offer them another drug. "How about this?'

> Angelina: Yeah, yeah. Like, that's what you have to do. I went to my house; I got Vicodin® [an opiate] and came here right away 'cause I heard it in her voice, that she was just like not gonna go to sleep she was . . . so upset, thinking about everything, and I was just like, "You need to go to sleep," and there's – you're not gonna fall asleep on your own, 'cause you're that coked up. So I came here and brought her Vikes [Vicodin]

> MaryJane: It let her sleep.

Preventing Harm

Knowledge of the pharmacological properties of the drug also allows users to avoid negative effects of certain drug combinations. As SickKid explains it:

> People doin' drugs don't know how to mix the drugs. They're passin' out. They're dyin.' Like GHB, K, Ecstasy, ya know whatta I'm sayin'? Like if you're gonna do drugs, you gotta know how to mix the drugs, ya know whatta I'm sayin'?

For example, most club kids know that the effects of depressants are exacerbated when consumed with alcohol. Often, that user can have no recollection of the episode's events. Furthermore, the adverse effects of GHB are further amplified when taken in combination with ketamine. Having such knowledge compels many, like Ralph, to refrain from mixing GHB and alcohol even when they are available:

> There was [G] but I wasn't doin' it, 'cause I was drinkin'. You can't mix the two. It's very dangerous. So we went back to my boy's house

after the club for after hours, hung out there all day. Some people were drinking, we were all doing meth, fuckin' bumps and shit. And then um, since I didn't do any alcohol over 3, 4 hours, I started doing G.

While out for breakfast, Osiris refused to drink the free mimosa that came with his meal:

Osiris took a big swig of G at the table, as he states, "it makes the food taste better." A mimosa or bloody mary came with the meal. I ordered a mimosa. Even though Osiris was unsure what it was, he ordered the same. I informed him it was a drink with orange juice and champagne mixed. He asked about the alcohol content in the Mimosa, as while on G, he cannot consume drinks containing "more than 40% alcohol." I inquired the amount of alcohol in the champagne the restaurant was serving. The waitress stated it was about 4%. As he states, "to be on the safe side," he decided not to drink it anyway. (November 14, 2004; field note)

Importantly, while these club kids are aware that certain drug combinations can be harmful, some use any drug that becomes immediately accessible. As MaryJane discusses:

I just can't learn to say no. Like, I'm the type of person that won't go and look for it, but if it's in front of me and someone gives it to me, I'll do it. "Give me, I'll do it," whatever . . . I've done everything sometimes. Took some crystal, a bump of K here, some coke (laughing) . . . That happens to me, whateva falls in front of me, I'm like, "okay I'll do that." "Can I have a bump?"

George's drug patterns are similar to MaryJane's:

When I go out I have a problem sayin' no to drugs. If someone puts a bump or a cap of G, or-or sometin' in my, ya know, someone offers me sometin', I have a hard time sayin' no to it . . . I'd rather eliminate myself from the whole entire picture then have to say no, ya know whatta mean?

Likewise, while these club kids have yet to experience the harm of multiple combinations of drugs, such mixtures as Angelina and MaryJane's prescription for Lucille's panic attack are alarming, and can be damaging.

SET

Zinberg explains that an individual's set – personality, mood and attitude – influences both drug preferences and drug experiences. Personality traits, such as being outgoing or shy, often determine the experience the user seeks. For example, shy users are more likely to consume substances that increase their sociability. An individual's mood before and during the drug-consumption event also influences the drug of choice and the drug experience. Users who tend to be depressed consume substances that would create an uplifting mood, and users often discuss the importance of being in the "right frame of mind" to engage in drug use. Positive ideas about the drug experience prior to drug consumption shape the actual experience of the drug. Over time, users develop expectations of drug effects, which influence their interpretations of the experience. For example, negative effects of a drug, such as diarrhea, may ultimately become a welcomed indicator of what will become a positive drug experience. Others who interpret such experiences as negative may refrain from using that drug in the future.

Personality

Many club kids compare their contrasting drug use preferences to that of their friends' and point to individual personality differences as determinants. Angelina, who prefers ketamine, and Lucille, who prefers cocaine, explain:

> Angelina: The reason why there's a big difference between us and me is because I do K and they coke . . . I think that just on a regular I'm typically an energetic person and . . . if I'm going to put something in my body I want it to have the opposite of what I am.
> Lucille: Where's with me I'm quiet, and I wouldn't say a word all night, but give me that [cocaine] and I talk.
> Angelina: And she does coke.

Betty Cool chooses to avoid "sloppy behavior" and thus, refrains from alcohol use:

> I don't drink too much when I do this stuff [crystal]. Ya know, I might have one or two drinks because number one, I'll get sick, I'll throw-up. I'm very sensitive. And number two, like I said, I don't like to get sloppy, and I think people who do that, who drink a lot with drugs, uh, they get very sloppy . . . alcohol does it to you by itself generally.

Mood

The club kids also discuss the role mood plays in consuming drugs. Ariel discusses how a "happy state of mind" is an ideal set prior to drug use:

> I feel that with drugs you have to always be ina happy state of mind.
> What happens is, if you're in a negative state of mind, you'll start
> seeing, like your mind controls like, you'll start seeing spiders – well
> if those were scary to you. Because if you're in a bad mood and you
> start to see like crazy scary things you get very scared and that's how
> people freaked out . . . It's very controlled by your mind. And people
> always told me that. That you have to be very careful. Don't think
> about bad things.

Tina agrees with Ariel, explaining that the experience on drugs is "totally
where your mental status is at."

Negative experiences with drugs, including ecstasy, ketamine, and LSD,
are also attributed to the mood and the emotional state of the user.[39]
Angelina agrees, as she explains her experience with cocaine:

> I was just doing, bump after bump, after bump, after bump, after
> bump [of coke], and I was a disgusting sweaty mess and when I think
> of the experience it turns me off to coke altogether, and maybe it's
> mental and that's why my stomach turns and I get tired and I get
> sick. 'Cause I think drugs are all about mental capacity and where
> you are. If you're in a good mood and you take a hit, you're gonna
> have a good trip.

Here, Angelina shows how set is an important factor in the drug users'
experience. Because of her excessive use of cocaine, Angelina developed
taste aversion to the drug. She created a mindset in which her "stomach
turns" when she consumes cocaine. Furthermore, Angelina explains that
mindset and mood also impact drug reactions.

Expectations

Many club kids possess preconceived ideas about what to expect from the
drugs. They often convince themselves that the drug experience will be
enjoyable, and tend to describe the positive effects of the drug as out-
weighing any experienced negative effects.[40] Occasionally, they turn potentially perceived negative effects into positive ones.[41] For example, Tyler
describes the undesirable ketamine "drip" (when ketamine is snorted, it
turns to liquid and "drips" down the throat) as an acceptable, welcomed
and enjoyable effect:

> *Dina: What about immediate side effects? Like the drip?*
>
> Tyler: That's not a side effect, that's part of the process. Dude, if you
> do it for more than like 2 or 3 times you learn to like the drip. That's
> how you know you've got it up your nose far enough that it's gonna

kick in. And you just have to live with the taste. Even the taste can start out as foul like lickin' a urinal cake, but after awhile, you get to like it.

Because Tyler, like other users, has a set of information regarding ketamine, he knows when a certain effect should happen. This reduces any anxiety that might otherwise occur, and transforms an undesirable effect of ketamine to an acceptable, welcomed and enjoyable effect. Michelle and Jack have had similar experiences with ecstasy:

Michelle: I used to remember, like I would always crap at the clubs, and it's so embarrassing. But you knew you had to go.

Jack: But we all did that. That was an E thing. There's serotonin receptors on your intestinal wall, god knows what the fuck they do, but I certainly know what happens when you, uh, take a lot of it [ecstasy].

Drug experiences, such as Michelle's and Jack's, provide users with knowledge, attitudes, and hence, a set, which influences future drug use behaviors.

SETTING

Zinberg identifies setting as the least investigated but most important component of his theoretical framework. For Zinberg[42] it is the setting that allows users to bring their "illicit drug use under control." The setting includes social rituals and group norms regarding drug use behaviors, and the immediate environment in which the drug is experienced. Research indicates that people initiate drug use with friends who show them how to use the drug, where to use the drug, and the overall conditions that favor positive drug-using experiences.[43] Together, these users establish rituals of use and norms of behavior, which become "values and rules" of drug conduct.[44] Additionally, user groups tend to disseminate information to novice users to help define the experience and avoid negative consequences associated with use. Sharing such information informs the user's set. For example, Becker's[45] research on marijuana users, Davis and Munoz's[46] study of the Haight-Ashbury hippies, and Feldman et al.'s[47] investigation of PCP users indicate that consuming the wrong dose, in an inappropriate setting, without proper knowledge of how to address particular reactions could fuel negative reactions to the drug.

Interviews with the club kids also indicate that the setting is the key element shaping their drug experiences. Five features within settings can foster controlled drug use: (1) group norms, (2) social rituals, (3) the setting's environment (i.e., lounge, bar, dance club, outdoor activity), (4) the sharing of drug knowledge, and (5) informational resources.[48] By implementing group norms and social rituals that regulate drug use and harms, using in safe environments and sharing information on the drugs used, these club kids – for the most part – are able to control their use, experience pleasurable drug-induced effects, and avoid criminal justice detection.

Norms of Use

The club kids distinguish and categorize certain drugs and drug behaviors as acceptable, while disliking and avoiding others, and many individual club kids consume substances accordingly. For instance, SickKid and David are the only club kids to try heroin (they both smoked it). The other club kids, like most club drug users around the world,[49] disapprove of heroin as well as crack. Many agree with George, who states: "I won't ever touch certain drugs, like heroin or crack." Tyler, for instance, explains that these drugs are more dangerous than the drugs he and his friends consume, such as marijuana, ketamine, LSD and ecstasy:

> There's really nothing that we do that's gonna fuck you up for life or send you to the hospital, ya know? No one's doin' heroin. No one's gonna overdose and die. No one's doin' crack.

Marijuana, which all the club kids (aside from Betty Cool, George, Isaac and Monica) smoke throughout the week, is perceived as the least harmful of all drugs. Many do not consider it a drug, and they disagree with its current prohibition legislation. Tyler, for instance, thinks marijuana "doesn't count as a drug as far as I'm concerned." David agrees and elaborates:

> Why is it that you're allowed to drink alcohol and get completely wasted out of your mind, but you're not allowed to smoke a fuckin' joint? I mean isn't that Chewbacca [ridiculous; irrational]? Doesn't that make no sense at all? Aren't you completely of like, incapable of functioning on alcohol compared to weed? So why should one be legal and the other illegal?

Club kids also tend to frown upon excessive use of drugs. Ralph, for instance, does not associate with some drug users in the clubbing scene, such as heavy methamphetamine users:

> . . . that I never witnessed or experienced in my life. Like that's, that's out of control. That's fuckin' drug addicts, straight-up meth. I've

never experienced, like me or any of my friends . . . we wouldn't hang out with people like that . . . But I've met a couple of people who have shown traits or specific, ya know, or specific weird behaviors that you've seen in that movie [Spun][50] . . . I've met them, hung out with them for ten minutes, and said, "Yo, this fuckin' guy's a wack job, I'm out', ya know, I don't even wanna be sittin' next to this fuckin' guy."

Angelina, MaryJane and Lucille also separate themselves from those who use drugs excessively:

MaryJane: But we don't get sloppy either. We're not like those people that sit and do three day binges.

Angelina: Yeah, we won't go on binges.

Lucille: Like, just like a recreational thing.

Betty Cool explains the norms of her group, and how she learned "moderation:"

We don't go out and take, ya know, ten pills, and do a bag of crystal, and drink, ya know, five glasses of alcohol, and ya know, shots [of alcohol]. Like, we use in moderation, I guess you could say. And not even, I wouldn't even say moderation, I would just say, we know how we feel, we know what feels good. If I'm feeling good then I don't need to take another one. Ya know, I'm not gonna take another one just to take another one. Um, I'm gonna take one if I don't feel anything, or if I'm comin' down . . . I'm not just gonna take three pills just because.

These norms of drug use are external controls, which often become internal controls restraining many club kids from engaging in excessive drug use. However, while these club kids seek to minimize harms associated with their use, a few periods of excess use and some ironies resonate within the data. For example, while Angelina states, "We won't go on binges," she also describes a few months when she excessively and repeatedly consumed cocaine. Similarly, while Ralph separates himself from those users who frequently and desperately consume drugs, he also went through a period of daily ketamine use, in which he diagnosed himself as an "addict:"

I went through a stretch where um, in college when I was doin' like K on like a daily basis with one other kid, or just like two other people. But with that, like that kind of drug is very like introverted kind of thing. You just do it, and you just kind of like sit there and like stay to yourself, keep to yourself. But um, there was a time where like ya know, I'd been doin' it like by myself, like on a daily basis, like, when

I shouldn't've been for a couple a months straight, when I was like, "fuck, what am I doin'? This is disgusting. I'm a drug addict . . . ."

Social Rituals of Use

Peer norms also coincide with social rituals of use, as most club kids have certain drug-using routines. Through group rituals of use, anticipating the risks and the excitements during the night are rarely experienced alone. Michelle and Jack explain their social ritual of drug use:

> Jack: We were really organized. We had to assign someone to roll the joints, and we had to assign someone the jar of K, and we all knew who had joints, who had K. And I would always wrap up everybody's E, because no one else had aluminum foil.

> Michelle: Not only that, it would be a lot of us going out in a big night, so we'd make a big purchase. So it's usually one person and then you'd have to divvy up, like, "alright I bought them all this time. I gotta give you three, you this–" It was dividing it up; figuring out where we're gonna put it [hide the drugs to easily sneak them into the clubs].

The following interview excerpt describes Monica's and her friends' ritual of preparing for their night out of mainly ecstasy consumption:

> One, where we all gonna meet before? Met at a friend's house. Who had the stuff? How many does everybody want? Ecstasy: we call them DBs, disco biscuits. "How many DBs? How many DBs do ya want? So it's a matter of who's coming, how many should I get – 'cause you never wanna get while you're inside . . . So while you're getting – "I want two DBs and one Ambien® [sleeping pill]. That's your make-up for the night . . . The Ambien®, we'll . . . leave at home; the pills, um, in the bra. I'd say, under the boob fat, the boobs. "They're goin' in the boobs" . . . We'll have drinks . . . talk about work, talk about uh – one girl's getting married; I'm the maid of honor – talk about wedding plans, and then we'll go out . . . You get there at what? 12:30-1[am]. You take it [the first ecstasy pill] at one. Then you wait an hour and an half, so you're looking at 2:30 [take the second] and then after the second, it's whenever . . . [but] don't take it past four. It's just a sign of bad things to come.

The club kids' drug-using rituals reduce the anxiety associated with using drugs, and additionally minimize potential harms that could occur. For example, Monica states above the importance of refraining from ecstasy use after 4am to prevent harmful consequences. However, many club kids, like Betty Cool, often violate their peer/self-imposed rules for the night:

We would go out saying, "alright we're gonna go to this club and that's it." Ya know, "we're gonna do a pill and hang out." And we wind up in afterhours and coming home the next day and doing a little more E than we expected and spending a little more money than we wanted to.

Environment

As in other drug studies,[51] the club kids describe certain social environments or settings as more appropriate for the use of certain drugs. As George states: "It all depends on the setting I'm in." Most of the club kids have particular preferences, with some similarities. Most club kids will not consume LSD (acid) or psilocybin mushrooms (shrooms) inside dance club venues. Rather, they consider dance clubs better suited for ecstasy or crystal methamphetamine consumption. For example, when MaryJane and George were asked about their decision to refrain from hallucinogens in clubs, they stated:

> MaryJane: I'd bug out too much, and it's too much, you gotta sit . . . and like sometimes you're so fucked up you're like, "what the fuck is going on?"

> George: I probably won't do shrooms or acid in a club anymore. Only because they're not really, I don't really don't consider them club drugs anymore. They're too much of a high. Like you wanna be out, and-and-when I-when I do shrooms or-or acid, like I wanna go on missions. I wanna go like walk around. I wanna like . . . not be cooped up in a club for too long, ya know whatta mean? So I'd probably hold back on doing acid or like mesc [mescaline] or shrooms in a club.

The intense effects of these hallucinogens are avoided in certain settings, such as dance clubs.

Similarly, many decide not to use ecstasy or crystal methamphetamine in certain types of venues. Ralph, for instance, would not consume these drugs in a lounge:

> I'm not gonna go to like a lounge and do a fuckin' bump [single dose] of meth. I'm gonna have a drink and that's it. It [meth] just doesn't fit; ya know what I'm sayin'? 'Cause like, you need a big place, lots of space that you could run around and do whatever you feel like without gettin' looked at like you're a maniac. You can't do that in a lounge.

Ariel discusses the ideal setting for her use of ketamine:

I like to do K and actually get into a K-hole . . . I don't want to do it in a club. I like to be like in a room with music, and it's dark. I like to lie down and basically be at ease to like be in a K-hole. I don't like to do it in a club, because . . . I'm really dizzy. I don't like standing up. I don't like all the noise . . . It's just not the right experience.

Using drugs in the appropriate settings is important for a positive and safe drug experience since – as many of the club kids often describe – the effects of the drug vary depending on the environment in which the drug is used. For example, Monica compares her experience using ecstasy at home to using drugs in a dance club:

When I first started doing E, I would prefer to do it at home, with friends. Now, I almost feel like if it's at home and with friends, I feel like, you're staying to yourself . . . If I'm looking, I'm standing outside and looking in like, "why are the five of us all sitting at five points to the room or just laying on the floor listenin' to music?" . . . When I'm at a club it's more interactive, more fun, more, dancing, and I don't need to be that like, to myself type feeling.

Ariel also has different experiences on ecstasy when she is at home compared to when she is clubbing:

At a club, because there's all these people around you and everybody's all antsy and excited and more talkative. And when you do it with like someone else in a room, you're still very talkative but you're much more sexual. It's a very different setting . . . It would be me and my boyfriend and music. And we'd do E and basically, it would definitely intensify the actual experience a lot. It would just be more like more touching. There would be lots of foreplay.

The influence of the setting on the drug experience also emanates from the discussion surrounding ketamine and GHB, as Ralph's comment exemplifies:

When you're on K by yourself, like outside of a club, like in a quiet room or something like that, it's like very, I'm not gonna say spiritual, but . . . you see people. And, ya know, you have conversations. And you could . . . visualize like actual like occurrences . . . it just being like you're in a fuckin' video game, and you don't know what the hell is goin' on, ya know? . . . But let's say I wanted to, ya know, do like a cap of G, get a little twisted, and hang out with a girl, whatever. It would enhance it, be sexual . . . We'd be hangin' out, touchy feely, whatever. And then once all is said and done, it's one o'clock in the morning, you go to sleep . . .

The setting of use can also exacerbate the potentially adverse physical effects of drugs – especially those of MDMA,[52] LSD[53] and ketamine[54] – as well as potential involvement with criminal justice agencies. Because MDMA increases one's heart rate and body temperature, consuming this drug in poorly ventilated, crowded venues with extensive dancing, could amplify these effects. Such consequences prompted many ecstasy users to consume water throughout their experience. Ironically, some users learned that too much water could also be harmful. Tyler and Jack describe their friend's experience:

> Jack: We knew to stay away from too much hydration, drop your sodium too low and get really sick. One of our friends actually wound up in the ER, she seized because she was doing E, and E can occasionally have a strange effect . . . just by itself . . . cause your kidneys to piss out all your salt, and then if you drink water on top of that – I think that's what happened to her . . . from over drinking water, you could seize and wind up in the ER. That's not cool; it's embarrassing to wind up in the ER.

> Tyler: She was like 90 pounds or 80 pounds, whatever, had too much E for her fuckin' body weight drank like 15 gallons of water and got all fucked up, ended up goin' to the ER – in the same hospital we all worked at – for like hyponatremia. She had gotten her electrolytes so far out of balance that she was screwed.

Jansen[55] explains a similar occurrence with ketamine, in which "the real physical dangers arise mainly from the setting" in which the drug is used. For example, ketamine makes walking and balancing difficult and blurred or double vision can also occur. Consequently, falling is common. While consumed in dance clubs, the lights, the crowd and the many staircases can exacerbate these difficulties. David explains: "if you're doing K you have to be prepared to hold on to some corner of the room, or something, or have a couch or something." Often changing the setting can remedy a negative effect. Ariel explains:

> There have been times where like they [friends] have not felt good, like they've just been sick or they just can't – usually, like a couple of us would leave. Usually at least one other person goes with this person to take them home, make sure they're okay, and usually no one's ever gone to the hospital. Usually when they take them home, they're much happier because it's quiet and they can lie down in their own bed.

Using drugs in certain settings also reduces the likelihood of criminal justice contacts and legal ramifications. The club kids consume drugs primarily behind closed doors of hotels, private homes or dance clubs where arrests are less likely. Essentially, their drug use is outside of public view and simple police detection. When entering dance venues, these club kids share information on the best methods of concealing their drugs. For example, Monica phones a friend to gather information on the security measures at different venues:

> I called my friend; I said what's the security like in the place, because I wanted to know where I need to hide my stuff. Birdland, seems like you don't need to hide anything. Other places, they're giving you, uh, ya know, cough and turn your head type check, or I'm expecting dinner after they search me, 'cause it's really quite invasive.

The invasive search Monica describes is more likely at high profile, frequently policed venues that are consistently in the media. Tina, who hid jars of ketamine in her vagina, explains a similar experience when she was searched at the Plant II:

> I'd put fuckin' jars inside me . . . 'Cause we were like, "oh, we wonder what's NRG gonna be like?" And we did that. That wasn't fun, but you, ya know, you have to do what you have to do . . . We put it in like a bag and put a string . . . Yeah, made a tampon outta jar . . . I mean one time I was fingered at the Plant II, by the security girl, and I was nervous then, I was very, very nervous . . . I took the jars and I just put it inside me, but I put inside me that I could grab it. And the girl went like this [palm up, pointer and middle fingers extended, ring and pinky fingers bent towards palm, and slid her hand], and I said, "be careful," 'cause I wasn't wearing anything underneath. I had this short dress on and I wasn't wearing anything. I was like, "be careful," ya know? So she's like, "hold on," and she went like this [palm up, pointer and middle finger extended, ring and pinky fingers bent towards palm, and slid her hand] and went like that [elevating the middle and pointer fingers grazing her vagina] and she shoved it up me more . . . and I'm like "I don't have anything! And you just fingered me!" . . . And she's like, "wait, let me again." . . . I'm like, "you're not checking shit again!" She wasn't wearing gloves!

In contrast, at some venues, club bouncers and owners are more concerned about violence in their clubs and simply conduct a "pat down" in search of weapons. The following field note of a security search at club NRG describes such an incident:

> Jess commented that he hoped they weren't going to search much, as he had tons of bottles of G in his sneakers by the laces of his sneakers. He also threw a Visine bottle filled with G in the hood of his sweatshirt. Jess thought that if he saw the bouncers thoroughly searching those before him, he'd simply leave, return the bottles to the car, and come back . . . We went to the line. Since I was with two

guys, they let us right in. They checked each of our IDs and we walked to the entranceway. The search was quite brief, almost like they were searching for weapons, not for drugs. The two bouncers did a quick pat down asking us to hold our arms out and spread our legs. They searched purses, but did not do a detailed search of shoes or pockets. Jess safely entered the club with his G. (May 15, 2004; field note)

When officers make an effort to heavily police venues, these club kids indicate they can identify narcotics officers inside a venue. Jack explains:

They had narcs running around the crowd, like offering to sell weed at Plant II . . . These narcs were basically like hired thugs that stuck out like sore thumbs and like, you know, were watching everybody and milling around and checking people. And literally like bumping into people just 'cause they were beefcakes.

Additionally, the clubbing experience deteriorates when security measures interfere with the night:

As we entered the club Plant II, we were searched by what appeared to be police officers. The female was friendly to me. They searched very thoroughly. She had a box of confiscated items on the floor. Ironically, you weren't permitted to bring in gum, but you were able to obtain free blow-pops in the bathrooms . . . Inside, bouncers were canvassing the entire place, walking around the dance floor, shining flashlights on patrons. If someone was sitting down, a flashlight was shined on him or her. No wonder the club was fairly empty. (April 3, 2004; field note)

George has similar experiences at Plant II, which eventually closed down:

I've had numerous nights at the Plant II, like where security's just breathing down your fuckin' neck. And you-you just feel paranoid to do anything at any part of the club, ya know whatta mean? Like, there's been plenty, there's been plenty of parties I've been to that are just garbage that I've walked in and walked right out, ya know?

As George indicates, venues with heightened security measures are often avoided.

When inside the safety of their hotel rooms, these club kids are very aware of hiding their drug use from hotel employees. The following field note describes one particular incident at Hotel Castle:

There was a knock on the door of the hotel room. Dan looked in through the peephole and noticed that it was room service. He told the guys to clean up. They threw away the marijuana roach, and wiped down the table. George grabbed the "tina" and held it in his hand. The guy placed the food on the desk/counter, and went to give George the bill. George asked the price and said, "one second," since he had drugs hidden in his hand and didn't want it to be seen. He came back and gave the guy $40. (March 7, 2004; field note)

Since these club kids have thus far avoided arrest and hence, criminal justice stigma, these measures to conceal and evade criminal justice contacts have been successful.

Drug Information Resources

In addition to sharing information on methods to conceal drugs, in these settings, drug users share drug knowledge based both on drug experiences and information obtained from various resources.[56] Drug knowledge gained from books, articles, Internet sites, trial and error practices, and experience is also known as user "folklore."[57] Among drug users, folklore serves as a reference guide to monitor the effects, maximize the experience, and address negative reactions to the drugs.[58]

Many club kids largely distrust the media's depiction and doctors' knowledge of the drugs, and disagree with drug legislation.[59] Most believe that the published information regarding the effects of club drugs is exaggerated, missing or incorrect, as it is contrary to their experiences with the substances.[60] For them, such information is read cautiously. For instance, throughout the research, Osiris repeatedly phoned me in search of a book or website that had unbiased findings on the effects of drugs. He consistently searches the Internet for new books on drugs. Osiris's comprehension of, and disagreement with, the readily available information regarding GHB provoked him to argue with doctors after he awoke in the hospital from consuming excessive amounts of the drug. The following field note contextualizes this account:

Osiris was at the pool party in Miami when he ran-out of GHB. He began to ask around, and bought a bottle for $30. When he never experienced the effects, he realized it was a fake and left the party. He met Jesse at a restaurant who sold Osiris some GHB, of which he quickly ingested a "few swigs [sips]" at the restaurant. He decided to meet his cousin at a strip club, left, and "jumped in a cab." He started to "feel funny" in the cab, and asked the driver to stop the car, as he didn't want the driver to think he was "vulnerable and take advantage" of him. When he got out of the car he "stumbled around" until a cop car stopped him. The officers handcuffed him and took him to the station. He recalled sitting at the station, and believed he "must have passed out." He awoke in a hospital bed, while the doctors were trying to put a catheter in his penis. He began to "freak out" . . . The doctors were standing over him trying to explain that everything was going to be "okay." Osiris told them that all he did was GHB. The doctors responded, "That stuff could kill you!" Osiris argued that GHB cannot kill you, and that the doctors have been "misinformed." He insisted they "review the research" on the drug. He further exclaimed that he was "fine" and was "able to go home." The doctors told him that he wasn't well and had to stay. He made a deal with the doctors that if he could walk to the end of the hallway, he could leave. He got off the bed, walked down the hallway, and left the hospital. (April 2, 2005; phone conversation)

Despite Osiris's "folk knowledge" about GHB, he was taken into custody, passed out and awoke in a hospital.

Many club kids, like Osiris, view the Internet as a resource for drug information. Monica, for instance, states she obtains information about club drugs "off the Internet." Similarly, George affirms that, "You can find plenty of information on it [drugs] on the Internet." These club kids also actively seek information on club drugs by conducting research and reading published books:

At Barroom, Estevez discussed a few studies he conducted in college on GHB . . . stating GHB puts your body in "REM sleep," so your muscles can rebuild themselves . . . He claimed that it is a myth that GHB is an amino acid and that it "causes the heart to stop." Rather, when mixed with alcohol, your body and mind enters REM sleep in an "unpredictable manner." "People can fall asleep at the wheel or while they are walking." This is why it is dangerous. He explained that this is exacerbated when "GHB is taken in cap form [pouring GHB into a water or soda bottle cap. A cap is one dose of GHB]" . . . [since] the person is unaware of how close he/she is to the last stage of REM sleep . . . [which is when] "you are completely asleep." When the person consumes too much GHB, he/she is in a "dead sleep" . . . He continued explaining that "E doesn't kill anyone either." Rather, "dehydration kills people." He also discussed "moral panics," and how "Americans and the news media exaggerate everything." According to him, "the public is very stupid." (May 31, 2004; field note)

Since Tyler and Jack are medical school graduates, and David has a PhD in neuroscience, they have access to a variety of medical reports regarding drugs. Both Michelle, Jack's wife, and Ariel, a close friend and clubbing buddy, indicate that using drugs in their presence is comforting. Michelle states:

It definitely helped ease my worry in the beginning, um, because I was probably more comfortable doing drugs if I knew he – like, knowing so much information about it . . . I was concerned about long-term effects . . . like what would happen to me now. And ya know, once it was explained to me, and ya know, I knew he had done his research so, I was definitely willing to try some things. So I would say if anything, it just kind of eased some of my worries, 'cause I kind of knew, "hey if I get sick, the doctor's right here," ya know? I knew they were watching out for me, and I kind of knew that he wouldn't do anything that was that bad, ya know . . . At the same time the knowledge has helped us not to go too far. Like none of us would really ever, we look down on, ya know, coke and heroin.

Jack's experience working in a hospital has influenced him to refrain from cocaine use:

People with, that do cocaine, get into, ya know, tons of trouble with their heart. They have strokes; they have heart attacks. Ya know, we see people all the time, like 20-year-old kids with heart attacks from doing cocaine, ya know? It's just not worth it.

Another source of information is experience (i.e., trial and error). The adverse effects from drugs decline as both the knowledge regarding the drugs and their use increases.[61] For example, Ralph and his friends learn both the dangerous and appropriate ways to counteract negative reactions to GHB or "G"ing-out:

. . . the first time . . . if somebody we know was G'ing out, somebody was like, "Yeah, give him a bump [single snorted dose] of meth." So I was like, "Alright, I guess that makes sense, he's about to go to sleep, give him a fuckin' bump of something that'll get him up." We tried it. It didn't do nothing, but make the fuckin' kid twitch while he was sleepin'. So I was like, "Yo, it doesn't work." . . . People have like these, and everybody keeps bein' like, "Yo, give him a bump of meth." "Yo, don't give him shit, just let him go to sleep and that's it. He'll be alright." So I mean it's just something that you learn . . . for instance . . . at an afterhours, if somebody you know that does like, does too much G, ya know what I'm sayin'? You lay them down on the couch. You fuckin', you make sure he's alright. You make sure he's breathing; you make sure he doesn't throw-up on himself. And then, ya know, you let him sleep for three-four hours, and then he's good. That's it. I mean it's just . . . trial and error. Through experience, that's it.

Sharing Folklore

The club kids, as George indicates above, share this information on where, when and how to use drugs in these settings, and help each other address adverse reactions to the drugs. For instance, many develop nostril conditions, such as bloody noses or growths, from drug snorting practices. The following field note excerpt describes how the information to alleviate such problems is shared:

> As the guys were getting ready to leave the hotel room, they started to discuss their nostril problems from "sniffing tina" [crystal methamphetamine] . . . Todd complained about the growth he had inside his nose. Ralph suggested putting Neosporin on it. He went into the bedroom to get some. Mike suggested saline, and George agreed with that method. Mike said, "You should clean your nose before you go to sleep because you don't want that shit lying in your nose." Mike added that he almost "choked once from inhaling water" when trying to clean out his nose. Ralph brought Todd the Neosporin and Todd applied it to the inside of his nose. (March 5, 2004; field note)

Among these club kids, seeking or giving help to friends is part of the "unwritten code" of using drugs.[62] Betty Cool discusses the importance of friends as monitors of behavior:

> If anybody is not feeling good, or somebody does get sick and like throw-up like I have, then we help each other. We don't just sit there and leave, ya know? "Okay, you go. Go throw-up in the corner there. I'm goin' to the dance floor now." Ya know, we help each other.

Ralph also stresses that unwritten rule:

> I mean, lucky enough . . . we all have, uh, the responsibility enough, and the decency enough to know like our limits, and we don't fuckin' go over it . . . I mean we have a crew. Like, our crew's pretty tight. We don't really hang out with stragglers. When we go out to a club, we hang out with who we go out with and that's pretty much it. Like, we've seen other people that, I mean, that I've known, but yo . . . we consider ourselves like a family, a family. We're about, like if you see somebody you know, you go tell one of yo, his boy, "yo, Mikey!" You know what I'm sayin'? "Your boy over there's a fuckin' mess go take care of him," and it's his responsibility to go take care of his boy. Ya know, it's kind of like the unwritten code of like friends, ya know what I'm sayin', especially in that scene and the kind of shit that we do, ya know?

Notably, however, while most friends look out for one another, some can neither be relied upon nor trusted. For example, a friend gave Tina GHB while she was under the influence of ketamine. Tina had a negative reaction to this combination. When her friends' relied on their folklore to address Tina's "horrible" experience, additional harm resulted. Tina explains:

That time that my friend put stuff [G] in my drink, it was at the S and M party . . . ya know, you're not supposed to mix all that stuff, you're not supposed mix G with anything, and especially K, and that was my least enjoyable night . . . I realized, I mean these people are not your friends. Like this guy just blatantly switched it, and I mean I was throwing up in there, and everyone who saw me, like saw I was like a mess, like falling and like, they brought me to my friend and he clearly saw, he's like, "that's not like her," ya know. They sat me down, and it was a horrible feeling. It was horrible because my friends who were with me were like, "take some more drugs. Give her something to wake her up. Like don't keep given them more drugs. The person who did it had balls, because they know me, ya know. I'm on something else, and you just shouldn't do that. Like offer it to me, if I want it I'll do it. But people know with G, you just lose it. You're just like, welcome to anything. And it's a shame because you're really, really are. And that happened, and I mean that was like my horriblest night . . . I mean, I just kept throwing up. I don't know what kind of stuff this was, I was just like throwing up and throwing up like gross . . . I mean I know that night I fell asleep and my friend was trying to pick me up and I just wouldn't like really get up, and then all of sudden he said I got up and I just threw up, and I didn't know I threw up. I found out like the next day, "like you were throwin' up like violently like pushing me and everything." And like I–I don't remember doing that. At first I woke up and I'm like, "when did I fall asleep in here?" And then that's when I realized like, this isn't safe, ya know, this isn't safe, if you don't know how you get somewhere. You can't really trust people.

Furthermore, friends are often under the influence of drugs, which can reduce their ability to assist a friend in need, as David and Tyler's experience exemplifies:

Tyler: Robert has problems with chronic nosebleeds. And our friend Caesar, totally fuckin' drunk, comes over and has some K . . . So first Robert snorts a big one, and thirty seconds later blood erupts from his nose. And he's like, "UUUUAAHHH," and he runs away screamin' 'cause he's bleedin' everywhere and he can't make it stop. Meanwhile, Pup snorts a massive lump of K off the mirror and within 30 seconds he's like, "oh no, oh, OH, UUH," and in about 5 minutes later he's lyin' on the futon goin', "I need my mommy, I need my–" And then Robert comes back with like a tissue stuffed up his nose, and he's like, "well I just like sneezed and vomited all that K." And Pup, "I need my mommy."

David: First he [Pup] went to my fuckin' bathroom on the first floor and puked . . . Dude, he just started pukin' . . . and like these guys like didn't know where to take him so they took him to the shower, so he was pukin' on the shower and I think outside the shower too.

Tyler: Dude, you gotta, you gotta remember Robert's like bleedin' to death from his nose, and I am in the biggest, ya know, I'm in a big fuckin' K-hole.

David: I was in a K-hole too.

Tyler: I was like no, hold him up. No, put him there.

David: Well, when I finally like was able to leave my room to check on what was goin' on in the bathroom, when I got there, like uh, all I saw was like Pup throwin' up on the shower, uh tons of tissue – we're talkin' about like millions of tissues of paper, like a mountain, like surrounding all of them . . .

Tyler: And I'm like sittin' on the radiator, bein' a good catholic, just starin' at blood fuckin' runnin'. Oh, my god . . .

Clearly, these immediate, short-term harms that the club kids experience in these settings are alarming.

THE CLUB KIDS' DRUG USE AND DRUG, SET AND SETTING

Zinberg and Harding[63] state that "at any one time variables from each of the three groups [drug, set and setting] interact in complex ways to determine who uses an intoxicant, how it is used, and what its effects are." Together, the pharmacological properties of the drug, the individual personality, the user's knowledge of the drug, and the place in which, and the peers with whom, the drug is consumed influence patterns of use and effects of the drug. Tina and Ariel describe this interaction:

Tina: Well, I've noticed when you're in the club you have the loud music, the lights, ya know, you're having fun, you're talking to people, you're drinking. Um. And then when you're home . . . , I mean if I was home doing coke . . . a lot of times I'm always alone. Usually, um, you -you're by yourself, I mean anything could just change your mood or you could just think about something, ya know? If I think about something and then I do drugs, ya know, I have to make sure my mental status is clean . . . Also people I hang out with, like a lotta the girls I do hang out with they don't do K, and it's so hard when you have two vibes going, like there's that K vibe, and there was that coke . . . You kinda wanna stay with same energy.

Ariel: I feel that with drugs you have to always be ina happy state of mind . . . Because if you're in a bad mood and you start to see like crazy scary things you get very scared and that's how people freaked out. But usually I find that if you start to feel that, just move to another part of the room that you find more pleasing and then you'll just seeing happier things with brighter colors . . . I always try to think about happy things and if I do see scary things, I'm like oh, I should move over here and have happy thoughts.

The interaction of drug, set and setting can either prevent or exacerbate potentially harmful drug-related experiences. Monica's response to the interview question, "Do you think drugs can be harmful?" further exemplifies this point:

Sure . . . given to the wrong person, at the wrong place. It's all about circumstances; it's all about environment. It's all about, um, knowing when is enough, knowing when the party's over. Ya know? Having a balance. Otherwise, you could really get yourself in trouble.

Understanding drug, set and setting is the basis for controlled and safer drug use. When users understand the pharmacological properties of the drugs, establish drug use rituals, have a clear mindset and obtain knowledge on the drug's risky combinations and negative effects, they can usually minimize harmful experiences and maximize the pleasurable ones. Zinberg's framework for understanding drug use indicates that the immediate social environment in which the drug is used greatly affects the drug experience. Because these club kids recognize the importance of (a) being in a particular mindset when consuming drugs, (b) being in the appropriate place surrounded by caring friends, (c) using the drugs in hidden and private spaces outside of police and public view, and (d) being aware of the potential harms associated with the drugs and drug combinations, they have the tools to control their drug-induced experiences.

During drug-using events, many club kids act as scientists as they mix substances to regulate their mood and refrain from combining certain substances, such as alcohol and GHB, to avoid possible consequences. Access to information regarding the pharmacological properties of the drug, their knowledge of the drugs they consume, which they share in multiple settings, as well as the norms of use they create in these settings, permit these club kids to engage in controlled drug use. However, social rituals, norms of behavior, and folklore to which are not always adhered, and are occasionally ineffective. The negative experiences described above as well as staying awake for days, not being able to eat (see also Chapter 2), and losing large amounts of weight in a short period of time (see also Chapter 2), are unhealthy behaviors that cannot be ignored. While controlled drug use does occur and users are conscious of the potential harms, these other patterns of use and their harmful side effects suggest that the club kids tend to ignore or disobey their sanctions and rules of drug use. Nonetheless, these club kids establish processes to regulate potential harms, and most importantly, they remain outside of criminal justice scrutiny and stigma.

The inconsistencies within the club kids' drug using patterns – successful harm avoidance and the unsuccessful harm experiences – exemplify two issues: (1) the larger contradictions within the club kids' lives, and (2) a problem with Zinberg's framework. The club kids live in a culture of excess in which conspicuous consumption is considered normal (see Chapters 2, 3 and 4). However, the club kids also live in a culture of control, in which they are informed of the appropriate modes and times to escape and consume – on weekends and holidays so long as it does not interfere with work. These club kids aspire to success – college graduation and well-paying occupations (see Chapters 2 and 3). Their pleasures and escape, then, ideally must be within the confines of "controlled loss of control,"[64] and for the most part the club kids' pleasurable escapes are. The club kids' consume drugs within controlled environments (dance venues, hotel rooms, lounges, or homes), and they mostly engage in methods of behavioral control. However, as George indicates, sometimes the club kids' also "stretch it" and engage in excessive consumption:

> . . . believe me, I do shit to extreme, but I try not to get it to the point where it's like outta control like that. Ya know whatta mean? I've been in some places where I've seen girls just passed out in the corner. I've seen guys like, that are fuckin' getting carried out of the place that are pukin' outta their minds. I look at it, I'm like, "Ya know, there's a point where you can't go, too, too, terribly far. I mean, you could stretch it every now and then, but that's just outta control."

While Zinberg identifies the immediate social environment in which drugs are used, Zinberg neglects those factors that occur in the drug users' lives outside of the drug-using settings. Incorporating timing, a structural-temporal element, into Zinberg's framework, with a particular focus on life-course factors – such as employment and relationships, and capital (i.e., social, human, cultural, and economic) – provides an enhanced understanding of set, setting, drug use, drug use patterns, and drug using contradictions (see Chapter 6). This is the topic of the next chapter.

NOTES

1. Some of the material has previously appeared in Perrone, 2006.
2. 1984.
3. 1963.
4. Becker, 1973.
5. e.g., Jackson-Jacobs, 2004; McElrath and McEvoy, 2005; Shewan and Dalgarno, 2005; Shewan, Dalgarno, and Reith, 2000.
6. e.g., Biernacki, 1986; Robins, Davis, and Goodwin, 1974; Waldorf et al., 1991.
7. e.g., Duncan, Dreyer, McKenna, and Whitsel, 1982; Earleywine and Martin, 1993; Freese, Miotto, and Reback, 2002; Jonville-Bera, Bera, and Autret-Leca, 2005; Logan, 2002.
8. e.g., Johnston et al., 2005.
9. Kuhn, Swartzwelder, and Wilson, 1998; Weil and Rosen, 2004.
10. Weil and Rosen, 2004.
11. Kuhn et al., 1998, p. 202.
12. Kuhn et al., 1998; Weil and Rosen, 2004.
13. Weil and Rosen, 2004.
14. National Institute on Drug Abuse (NIDA), 2006.
15. Kuhn et al., 1998; Weil and Rosen, 2004.
16. NIDA, 2002.
17. Kuhn et al., 1998.
18. Grinspoon and Bakalar, 1997.
19. Kuhn et al., 1998.
20. Kuhn et al., 1998, p. 83.
21. Kuhn et al., 1998, p.100.
22. Kuhn et al., 1998, p. 86.
23. Kuhn et al., 1998.
24. 1998, p. 87.
25. Doblin, 2002.
26. Kuhn et al., 1998.
27. Beck and Rosenbaum, 1994; Hammersley, Ditton, Smith, and Short, 1999; Hammersley et al., 2002; Hansen et al., 2001; Lenton and Davidson, 1999; Measham et al., 2001; Ter Bogt et al., 2002; van de Wijngaart et al., 1999.
28. Jansen, 2001.
29. Kuhn et al., 1998.
30. Jansen, 2001, p. 43.

31. see Freese et al., 2002; Jansen, 2001.
32. Freese et al., 2002.
33. Ibid.
34. Smith, Larive, and Romanelli, 2002.
35. see Freese et al., 2002.
36. e.g., Asante, 1999; Jones, 2001; compare to Jenkins, 1999.
37. Jansen, 2001.
38. e.g., Hammersley et al., 2002; Hinchliff, 2001; Joe-Laidler, 2005; Levy, O'Grady, Wish, and Arria, 2005; Measham et al., 2001.
39. see Hansen et al., 2001; Jansen, 2001; Zinberg, 1984.
40. see also Kuhn et al., 1998; Shewan et al., 2000.
41. cf., Becker, 1963; Kuhn et al., 1998; Sherlock and Conner, 1999; Shewan et al., 2000; Zinberg, 1984.
42. 1984, p. 5.
43. Becker, 1963; Grund, 1993; Zinberg, 1984; cf., Akers, 1985; Sutherland and Cressey, 1966.
44. Zinberg, 1984, p. 5.
45. 1963.
46. 1970.
47. 1979.
48. see other club drug user studies, such as Beck and Rosenbaum, 1994; Flom, Friedman, Jose, and Curtis, 2001; Latkin, Forman, and Knowlton, 2002; Measham et al., 2001; Shewan et al., 2000; van der Rijt, d'Haenens, and van Straten, 2003; Warner, Room, and Adlaf, 1999.
49. see Beck and Rosenbaum, 1994; Forsyth, 1996; Hammersley et al., 2002; Hansen et al., 2001; Hunt and Evans, 2003; Joe-Laidler, 2005; Measham et al., 2001; Ter Bogt et al., 2002; van de Wijngaart et al., 1999.
50. Akerlund, 2002.
51. e.g., Cleckner, 1979; Forsyth, 1996.
52. Gowing, Henry-Edwards, Irvine, and Ali, 2002; Hammersley et al., 2002; Hansen et al., 2001; Shewan et al., 2000; Spruit, 1999.
53. Zinberg, 1984.
54. Jansen, 2001.
55. 2001, p. 47.
56. e.g., Becker, 1963; Brewer, 2003; Decorte, 2001a, 2001b; Grund, 1993; Jansen, 2001; Kelly, 2006; Panagopoulos and Ricciardelli, 2005; Riley and Hayward, 2004; Sherlock and Conner, 1999; Southgate and Hopwood, 2001; Zinberg, 1984.
57. Becker, 1963.
58. Becker, 1963; Brewer, 2003; Cleckner, 1979; Decorte 2001a, 2001b; Grund, 1993; Heather and Robertson, 1981; Kelly, 2006; Panagopoulos and Ricciardelli, 2005; Southgate and Hopwood, 2001; Zinberg, 1984.
59. cf., Coomber, Morris, and Dunn, 2000.

60. see Jenkins, 1999; Kuhn et al., 1998.
61. Becker, 1963; 1973; Zinberg, 1984.
62. see also Hansen et al., 2001; Lenton and Davidson, 1999; Shewan et al., 2000.
63. 1982, p. 16.
64. Measham, 2004.

6.   TIMING AND CAPITAL[1]

Zinberg's[2] "drug, set and setting" framework recognizes the importance of the social context of drug use at the time of the drug-using event in understanding drug use patterns (see Chapter 5). The addition of the perspectives of life-course criminology – understanding a person's social context and how this context is dynamic throughout an individual's life – greatly improves the conceptualization of the set and setting of drug use. Considering the point in that individual's life (i.e., "timing"), such as being a college student or a newly hired employee, leads to an enhanced understanding of the individual's mind*set* at the time of the drug-using event. The amount and type of resources that the drug user can access, and that accrue over the life course, influence the settings in which drugs are used (i.e., public or private). To further explain individual set and setting, in this chapter I explore the effects of *timing* (stages in the life-course trajectory) on individual drug-using patterns. I give particular attention to how life events are mediated by the possession and accumulation of various forms of *capital* (social, human, cultural, or economic), which – in addition to the control of drug, set, and setting – can insulate these users from harmful drug-related experiences – including problematic drug use, loss of employment, arrest, physical sickness, and overdose.

Life-course perspectives suggest that as people age, their increasing bonds to conventional society reduce their likelihood of engaging in illegal and illicit behaviors, including drug use.[3] New family responsibilities (e.g., having a child) and new employment responsibilities are "transitions" (i.e., life events) in individual lives that can cause a "turning point" (i.e., change in the life course) in which the individual refrains from illegal behaviors. A person's social investments in family, work, and/or school act as informal social control mechanisms that buffer involvement in illegal behaviors. Because individuals fear the risk of harming those social bonds and investments, they refrain from such behaviors.

Pathways throughout the life course, especially transitions, are influenced by capital. Bourdieu[4] conceptualizes four types of capital that an individual can possess and accumulate. They are economic (money and assets), human (educational accomplishments and skills), social (networks through which resources could be accessed) and cultural (dominant class norms and tastes). Socially embedded individuals have access to resources and opportunities within social networks that can be utilized to improve life chances. High levels of the forms of capital provide access to employment and educational opportunities and tangible financial resources, which permit smooth transitions, meaningful social investments, and hence, either the preservation of one's current status or movement upward on the social scale. In sum, capital enhances the likelihood of available support for the welfare of the family, economic prosperity, physical health, and overall life well-being.

The club kids discussed the importance of life-course transitions and social and economic resources in shaping their decisions to engage in excessive drug use and use reduction and cessation. As documented in other studies of drug use[5] and club drug use in particular,[6] many life-course factors triggered these club kids' decisions to reduce, alter and ultimately control their drug use. For example, as the sample aged, many experienced an increase in work and financial responsibilities and their bodies' decreasing ability to manage going out all night and using drugs. Consequently, many chose to cease, greatly limit or alter their drug use patterns to be able to complete daily tasks that were necessary to fulfill occupational and educational responsibilities. For most of these club kids, their drug use is temporary and is limited primarily to the adolescent and emerging adulthood[7] developmental stages (see also Chapter 3). When the club kids leave these stages and enter adulthood, their drug use patterns change. Many have reduced or desisted entirely from using drugs.

Because this sample of drug users had high levels of capital – economic, social, human and cultural – their life-course trajectory was, for the most part, a privileged one. Most experienced social and economic stability and prosperity throughout their life course, and had ready access to educational and professional opportunities. Most of these club kids experienced traditional, conventional, life-course transitions (e.g., high school and college graduation, graduate school, professional employment, and stable family relationships). Their social and economic privileges insulated them from harms typically associated with drug use. For example, the club kids' social capital gave them access to information regarding how to consume drugs safely, and their economic capital kept their drug-using activities sheltered from police drug busts that are often targeted in low-income areas.

Because life-course transitions and the possession and use of capital are linked, in this chapter I discuss how both factors affect changing patterns of drug use and their relationship to harmful experiences among the club kids. I first discuss life-course theory, and I follow that discussion with an explanation of how various macro-level factors, including capital, shape both transitions and drug use patterns. Essentially, in this chapter I demonstrate how life-course transitions and access to capital shape the club kids' drug-using behaviors.

TIMING: DEVELOPMENTAL AND LIFE-COURSE PERSPECTIVES

Developmental and life-course perspectives are similar approaches to understanding criminal behavior.[8] These perspectives seek to understand the development of criminal behavior and explain the relationship between age and crime. The age-crime curve illustrates that in large populations throughout adolescence crime rates rise rapidly. In the late teens or early 20's, crime rates peak and then subsequently begin to steadily decline. Life-course and developmental perspectives have sought to explain this phenomenon by paying particular attention to those factors that influence onset, persistence and desistance[9] of delinquent and criminal behavior throughout an individual's life.[10] Prior to life-course criminology, researchers focused primarily on explaining juvenile delinquency, as the age-crime curve peaks in the teenage years.[11] However, in the late 1980s and early 1990s, many criminologists argued for a paradigm shift[12] toward a more developmental perspective, focusing on within-individual changes over time. As a result, many new theories began to emerge. Most notably, Sampson and Laub[13] postulated an age-graded theory of social control, which suggests that when people obtain salient social bonds in adulthood it triggers a decrease in offending behavior.

Life-course and developmental theoretical frameworks for understanding offending exist along a spectrum with ontogenetic explanations on one end and sociogenic explanations on the other.[14] Theories closer to the ontogenetic end of the spectrum explain criminal trajectories in relation to individual traits (i.e., psychological/cognitive impairment) and family influences (i.e., early socialization). These theories point to inter-individual persistent differences, such as low self-control[15] or neuropsychological impairments and poor executive functions,[16] as explanations of the age-crime relationship. Since such conditions are fixed throughout the life course, theories near the ontogenetic end of the spectrum tend to emphasize the continuity in criminal behavior.[17] Physical aging is another ontogenetic condition that is associated with desistance from criminal activity. However, unlike other ontogenetic factors, aging is dynamic. In contrast, the life-course theories closer to the sociogenic end of the spectrum focus on social factors (i.e., neighborhoods, social bonds and social class) noting that with increasing social bonds, for example, desistance becomes more likely.[18]

The club kids' changing drug use behaviors can be explained through a combination of ontogenetic and sociogenic factors. Both individual factors (i.e., human agency or will and physical aging) as well as social factors (i.e., bonds and capital) account for the shifts in drug use over the club kids' life trajectories. Many club kids describe the biological/physical changes their bodies' endure with aging that impede drug consumption and club-bing activities. Moreover, as the club kids enter new stages of their life course they experience increasing responsibilities, which further obstruct their clubbing and drug-using lifestyles. In this section, I examine both continuity and change in drug-using behaviors over the club kids' life course.

Life-course criminologists within this paradigm indicate that the follow-ing five factors are important for understanding such behavioral patterns over the life trajectory: (1) macro-level effects (e.g., capital), (2) transitions, (3) the quality of those transitions, (4) human agency (or consciously willed decisions), and (5) society's responses to their behavior (e.g., arrest, incarceration and stigma). Each of these factors has a gradual and cumula-tive influence as well as a reciprocal relationship with behavior. Each factor also greatly influences other factors in the model. To clarify, macro-level factors in society, such as historical periods of affluence or of delayed transitions into adulthood, influence the quantity, type and quality of transi-tions experienced by individuals, affecting the probability and the types of responses to drug use or criminal behaviors. Transitions to new stages in the life course (such as adulthood) may enhance and increase the level of people's capital, while criminal justice responses to drug-using behavior could reduce their capital. The quality of transitions influences their sali-ency in the life of the individual, and both the quality and the presence of a transition may influence a person's behavior. The possession of resources (capital) and transition experiences (timing) can also inspire an individu-al's willed decision (agency) to change his/her behavior. Human agency may then provoke the drive toward new transitions, such as obtaining a new job, which can increase the level of capital. Capital, agency and responses to behavior also have direct influences on behavior. Furthermore, engaging in offending behaviors can increase or reduce capital and can influence the addition or removal of certain life events (e.g., loss of employment).

For these club kids, the high levels of capital they accumulate over their life course (see Chapters 2 and 3) permit smooth transitions and insulate them from criminal justice responses to their drug-using behaviors. This increases their capital, provokes the addition of other smooth transitions through adulthood, and further protects their drug use from criminal justice stigma. Moreover, their high levels of capital and social bonds throughout the life course provide them with the power and the reasons to willfully change their drug use practices so as to prevent jeopardizing their ties to conventional activities.

Life-Course Trajectory and Transitions

Onset and Use

The onset of offending usually occurs between ages 8 and 14 years. Typically, offending behaviors peak between the ages of 15 and 19, and most offenders desist between the ages of 20 and 29.[19] According to Caspi and Moffitt,[20] 85% of offenders desist by the age of 28 years. The pattern of onset tends to be very similar among different generations, and within different social and economic classes.[21] Less serious offenses tend to have an earlier peak in the age of onset.[22]

The onset of drug use, excluding marijuana and alcohol use in the general population, is much later than the average onset age of criminal behavior. The National Institute of Drug Use and Health[23] indicates that the average age of initiation is 20.7 years for ecstasy, 19.7 years for cocaine, and 18 years for LSD. Similarly, the average age that the club kids started consuming drugs, excluding marijuana and alcohol, was 19 years (see Table 6.1). Five of the club kids (Ralph, Mike, George, MaryJane and J. Masters) started using as high school students. The other club kids, with the exception of Betty Cool, started using drugs in their early 20s, mainly while in college.

The first drug used, aside from marijuana and alcohol, is linked to the year in which that club kid began to use drugs (i.e., a cohort effect).[24] Bachman Johnson, O'Malley, and Schulenberg.[25] state that "specific drugs have risen and fallen in popularity at different times during the past several decades." User drug patterns often vary depending on the time period in

Table 6.1: The Club Kids' Drug Use (excluding marijuana and alcohol)

Name	Age (Years)	Age Onset (Years)	First Drug Used	Drug Preferences
Angelina	26	20	ecstasy	ketamine
Ariel	25	19	ecstasy	ecstasy
Betty Cool	33	25	ecstasy	crystal meth
David	30	19	LSD	ketamine
George	22	15	cocaine	crystal meth & GHB
Isaac	34	unknown	unknown	current non-user
Jack	29	19	LSD	ecstasy & ketamine
J. Masters	30	15	LSD	cocaine
Lucille	25	19	ecstasy	cocaine
Mary-Jane	25	17	ketamine	cocaine
Michelle	28	18	LSD	ecstasy & ketamine
Mike	26	16	LSD	crystal meth
Monica	28	21	ecstasy	ecstasy
Osiris	28	24	ecstasy	GHB
Ralph	25	16	LSD	crystal meth & GHB
SickKid	27	unknown	unknown	ketamine
Tina	22	20	ketamine	crystal meth
Tyler	28	23	LSD	ketamine
	AVG: 27	AVG: 19		

which the individual begins and continues to use drugs. With the club kids, those who began using drugs in the early 1990s primarily started with LSD. Those, however, who began using from the late 1990s into 2000 began with ecstasy (see Figure 6.1).

The club kids' patterns of drug initiation fit within the larger national trends of drug use. Both the Monitoring the Future (MTF) study[26] and the National Survey on Drug Use and Health (NSDUH)[27] found rising

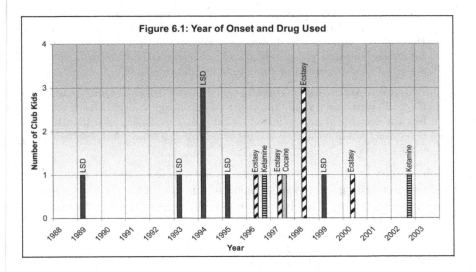

Figure 6.1: Year of Onset and Drug Used

prevalence and peaks in LSD use between 1994 and 1996, and rising prevalence and peaks in ecstasy use from 1998 to 2001.[28] The following quotes from Angelina, Lucille and MaryJane describe how they skipped the LSD era because they had a later onset of drug use:

> Angelina: But I feel like the reason why I didn't do acid is acid was before my time. I didn't start doing drugs until after it was normal, when people were doing ecstasy.
>
> MaryJane: Yeah, people were doin' that [LSD] in high school and I wasn't.
>
> Lucille: Yeah, we were later.
>
> Angelina: We were like 20, ya know?

While the majority of the sample had been using at least one type of club drug for about eight years, the fluctuating popularity and availability of drugs at particular time periods greatly influenced their drug use. The rise in the rate of cocaine use occurred in the late 1970s,[29] and rates of PCP use skyrocketed in 1989.[30] Since 2002, the NSDUH[31] and the MTF[32] have reported declines in the incidence and prevalence of ecstasy use. These secular trends are evident in the shifts in drug use in the club scene. Both George and Betty Cool described the changing drug patterns:

George: The acid just kinda fades out, 'cause ya know, it wasn't around anymore. Shrooms: shrooms, like those things kinda fades out. Mesc [mescaline]: you can't find mesc anywhere anymore . . . K faded out for awhile, but now it's comin' back . . . Like crystal and G right now are the E and K combo of the late 90s, ya know?

Betty Cool: When I started going out that [GHB] wasn't such a big thing. Ecstasy was a really big thing. K was a big thing. Those were like the two big things when I started going out. Um, now it's like G, crystal, ya know? Those are bigger things, ya know, at least from what I know.

While ecstasy is presumed to be the most popular drug in dance club settings, the primary drugs of choice among the club kids are ketamine (used by 6 club kids) and crystal methamphetamine (used by 5 club kids; see Table 6.1).

Use Patterns, Desistance and Transitions

As research on other offenses has found,[33] most substance use research indicates that drug and alcohol use tend to decline with age[34] – with cigarette smoking as an exception.[35] The club kids' patterns are similar, although they continued to use quite heavily through their late 20s, when the age-crime curve predicts they would have desisted. However, the overall decline in club kids' drug use patterns indicates that they are in the process of de-sisting.

Le Blanc and Loeber[36] indicate that desistance[37] is not an abrupt, spontaneous event. Rather it is a process, which occurs in three stages. First the frequency of offending or drug use is reduced (deceleration), then the types of crimes committed or drugs used become fewer (specialization), and then the offenses or drugs consumed become less serious (de-escalation).[38] Most club kids had begun to consume only certain drugs, and had reduced their use to weekends or holidays.

Life-course theorists closer to the sociogenic paradigm argue that "attachment to a conventional other, such as a spouse, stable employment, transformation of personal identity and the aging process" influence the desisting process.[39] Studies overwhelmingly demonstrate that life transitions in social ties, such as getting married and obtaining a steady job, can explain variations in offending patterns throughout adulthood that childhood propensities cannot.[40] Such transitions in the life course encompass bonds to conventional norms that promote non-deviant behavior and – with the exception of those with "pathological conditions" – permanent discontinuity of offending.[41]

Experiencing a transition may result in a turning point that shifts the life trajectory toward a more conventional lifestyle. Sampson and Laub[42] assert that the effects of turning points throughout the life course include:

> (1) a "knifing off" of the past from the present; (2) opportunities for investment in new relationships that offer social support, growth, and new social networks; (3) forms of direct and indirect supervision and monitoring of behavior; (4) structured routines that center more on family life and less on unstructured time with peers; and (5) situations that provide an opportunity for identity transformation and that allow for the emergence of a new self or script . . .

Merely experiencing a life transition is not sufficient to cause a turning point in the life trajectory. Rather, both the quality and the timing of the new bond or investment are important in determining the transition's effect.[43] For example, obtaining employment will not cause a turning point; rather the occupation must be both stable and important to the individual. Furthermore, at particular ages these transitions have greater salience than at other stages in the life course. For example, those individuals provided with stable employment after 26 years of age are more likely to desist than those with stable employment prior to age 26.[44] Between the ages of 32 and 45, marital attachment has "the largest direct effect" on behavior.[45] And, becoming a parent is a much stronger influence on behavior when the individual is between the ages of 28 and 31.[46]

Life events have a gradual and cumulative effect on individual offending patterns. Throughout the life course the effects of a transition, such as marriage, can vary,[47] and the ability to establish a bond like marriage can permit success in making future life transitions. Graduating from college (a positive life transition) increases one's life chances and provides opportunities for employment (another positive life transition). These transitions act as informal social controls inhibiting delinquent and deviant behaviors.

The importance of life-course transitions in influencing persistent use, use reduction (deceleration), switches in drugs of use (specialization) and desistance from use resonated throughout the club kids' interviews. Akin to Sampson and Laub's[48] arguments, changes in employment responsibilities, new familial obligations, physical aging, and romantic relationships shaped decisions of which drugs to use drugs, and when and where to use them.[49] Ralph summarizes most of the club kids' drug-using experience:

> As of lately, it's [clubbing] been decreasing . . . with my old age, it's been becoming like once a month, once every six weeks kind of thing . . . 'Cause as I'm getting older I find recovery time to be way great, and it takes a bit of a toll on my money making abilities . . . And it interferes with like, for instance, like I could be going out and getting like a number of freelance jobs instead of going out to the club. But because I go out to the club, I might not be. I may be tired; I may not wanna do it. So it has an effect . . . and because the fact that my sister's getting married, and I'm becoming more family oriented with age, and my youthful years of being able to go out carefree, without a care in the world, and say, "Ya know what? Screw school!" Or, "I don't have to go do this!" My irresponsibility days are over.

Employment and School Responsibilities

Robust research findings indicate that stable employment and commitments to college or school reduce offending[50] and drug use.[51] Similarly, as the club kids assume adult roles, they experience increasing responsibilities, which compel many to alter their choice of drugs and the appropriate times to use.

"Having responsibilities" is the most cited reason for reducing, shifting, and discontinuing their drug use. Angelina's experience illustrates the saliency of responsibilities in general:

> I just think that physically you can't do it any longer . . . It takes a toll on you. You have more responsibilities in your life. I used to be able to feel like shit on Monday and not really have that much on my plate to worry about. Now, I can't. If I know I'm going to feel like shit on Monday, I can't risk it.

Similarly, SickKid chooses to abstain from going to Miami to take care of responsibilities:

> They went to South Beach, they were like, "aagghhh, SickKid didn't come!" Ya know what I'm sayin', like people talking shit like, "oh, he's ghetto. He can't afford it." Meanwhile I had to do things. I had a meetin'; ya know what I'm sayin'? . . . I take care of responsibilities, I'm responsible. It's my turn now to look out for my moms.

On Monica's priority list as well, work and family obligations "come first":

If I have a big work week ahead of me, you're not gonna see me at [club] NRG . . . Ya know, it's not that big of a deal. Um, ya know, work is number one. If I have family functions, that on the weekends, they come first. Ya know, I remem-the first time I ever did E, the next day I was called into work to do someone a favor, and I was like, "oh, my god!" But I still made it, ya know. I never missed work because of it.

For Monica and many other club kids, employment responsibilities take precedence over a night out of clubbing and drug use. Many club kids began their drug-using and clubbing careers while in high school or college. Now that they were graduating and transitioning into employment, they took steps, such as refraining from drug use, to avoid jeopardizing their employment status. For example, during Jack's third year of medical school and as a resident, he had fewer opportunities for leisure. His previous frequent use of ecstasy and ketamine (every weekend for two years) had come to an end, and his consumption of drugs was now limited to special occasions:

Yeah, we probably averaged E every week for almost two years . . . when I started third year, I was really behind the rest of my classmates . . . when I got into like small groups and I never knew the answers to any of the questions, I was like, "Fuck, I should spend more time hitting the books," ya know? So I felt guilty going out after that, and I spent more time reading. . . . I mean if there's a good night that I'm not on call and I'm not broke, I'll go. I probably won't do E anymore – well, I'll do one hit for sure, if I have a full day off of work the next day.

MaryJane refrained from going out during the week, as her job required her to be "on her toes":

Monday I'm responsible for six kids and I have to be on my toes, you know what I mean? Like I can't, I hate, like I won't go out during the week when I have work 'cause it's not worth it. If I go out I can't touch anything, or anything–or I have to be home early. Like you just have responsibilities now. You have to save up for better things. I have bills to pay.

Like the other club kids, Betty Cool also attributed her reductions in drug use to increasing responsibilities:

When I started living on my own and had bills to pay and couldn't afford to go out as much as I used to. . . . I did get my [nursing] license and I started working . . . fulltime, in a job that I had to work every other weekend [this] stopped me from going out as much as I used to. Because that's very big, ya know? As a nurse, you have to work weekends, every other weekend. So that stopped me from going out as much as I used to. And um, like I said, living on my own, bills, money, ya know, it's not as easy when you're living at home, and working part-time, you don't have responsibility.

While some refrain from drug use, others, like Tyler, limited their use to those drugs that have less intense effects:

We're all not in school anymore. We all have jobs that require us to work five times as hard as we ever did when we were in school . . . On a good night when there's people that are gonna go, and there's a good venue and a good DJ, I'll drop a couple of pills [of ecstasy] and I'll go, if I don't have to work. But something like acid that's gonna fuck me for 36 hours, or a mediocre night where I gotta be in the lab at 6 am, it just doesn't happen anymore. It's not worth it.

Transitions throughout the life course influence drug use primarily when the club kid values that bond. For example, during a period of time at his place of employment as a temp, George would often call in sick to recover from his weekend of partying:

Thursday was [club] Wings, uh, I go to work Friday on like two-three hours sleep, come home, shower, shave, go get a haircut, um, then go to work at the [club] Plant II Friday night. After the Plant II – after work – I go to fuckin' Wax for DJ Italian Stallion. Um, I usually hangout all day Saturday sleep like a few hours Saturday night, wake back up, um, go to work at-at the Plant II for DJ Boy, and then go right to the [club] Plant. After the Plant fuckin' go hang out and go to [club] Wild on Sunday and then hang out Monday. And then fuckin' finally die Monday night and sleep till ya know, fuckin' go to work Tuesday miserable. Ya know but, I would work. The recovery time was a lot shorter then. If I could sleep a few hours, I'd be fine. I'd-I'd ya know, go to work early Tuesday, stay late Tuesday, Wednesday, Thursday, ya know, Friday. So like I did my work when I was workin' . . . I didn't call-I-I didn't call every Monday. I would sometimes even go back, shit-I usually go fuckin' Friday, Friday, Saturday, Sunday, Monday straight up and go to work Monday all like tweaked out like on fuckin' crystal . . .

When his job status shifted from a temp to a full-time employee, his work increased in importance, and his pattern changed:

I partied all summer, and I was working with them as a temp. I called out every Monday, I was, I was a wreck . . . So, I'd say from like, we'll say the end of '99, 2000, 2001, I was doin', I was heavy–heavy into drugs . . . then I started doin' G and crystal, and had sex. 2002, like mid-2002 I think that's around the time I started-I laid-off goin' every weekend . . . I just realized it was time to fuckin' slow it down a little bit. I was goin' strong for three almost four years. And goin' strong, out every weekend, ya know whatta mean? And I wanted to get my shit straight with my . . . with uh, work. Ya know? I did.

However, on occasion, George and a few of the other club kids mentioned the occasional use of club drugs during the week in order to facilitate an effective workday.[52] For instance, George usually refrained from drug use throughout his workweek, but consumed crystal methamphetamine and GHB on Mondays after a long weekend:

I'll party straight through till I have to go to work Monday morning. And then once I get to work . . . I usually bring a little crystal with me to work, a little G with me to work, and I'll-I'll do a little bit, not to get high, but just to give me enough energy, a boost to stay awake, and not be miserable and grouchy, and edgy, and paranoid, ya know?

Likewise, Angelina and a friend in college consumed cocaine every night for two months to complete all the necessary term papers so the friend could graduate, and J. Masters used cocaine to manage his busy schedule during his senior year in college:

Angelina: There was a two-month period of time when me and a friend did it [cocaine] like every fucking night for like two months.

Lucille: I remember you coming into the Plant like, "We just wrote a paper, and we did this and we did that."

Angelina: This girl, like one of my best friends, two years younger than me, needed to graduate college, and was not doing well and I slept at her house for an entire semester. She got me coke and I did all of her papers for her.

J. Masters: When I was in college, I wasn't bad until like my senior year . . . I did coke for an entire year, like nonstop. It was crazy. At the time, I was taking classes and I worked for [a politician], and I tended bar at night. So I'd get up, I would go to school, I'd go to work for them, and then went to the bar . . . I mean I could do coke all day long and work and be fine, which a lotta people do do.

Aging

Another process that influences shifts in, and desistance from, offending through the life course is the ontogenetic process of aging.[53] Merely getting older decreases the body's ability to engage in certain activities. Specifically, going clubbing and using drugs takes skill and energy, much like being a successful thief.[54] Aging significantly reduces the body's ability to perform and manage such activities. Matsueda and Heimer[55] explain that within the life course, offenders will reach "a point in which the physiological effects of ageing begin to hamper adequate role-performance and therefore, attainment of rewards." The club kids' increase in age, coupled with their body's decreasing ability to dance and party all night, are often cited as reasons for alterations in drug use. Thus, SickKid, Monica, and Ariel explain the toll these factors have taken:

> SickKid: But like I feel it man, I feel it in my body. I'm gettin' old, man. I don't got energy like used to; ya know what I'm sayin'? It's not the same no more . . .

> Ariel: I've outgrown it a lot . . . And ya know like, it's exhausting the next day. You stay up all night long, and you dance and you party and meet lots of strangers and you're very happy, and the next day though it's really like exhausting. You're exhausted and basically your entire weekend you like come down. So I can't do it anymore, it's too exhausting.

> Monica: Its different back then, I stayed out much later. Um, now, I'm more concerned about what my hangover's gonna be like. Back then, I didn't care, and I dealt with the hangover. I cannot deal with a hang over, whether it be from drinking, or even overeating. That's what I think keeps me most in check.

Managing the day-after effects of consuming drugs and partying all night, as Monica indicates above, became increasingly difficult as the club kids moved through adulthood. As Robins[56] states: "[p]hysical decline is surely one explanation for why there is so clear a relationship between desistance and age." Angelina, MaryJane and Lucille described the day-after effects of consuming ecstasy:

> Angelina: Yo, you know what it is? It's the day after it's like . . . you're possessed by the devil.

> MaryJane: You can't go to sleep, it's like you need Xanaxes, like you need something to put you to sleep.

> Angelina: You can't eat for like a couple days after.

> MaryJane: Yeah, you got to re-teach yourself how to eat . . .

> Angelina: I just think that physically you can't do it any longer.

> MaryJane: I can't.

> Lucille: You can't.

> Angelina: It takes a toll on you.

David and his friends provided similar reasons for their reduction in ecstasy use:

Honestly, one of the reasons why I think we stopped going and getting fucked at all those clubs was because E, . . . MDMA, gets to you. . . . basically you do E and the next day you wake up feeling like absolute shit, at least I do sometimes. And um, basically you feel depressed and you uh, you feel really thirsty and your whole muscular system might feel fucked up, kind of like you're about to get fucked or something like that. . . . so I think that's part of the reason . . .

The club kids who discontinued regular use of ecstasy and instead consumed GHB cited the "following day" as their primary reason for switching drug preferences. Unlike the day after a night's use of ecstasy, users claimed that GHB did not leave them depressed or exhausted. In fact, subsequent to a night's rest after using GHB, they claimed to be "refreshed" and "ready" for a new day. At club Barroom, Estevez described this feeling:

Estevez said that GHB puts you in deep REM sleep. He said, "When a person awakes from REM sleep that person feels "refreshed" and "ready to go." When we take short naps, we tend not to feel refreshed because we didn't get deep within REM sleep." Estevez tends not to use ecstasy anymore, or at least uses it a lot less, because he said he could not handle the two days needed for recovery. G, on the other hand, has no recovery time. Once you sleep, you feel "brand new" when you awake. (May 31, 2004; field note)

Ralph contrasted the after-effects of consuming GHB with those of alcohol:

It's [GHB] not like alcohol where you're gonna fuckin' get hung over, throw up, if you do too much . . . Let's say I was gonna go out and do it tonight . . . do like a cap of G, get a little twisted [high from GHB], and hang out with a girl, whatever. . . . then once all is said and done, it's one o'clock in the morning, you go to sleep, you sleep fuckin' nine-ten hours like you normally would-you'd wake up the next morning like nothing ever happened. It's not like alcohol. You won't be hung over or anything like that.

Romantic Relationships

Studies show that recreational activities and drug use behaviors are linked to romantic partners and peers.[57] Life-course research indicates that, for the most part, when an offender marries a non-offending partner, the offender significantly reduces his/her engagement in criminal behavior.[58] However, using marital status as an indicator of change can be misleading, as dating and cohabitation often precede marriage.[59] Increasingly, young people throughout their 20s are "choosing to cohabit or steadily date rather than marry."[60] Hence, participation in a romantic relationship can be equally as salient as marriage when understanding patterns of behavior.[61] It is important that life-course criminologists understand the changing nature of romantic relationships before, during and after marriage.[62]

While only two of the club kids were married, many club kids indicated that not having a significant other (i.e., being single) compelled them to club and consume drugs more frequently. Betty Cool described her experience:

> Ya know when we [her and her friends] first started going out it was like four of us, all tall, blonde. They used to call us like the blonde ambitions. At that one period in time, we were all pretty much single at the same time . . . I was single for two years, and um, then I met my boyfriend that I'm going out with now who also likes to go out. So we go out together. But for two years, I was single, and um, that's when I can say I was really like in the city [partying at clubs] at least three nights a week . . . When I was 27, I've just come out of a six-year relationship, I was single for the first time in 10 years, and I was like let loose, ya know. I was let loose, I was hurt, I was ready ta, ya know, just go and have fun, and that's it.

J. Masters had a similar experience:

> I normally, I mean, I used to go out every now and then or once a month or once every coupla weeks. I'm out almost every weekend. At least one night a weekend . . . Ya know what? Not havin' a girlfriend is a big, big part of it . . . I did nothing with my ex-girlfriend at all, smoked pot once or twice. That's about it. I mean we would go out but we wouldn't go clubbing. We would just go, ya know, do like girlfriend/boyfriend type things, ya know . . . And, I mean I dated a lotta girls in between, whatever it may be . . . So throughout the course of like, within each year or so, there was a time when I did coke every weekend for a little while. And then it changed because, really, ya know why it changed? Honestly, it changed because I stopped hangin' out with one girl that I was always hangin' out with, and at that point it changed. It's like I didn't need, it wasn't around as much. Which is kinda weird but, I don't wanna say a girl affects what I do or what I don't do, but it was definitely the issue with that.

As the quote from J. Masters indicates, being tied to a romantic relationship can have an erratic effect on the club kids' drug-using patterns. Some relationships cause reduced drug use and others incite excessive use. Michelle and Jack, while married in May 2002, continued to consume drugs, and George increased his ketamine consumption when he was dating a particular woman:

> Usually when I'm with this girl, like we're kind of seeing each other, but at the same time it's just like basically casual sex, ya know like,

so-there's-there's feeling there, but neither of us are gonna admit it, and it's probably good thing that we don't. Um, Sunday after [club] NRG I ended up goin' home with the same girl I was with. Her and I came home together and we slept like four-five hours, and then we're doin'-was doin' K all fuckin' day. It's disgusting . . . just doing K all day; you're just like, "ew!" I don't know, it's just, I can't do K by itself, but just 'cause I'm with her, like I do things I don't normally do, like drug wise . . . I'll smoke weed, I'll have some K. She loves K . . . I'm like, "fuck it, I'll do it."

The unpredictable effect of romantic relationships on drug-using patterns was largely attributed to the drug-using pattern of the partner. And, for many club kids, locating, dating and marrying someone who was not a member of the clubbing and drug-using scene was difficult, as MaryJane, Angelina and Lucille point out:

MaryJane: Half the time I try to date people who don't do drugs, and it's bad because I look like – I think they're scared of me –

Dina: Could you be with someone who didn't do drugs?

MaryJane: I've tried it, it doesn't really work.

Lucille: I think if they still went out [clubbing].

Angelina: No, because number one, we wouldn't find them . . . because where are we gonna find this person? Unless we met them in like the supermarket.

Such dating and marriage patterns are not unique, as relationships are not random. Rather, "homophily in partner characteristics is well established . . . "[63] Studies demonstrate that people tend to select partners based on taste and experience similarities.[64] Many club kids sought a partner similar to themselves. For example, Monica who did not smoke marijuana regularly, refused to date a frequent marijuana user. However, she would, and did, date an ecstasy user:

I would never date or go out with someone who's a big pot smoker. That might be hypocritical but, if they were into E, that would be okay.

The male club kids (all of whom self-identified as heterosexual) were less likely to date someone who, like them, used drugs and frequented clubs. As MaryJane's quote above indicates, many male partners were frightened of her use. The male club kids seemed to adhere to a double standard regarding drug use. Just as heterosexual men are often rewarded for sexual promiscuity and sexual activity while heterosexual women engaging in those same behaviors are derogated,[65] women who engaged in excessive drug use were demeaned by some club kids. George's comments explicitly demonstrated this:

> Ya know what? Any girls that I meet I'm not gonna even gonna give two shits about if I meetem in a club, ya know whatta mean? I–I tried dating people who-who I met . . . in the scene. It never works out, ya know whatta mean? . . . They're just, just not something ya wanna– . . . If I wanna fuckin' settle down, I'll go look for a girl in like, . . . I'll go to like a drinking crowd party, ya know whatta mean? . . . Not like an afterhours, grimy fuckin' drug party. It's just, yo, it's not gonna happen . . . Not that it can't but, I'm not gonna give it the benefit of the doubt.

> *Dina: But isn't that what you do?*

> George: That's what I do, but it's not what I'm gonna do the rest of my life, ya know whatta mean? . . . It's a known thing. You ask a lotta people who's been in the scene long enough will tell you, "If you wanna meet somebody to take serious, you're not gonna meet'em. And if you do it's a rare." Ya know whatta mean? "You're not gonna meet'em here."

Ralph, on the other hand, was more "open" to marrying a woman from the scene:

> *Dina: So, would you meet your wife in a club?*

> Ralph: I'm gonna say yes. I'm open to it. It's possible because just like me, I'm gonna say I'm a good person. I know I am, and I know there's other people similar in background and ya know, in wholesome and goodness to me. So I'm gonna say its possible. But everybody you meet in a place like that you gotta keep, um, at arm's length for a long time until you actually find out the real, the real person that they really are. 'Cause I'm gonna say 7 out of 10 that are shady individuals you don't want nothin' to do with.

As George stated above, many club kids anticipate discontinuing drug use and clubbing once they marry or settle down. For example, MaryJane states: "Once you get married, serious it's done. No more of this. Maybe I'll smoke pot, but all this shit's over . . . "

The above quotes demonstrate that many club kids alter their drug use patterns because of their changing romantic relationships. However, it is clear, as in the quote from J. Masters above, that most of the club kids greatly reduce or discontinue use because of the decline in time spent clubbing with friends.[66]

Parenting

Parenthood is an additional life transition that tends to foster desistance from criminal behavior and drug use cessation.[67] However, the club kids did not say they would discontinue use entirely once they become parents. Rather, most club kids claimed they would refrain from using certain substances and would avoid using them in their child's presence; however, they would continue to engage in drug use when their child was not in their care. For instance, Angelina said she would continue using cocaine when she is a mother, but would refrain from using ecstasy and ketamine:

> I don't think when I'm 30, like 35, I'd drop a bomb [ecstasy]. I'd probably do a little larry [cocaine] . . . Oh, I'm not gonna be doin' K when I have kids . . . No way.

MaryJane found parents who used drugs in the presence of their children to be appalling:

> MaryJane: I've seen people, like do drugs with kids in the room, and like that disgusts me.
>
> Angelina: I don't know. I would never.

Yet, Lucille said she would continue to use cocaine when her child is with a babysitter:

> Dina: Will you stop completely?
>
> Lucille: Eventually. You know, I think that when I'm in my 30s, if I'm still like going out every once in awhile, and if it's [drug] around I would do it. I don't think I'd go looking for it, the way like you do now. But let's say you were like, if we're like at a party . . . you're 33 years old and maybe you have a 1 year old baby at home with the babysitter, and . . . somebody was like, "Oh, I have larry" [cocaine] . . . You're gonna do it. I don't think it's gonna be like more, like such a habit when you're older. I think it will like stop, but if it's in front of you, I think you would do it for fun.

As Lucille indicates above, most club kids considered their use of drugs to be similar to others' use of alcohol. Just as many parents hire babysitters so they can go to bars or parties where they consume alcoholic beverages, many club kids also anticipated obtaining a babysitter and spending a night out consuming drugs. Monica's outlook exemplifies this view:

> I could see myself, ya know, I can't say that I'm never, ever gonna do it again 'cause that would be a lie. I don't know what would happen

if I have kids. Ya know? I would like to think, "ya know, the babysitter's here, and I get out a night out with my husband. And we can have a fun night. Not over doing it.'

In contrast, George claimed he would discontinue using drugs when he and his partner were trying to conceive:

Granted there will be a time in my life when a family and my career, in that order, will come first to my own wants, not needs. After all, I want to go and I want to get high. A family, most importantly, a child in my eyes is a fulltime dedication and I plan on taking at least a, one year to clean my body up (no steroids and no drugs) before I plan on getting my wife pregnant.

Isaac, the only club kid who had a child, described how having a son provoked him to discontinue marijuana, alcohol and cocaine use:

Ya know, I remembered at the time how bad I was when I was doin' coke . . . As long as I had it, ya know? It didn't matter. I used to stay up for long time, sleep, get up the next, back at it again. I just quit drinkin', takin' Xanax . . . I really had to . . . It was really important to me to not let drink and smokin' do anything anymore. Be sober again, ya know? I got a kid now. That's everything that my ex does. She drinks and smokes and does her shit. I don't wanna be like her, ya know? It's fine for my son to deal with her, but I don't want him to deal with me like that.

Summary

With some exceptions, the club kids were in the process of desistance. Many were engaging in specialized drug use patterns by (a) limiting their use to non-hallucinogens and/or (b) refraining from ecstasy use. Many were also deescalating the amount of drugs consumed by (a) refraining from using during a workweek, and (b) avoiding use when employment or family obligations arose. The club kids attributed theses changes in their drug use patterns to their increasing assumption of adult roles and their decreasing physical energy as they get older. These life transitions essentially protected the club kids from using drugs in potentially harmful and excessive ways.

CAPITAL AND TIMING: MACRO-LEVEL INFLUENCES AND STAGES OF THE LIFE COURSE

Most life-course research indicates that if youth are involved in heavy alcohol or drug use, their behavior is likely to have adverse consequences that create obstacles to the accumulation of capital and successful transition to adulthood.[68] Specifically, Krohn and Thornberry[69] state that, "delinquent behavior and drug use are related to failure to graduate from high school, teenage parenthood, and living independently from the family of origin before graduating from high school." Clearly this was not the case for the club kids. The contradictory findings may have occurred because many studies focus primarily on the individual behavior rather than the structural and social context of use. Most studies focus on lower-class individuals[70] who lack access to capital that can insulate them for criminal justice responses to their behavior and other cumulative disadvantages.[71] Company executives and other drug users in positions of power, such as these club kids, are often missing from these studies.[72]

The club kids experienced smooth transitions throughout their life course as they entered adulthood and escaped the harms typically associated with drug use primarily because of macro-or structural-level factors (e.g., coming of age during historical periods of economic prosperity and accumulation of wealth) within their lives. As Laub and Sampson[73] state, behavior "is a result of a combination of individual actions (choice) in conjunction with situational contexts and structural influences." Social, economic, cultural and political environments and resources influence the accumulation and experience of transitions.[74] Situational and structural factors limit available life choices, and changes in the economic and social conditions alter the timing of the choices available. Together, these factors govern the type and timing of life-course transitions. Individuals select, and are socially positioned among, particular employment options and educational opportunities and potential life-partners. Such factors are not randomly assigned. Rather, race, class, gender and historical events and circumstances external to the individual are important in understanding the patterning of life chances and opportunities.[75] Specifically, capital and the changing life-trajectories associated with changing social and economic conditions greatly influence the type, timing, and experience of life events.

Because these club kids were socially, economically and culturally embedded (see also Chapters 2 and 3), they had access to networks with educational and employment opportunities. Most importantly, they were better equipped (1) to avoid physical and social harms associated with their use and (2) to escape criminal justice stigma. Specifically, the club kids' social positioning (level of capital) provided them with bonds to institutions, protective assets, resources to finance their drug use, and access to private settings for drug use and information regarding the drugs they used. These life chances and safer drug-using options insulated them from arrest and other consequences of entering the criminal justice system, such as loss of employment.

Capital

The salience of capital resonates within many life-course theories because capital plays a significant role in the experience of life transitions.[76] Successful transitions are largely determined by an individual's access to the resources that his/her family, community, peers, and school possess.[77] Over time, this relationship between life-course transitions and capital becomes a reciprocal one. High levels of all forms of capital tend to create positive turning points, and smooth transitions throughout an individual's life and these transitions create and increase the strength of capital. As Sampson and Laub[78] state: "Among those in advantaged positions that provide continuity and social resources over time, both nondelinquents and delinquents alike are presumably not just more motivated, but better able structurally to establish binding ties to conventional lines of adult activity." The possession of high levels of capital and strong bonds to conventional activities also insulate many drug users from drug-related harms and criminal justice detection.[79]

According to Lin,[80] capital is an "*investment of resources with expected returns in the marketplace.*" Capital has many forms: social, economic, human and cultural.[81] To accumulate and reproduce capital, time, access and ability are required. Social and cultural capital are the "immaterial" forms of capital.[82] Cultural capital encompasses the knowledge and practice of elite norms, attitudes and behaviors, and economic capital includes assets and finances. Social capital comprises the embedded resources in social networks that can be accessed when needed.[83] For example, peers or family members who have connections or influence in labor and political organizations, medical facilities or industries – that the individual can access – provide social capital. Human capital includes educational background (i.e., college or postgraduate degrees), knowledge and labor skills.

In late capitalist societies, each function of capital is converted into economic capital and is measured in economic terms.[84] The value of an individual's human capital, for example, is assessed by the amount of economic return such a skill can warrant. The ownership of, or access to, any form of capital or commodity – including a college degree, an attractive physique, or a high-class car – denotes the individual's possession of capital. Matsueda and Heimer[85] explain:

> In a market economy, various forms of capital investment increase the likelihood of individual market success, including investments in *human capital*, such as schooling and job training, *social capital*, which inheres in social relations such as obligations and expectations, information channels, and norms, and *cultural capital*, defined as competence in elite status cultures, including elite attitudes, behaviors and habits. These forms of capital are resources that can be translated into material rewards through conventional institutions.

Experts on capital[86] stress the importance of both the quality and the nature of the capital investment. For example, Burt[87] demonstrates that having links to networks outside of one's immediate social network (i.e., structural holes) can increase social capital. Furthermore, if one cannot access his/her acquaintance's resources then that is not a beneficial network tie. Therefore, much like life-course transitions, the mere presence of capital in an individual's life may be of less importance than its quality.

The form and amount of capital of an individual's family, home community and to those whom that individual remains connected are the primary determinants of the individual's type and level of capital. However, throughout the life course, that individual can both accumulate and lose capital. Hagan[88] clarifies that, "We acquire at birth and accumulate through the life-cycle unequal shares of various kinds of capital that incrementally alter and determine our life chances." Family resources largely determine the neighborhood in which their children will grow up, the quality of their school, the medical and nutritional care they receive, the opportunities available to them, and the experiences they will encounter.[89] Thus, familial and social support and resources are equally important in childhood as they are in adulthood, "as advantages and disadvantages accumulate over time."[90] For example, possessing high levels of social and economic capital provides access to an education and hence, high human capital. Furthermore, human capital increases social and economic capital and, in combination, they permit access to yet another form of capital: stable, well-paying employment. And the cycle continues; capital and the life-course trajectory are innately linked. A favorable position in the social structure facilitates the accumulation of capital, and the possession of capital permits both the maintenance and the addition of advantageous adult bonds. Thus, the relationships among capital, transitions, and behavior are reciprocal and cumulative.[91]

Starting off with low capital can create weak bonds to conventional society, which may increase the likelihood of delinquency. Moreover, the ways to accumulate capital through the informal economy are often labeled as delinquent. Committing acts of delinquency, then, may further weaken or prevent bonds to conventional society, consequently reducing or limiting the delinquent's capital resources. This process, known as cumulative disadvantage, essentially creates a downward spiral of capital and social bonds, while increasing the likelihood of offending and drug use. As Thornberry[92] states: "while the weakening of the bond to conventional society may be an initial cause of delinquency, delinquency eventually becomes its own indirect cause precisely because of its ability to weaken further the person's bond to family, school, and conventional beliefs."

Hagan[93] indicates that those who possess and have access to high levels of capital are more likely to escape criminal justice and other official negative labels, and avoid the harms of cumulative disadvantage. These individuals are given more opportunities for conventional attachments and positive transitions, which being arrested and institutionalized could otherwise thwart.[94] Since most of the club kids already possessed high levels of various forms of capital, they worried less about the effects of cumulative disadvantage associated with arrest and being labeled as an offender.

Neighborhoods and families with higher levels of social, economic and human capital can provide greater access to networks for educational and employment opportunities. Often, early delinquency in these privileged circumstances is handled primarily in the home, outside of official labeling and punishments.[95] Delinquency, under those favorable circumstances, does not disrupt "the normal course of adolescent development and interfere[s] with the accumulation of human and social capital."[96] Possessing both capital and bonds to conventional lines of activity creates life responsibilities, obligations, expectations, and norms that act as informal social controls, which avert and reduce criminal behavior, drug use and drug harms.

In the United States, capital is highly correlated with race and class. Well-educated Whites tend to have more capital than other groups, and the upper class has the largest pool of capital, thereby increasing the overall life chances of members of these groups. As Sandefur Eggerling-Boeck, and Park[97] state: "Young people who are White, have highly educated parents, and who attend private schools are more likely to start off well during the early adult period than those who are Black, Native American or Hispanic, have less educated parents, and who attended public schools." Also, studies indicate that compared to other ethnic and racial groups, Whites are more likely to obtain a four-year college degree, which adds to their supply of capital.[98]

Capital and the Club Kids

The club kids discussed the importance of capital in influencing their behavior. With a few exceptions (SickKid, Isaac, and George), the club kids came from middle to upper class families with ready access to educational, economic and employment resources. Most were experiencing smooth transitions throughout adulthood. Their possession of economic and human capital greatly increased their life chances, while simultaneously keeping them "in check" regarding their drug use, as David and Ariel explain:

> David: We're, the whole group of friends here at [graduate school], we're, we're all pretty much professional. We have futures, bright careers, bright futures. So ya know, that kind of keeps you in place.

> Ariel: I don't think anyone would ever sit there and take 5 [ecstasy pills] all at once, ya know? They, they got their health to think about, they're own careers, they don't wanna be in the hospital. It's different from like someone in high school who has nothing to lose and doesn't really care . . . except I mean they do care. The worst comes to worst, their parents would find out, right? But like they're not gonna loose their job or career or anything like that.

Interestingly, Ariel's quote demonstrates the breadth of protection she felt from criminal justice detection. As a high school student, she perceived the worst response coming from her parents. Arrest, prosecution, and a sentence to be served in a juvenile facility were consequences absent from her mind.

For the club kids, access to resources via social capital helped many to finance their drug use, preventing them from resorting to other crimes to obtain money to purchase drugs. For example, George often relied on Mike's capital when George was low on money:

> The bank of Mike is also pretty helpful too. 'Cause all the trips went on Mike's credit card. We paid him back. Like, he just booked Vegas on his credit card. I gotta pay him back now. Bank of Mike, no interest.

Jack used a school loan to finance his summer of partying:

> I had to take out a loan to finance my summer (laughing). They [his medical school] offered computer loans for people who need to buy computers. I had a computer, but I just went and told them that I

need a computer. They gave me like 24 hundred dollars. I considered it like a vacation . . . Now, we can't just take out loans to finance our bad habits.

Life-course transitions and capital also shape harmful experiences associated with drugs, including physical harms and criminal justice responses to drug-using behaviors. Individuals with protective assets such as a privileged social position, Thornberry[99] explains, "are less likely to experience strong negative consequences brought about by feedback effects from delinquent behavior." Individuals from the middle to upper classes are better equipped through their social position to avoid negative consequences associated with their behavior. In particular, they can evade official labeling, and hence avoid suffering later problems when obtaining employment.[100] Capital and social bonds can insulate these offenders and drug users from arrest and other consequences from entering the criminal justice system.

The club kids' social and human capital also provided them with access to information regarding the harms associated with their drug use (see also Chapter 5). For example, Jack discusses the medical knowledge he obtained via his former medical school:

I've never seen anything convincing . . . I mean, as far as I know, there's no science saying that, ya know, any of these drugs cause like prolonged effects, ya know? There's really not that much science to go through . . . You can argue that we don't have long-term data on people, but I think that we have. The real study to do– see, this is the problem with science, is that you can do anything in an animal model, and it's, "is that animal model real? Is that result generalizable?" I think the real study to do is to do a population based study. Like, it would be retrospective so it wouldn't be the best thing in the world. But, you can do people who do, like people've been doing ecstasy since like the 80s now. Like you can do, population based, large group, thousands of people, like retrospective studies and look at the time course from the, ya know, onset of ecstasy. You can standardize among dosage and how much they took, and you can see if they have any cognitive impairment . . . Like I basically dismissed all the basic science studies in this area because they'll get a bunch of kids who are doing tons of different drugs, they'll make them stop doing E for a week, and give one group E for a day, and then, and then do cognitive testing – and show, "uh, hah!" Like, how do they conduct that? Like how do you know they're not just doing test after test after test until they get the result that they really want? Ya know, they're all small groups. . . . what about all the people that did acid in the 60s? I mean that's a huge population. Like, how do they compare to the rest of the population? I mean you have control, right? People who didn't do acid in the 60s. So compare them. How do they measure up? Like what are the important clinical outcomes? Like, brain imaging to me, like fine, what does that mean? Like to me, that's not important. Are there any clinically significant effects? That's all I worry about. In other words, you can change someone's physiology like by giving them a drug, but then do they have any benefit from it, right? Ya know, and the truth is that human physiology is so complex we never really understand it a hundred percent . . . You can do imaging studies from those who did acid in the 60s and show that there are cortical changes with this group compared to the control group. But then, ya know, if cognitively you can't find any real differences 30 years out, or there aren't any increased rates of Alzheimer's, Parkinson's, brain tumors, then what is that image you found on the MRI? Does it mean anything? I would argue that it doesn't mean anything . . . I've also been to Tox conferences, and New York City Poisons . . . and they don't really know, they're not aware of any short term or long term like harms of these drugs. Like people have called like 212-poisons and asked, ya know, "what are the risks of like doing ecstasy?" And they [poison control] just laugh. And these guys are the experts on drug abuse in the medical community.

To protect himself from driving under the influence of drugs, J. Masters, who possesses enough economic capital to afford a night in a New York City hotel, checked himself into a hotel when his drug use reduced his ability to drive home. He explained:

> We always have to figure out one person that's gonna drive home. Or we'll take a cab. Like when we're out there, we always take cabs. But get to the city, back: it's an expensive cab ride. I mean I've checked into hotels walkin' outta clubs sometimes. I realized I couldn't drive and I stopped.

Betty Cool attributed the drug-related harms she witnessed in the clubs primarily to social factors:

> I think a lotta of what has to do with the reasons for the clubs being closed down and what people do inside the club, has to do with what goes on in their life outside of a club. Ya know, whether it's family and whatever else, ya know? Ya know, I think a lotta of kids today – I don't think it's the club scene that affects them. I think it's what goes on home.

Summary

Most of the club kids had yet to experience a punitive criminal justice response to their drug-using behaviors. Rather, their salient transitions in employment and family life afforded to them through their high levels of capital had insulated them from criminal justice system involvement (such as arrest).[101] In contrast to other drug users, the club kids' capital allowed them to consume drugs primarily in private settings, such as clubs, hotels or private homes. They were less likely to use in the street, where they would be more susceptible to police observation.[102] Studies indicate that, after controlling for levels of drug use, Blacks and Hispanics are more likely to be arrested for drug use than are Whites.[103] Furthermore, possessing capital gave the club kids privileges that they did not want to lose, thus deterring many from excessive drug use. The following quotes indicate the value that the club kids' placed on their life responsibilities and achievements, and the privileges these afforded to them:

> George: If you're going to party, you have to be responsible first with other areas of life.

> Betty Cool: Who's better than me? I work. I have a good job, ya know? I come from a good family. I have good friends. And ya know, I could have fun.

Alterations to the Stages of the Life-Course Trajectory

The capital most of these club kids possessed had situated them within an affluent life stage in which they had experienced smooth and traditional transitions with few, if any, interruptions. However, many club kids had yet to experience certain markers of adulthood, such as marriage and parenthood. According to older life-course perspectives,[104] stages in the life course begin with childhood progress into adolescence, and then, at around age 18, the stage of adulthood begins. By the time the individual reaches age 25, he/she has already experienced the primary adult life events: marriage and parenting. Given this typical trajectory, all but one of the club kids would have been expected to be married and to have started a family. Accordingly, they would have greatly reduced or discontinued using drugs. Contrary to this scenario, only two of the club kids were married (they were married to each other) and they continued to use drugs during their late 20s. Compared to previous generations, these transitions into adulthood occurred much later in the club kids' life trajectories. Because of economic and social shifts, including globalization, a larger gap between adolescence and adulthood had resulted (see also Chapter 3). During this new stage of development, termed emerging adulthood,[105] or moratorium,[106] these club kids had the money (economic capital) and the time

– 192 –

to go clubbing and consume drugs.[107] However, as the club kids left this stage and experienced adulthood transitions (see above), many altered their clubbing and drug use patterns to avoid harming these transitions.

Emerging Adulthood

When life-course theories first emerged, developmental stages occurred at predictable ages: childhood continued until about age 12, adolescence until about 18, and adulthood began after age 18. Now, however, a new stage of life development between adolescence and adulthood, known as "emerging" or "early" adulthood, has surfaced[108] (see Chapter 3). Arnett[109] and Furstenberg, Rumbaut, and Settersten[110] point to macro-level factors, such as the rising need for post-high school and even post-college education and the changing nature of employment opportunities, as contributors to this new stage of development (see Chapter 3). During the 1940s and 1950s, young people in their 20s more or less socially mirrored those in their 30s and 40s, engaging in full-time employment, marriage, and children. During those earlier decades, adulthood began after a short adolescent period. Currently, in contrast, individuals in their 20s have much different experiences from past generations within the same age bracket. Those born in the 1970's and 80's experienced adolescence at much earlier ages and adulthood at much later ages, than previous generations. This has compelled many of them to rely on their parents well into their 30s. It is this period in the life course (specifically, between 18 and 34 years of age) that is referred to as early or emerging adulthood.

Childhood development experts indicate that biological maturation and sexual experimentation occur earlier among current generations. Children are now "growing-up" more quickly and "childhood as a period of life . . . is being squeezed."[111] Current generations of youth are also experiencing "unpredictable," "prolonged," and "disordered" sequencing of adulthood transitions (i.e., marriage, moving out of their childhood homes and completing school).[112] Thornberry[113] characterizes this transition to the adulthood stage as, "a volatile period of increasing freedom and independence . . . [with] a variety of living arrangements . . . [and] great transiency."

These shifting life experiences are primarily the result of economic and social changes, including globalization, resulting in the prolongation of higher education and the delaying of employment and settling down with a family for a decade or so later.[114] This trend has created a gap between adolescence and adulthood, in which "it is simply not possible for most young people to achieve economic and psychological autonomy as early as it was half a century ago."[115] Research indicates that without college and secure employment it is difficult to manage transitions in adulthood, such as financial autonomy.[116] Achieving a middle-class lifestyle is extremely arduous without possessing economic, human, cultural, and social capital. Consequently, many young people, like the club kids, seek a graduate education, engage in nonmarital relationships (see also Chapter 3), and continue to rely on their parents for economic resources and housing (see Table 1.2).

Young adults' extended reliance on their parents, into their 30s, places a strain on many families who also may have to support aging parents. Young people from middle and upper classes, such as most of the club kids, are fortunate to have resources and support, which are often unavailable to many of their peers from the lower social classes. "The ability of families to manage this long and complex period clearly varies greatly by the resources they possess or those they can access through formal or informal ties."[117] Individuals who come from highly educated, well-off families are more likely to obtain the support and resources necessary for professional and educational advancement.[118] For example, Ralph, who still lived at home with his family, explained the important role his parents play in his transition into adulthood:

> I pay rent, but they put it away for me, ya know what I'm sayin'? I can't complain. I got fuckin' great parents.

Similarly, when George was younger, his family cushioned his transition to adulthood and economic autonomy:

> Ya know, money's a big thing right now, ya know whatta mean? When I was younger I could hit up my father for money, or uh, my grandma's, some money, or my mother if I wanted money. Whatever I spend now, I earn, ya know whatta mean? I'm not borrowin' money from anybody. Nobody's givin' me money, so I have to pay my own way.

As George aged and acquired adult life responsibilities, he had to rely more on his own resources to finance his lifestyle. Likewise, when Betty Cool was living at home, she was able to take a year off prior to her nursing board examination and rely on her mother while she went clubbing and consumed drugs:

> When I was 27, I had just finished school, nursing school. But I hadn't taken my boards yet, and I kinda wanted like a year to myself to go

out and like have fun and my mother was like, "go ahead." I was still living at home, so I did.

As the club kids got older, most experienced the effects of aging and transitioning from emerging adulthood to adulthood. Their increasing responsibilities, afforded to them through their sources of capital, coupled with their decreasing physical abilities to dance all night and use drugs, meant that for most club kids, their drug use would eventually be discontinued. Such elements within the club kids' lives had already begun to lay the foundation for the need and desire (i.e., human agency; see below) to alter, and desist from, their drug use (see also above).

Human Agency

Human agency or will – a key component of the individual's mind*set* – is affected by macro-level elements, including changes in stages of the life course and capital. These factors influence the type, quality and value of available life choices. Within the confines of the available choices, individuals make decisions to either discontinue or continue deviant behaviors.[119] Sampson and Laub [120]state that, "individuals construct their own life course through the choices and actions they take within the opportunities and constraints of history and social circumstances." The club kids' high level of capital, conventional life transitions, and access to networks and resources to enhance life chances provided them with a variety of profitable life options that were unavailable to many other drug users. With such life chances available, these club kids – for the most part – made choices throughout their drug-using trajectories to avoid harming their ties to employment and family that would have placed their capital (social, human, cultural and economic) in jeopardy.

Life-course criminologists argue that certain life events may prompt individuals to reconsider the direction of their lives, and perhaps change their behavior.[121] Often, at a turning point, individuals change the direction of their lives as they reflect upon, respond to, and create new experiences and pathways.[122] For example, research indicates that many ex-offenders emphasize that desistance is a result of "voluntary actions."[123] Offenders who desist may experience changes in their personalities and self-concepts in which they develop greater concern for others and accept the need to take control of their futures.[124] Many drug users also discuss the importance of human agency in changing their patterns of use.[125] Likewise, the club kids, such as Ralph, often attributed shifts in patterns to their "common sense" decisions:

> I went through a stretch where um, in college, when I was doin' like K on like a daily basis, with one other kid, or just like two other people . . . I'd been doin' it like by myself, like on a daily basis . . . when I shouldn't've been, for a couple a months straight, when I was like, "fuck, what am I doin'? This is disgusting; I'm a drug addict." So I stopped . . . I had enough common sense to realize that ya know?

George explained that users must decide to prevent drug use and partying from consuming their lives:

> I mean I, believe me -I do shit to extreme, but I try not to get it to the point where it's like outta control . . . "Ya know, there's a point where you can't go, too, too, terribly far. I mean you could stretch it every now and then, but that's just outta control."

Notably, most club kids had the capital to shape their agency for change. But human agency does not occur in a vacuum. Maruna[126] stresses that focusing primarily on human agency, such as "moments of clarity" and "hitting bottom," is problematic. He states that, "randomly assigning identical turning-point experiences to addicts and offenders, in the hope that this would trigger self-transformation, might be a formula for disaster."[127] Rather, understanding the relationships among structural factors, life events, human agency and behavior is necessary to explain continuity and change in drug use patterns. Specifically, individual life options are "confined by a range of specifiable circumstances"[128] established primarily by that individual's possession and access to capital.

Understanding the Life Course

An individual's life course is affected by multiple levels of social ecology:[129] (1) the macro level – including drug trends (period or secular trends), cultural norms, and structural changes, (i.e., globalization, economic shifts, and educational requirements); (2) the meso level – including social institutions (school and family), networks and resources (capital); and (3) the micro level – including available individual options and decisions (human agency). These levels interact with one another to determine both the possession and accumulation of capital, to structure life-course transitions, and to govern the drug-using trajectory. Life-course and developmental perspectives indicate that capital and informal social controls, such as bonds to conventional norms, marriage, work and school, are key elements in explaining continuity and discontinuity in offending and drug-using patterns.[130]

During the club kids' life-course trajectories, they reported periods of excessive (daily or weekly) use, changes in drugs of choice – such as shifting from ecstasy to GHB – and reductions and cessations of drug use (see also Chapter 5). For most club kids, their excessive use of drugs was temporary. Because many of the affluent club kids were within the stage of emerging adulthood, they had the freedom, the time, the money, and the energy to be "weekend warriors," escaping into fantastical worlds and consuming substantial amounts of drugs. However, many of the club kids who entered adulthood have begun the de-escalation and specialization stages of the desisting process. They reduced or shifted their drug use to accommodate increasing responsibilities and their decreasing physical agility as they aged. Increasing financial obligations, obtaining new intimate partners as well as ending relationships with others, and, for some, becoming a parent were additional reasons for changing their drug-use patterns.

Many club kids also attributed their shift from ecstasy and ketamine use to crystal methamphetamine and GHB use to their increasing employment and family obligations and their bodies' decreasing ability to handle the day-after effects. However, the decreasing popularity of ecstasy and the rising popularity of crystal methamphetamine, both in nationwide trends and within the club scene, may also have accounted for these changing patterns of drug use.

While most of these club kids' drug-use patterns largely reflected the importance of social bonds in affecting behavior, SickKid's trajectory seems to have been an outlier. He never attended college, was employed part-time, and did not appear to be on the path toward desistance. Perhaps SickKid's trajectory typified Moffitt's[131] life course persistent offender, who was characterized by cognitive deficiencies. Or SickKid's low social status and few capital resources may have prevented him from achieving stable life transitions and desisting from drug use.

Nevertheless, many club kids had been using drugs for almost 10 years and all continued to use drugs through their 20s and even into their 30s; most of their use had not impeded their educational or career achievements. And, they had successfully avoided arrest and stigmatization as offenders or addicts. Their capital and life transitions protected them from these harms typically associated with drug use.

NOTES

1. Some of the material in this chapter has previously appeared in Perrone, 2006.
2. 1984.
3. e.g., Benson, 2002; Erickson and Cheung, 1999; Esbensen and Elliot, 1994; Sampson and Laub, 1993; Thornberry, 1987.
4. 1986.
5. e.g., Biernacki, 1986; Boeri, 2002; Esbensen and Elliot, 1994; Hamil-Luker, Land, and Blau, 2004; Robins, Davis, and Goodwin, 1974; Shukla, 2003; Waldorf, Reinarman, and Murphy, 1991.
6. Allaste and Lagerspetz, 2002; Beck and Rosenbaum, 1994; Hammersley et al., 2002; Hansen et al., 2001; Kelly, 2006; Measham et al., 2001; Ter Bogt et al., 2002.
7. Erikson (1968/1994; 1970) would call this stage a psychosocial moratorium or a delay of adult commitments. This period typically occurs between youth and adulthood, and the young adult in this stage often engages in "free role experimentation" (Erickson, 1968/1994, p. 156).
8. see Piquero, Farrington, and Blumstein, 2003 for a detailed description.
9. Loeber and Le Blanc (1990) prefer to use the terms activation, aggravation and desistance to describe onset, persistence and desistance.
10. e.g., Farrington, 2005; Sampson and Laub, 1993; Thornberry, 1987.
11. Cullen and Agnew, 2003.
12. e.g., Hagan and Palloni, 1988; Loeber and Le Blanc, 1990.
13. 1993.
14. Maruna, 2001; Matsueda and Heimer, 1997/2005; Sullivan, 1996.
15. Gottfredson and Hirschi, 1990.
16. Moffitt, 1993.
17. e.g., Gottfredson and Hirschi, 1990; Moffitt, 1993.
18. e.g., Sampson and Laub, 2005; Thornberry, 1987.
19. This finding dates back to the 19th century. For example, in the 1820s in France, crimes peaked between late teens through the mid-twenties (Quetelet, 1831/1984).
20. 1995.
21. e.g., Farrington and Maughan, 1999.
22. Le Blanc and Fréchette, 1989.
23. 2005.
24. Cohort effects are differences that affect a particular group who initiate or experience something together (Farrington, 1986).
25. 1996, p. 116.

26. Johnston, O'Malley, and Bachman, 2003.
27. Substance Abuse and Mental Health Services Administration (SAMHSA), 2003.
28. see also Golub, Johnson, Sifaneck, Chesluk, and Parker, 2001.
29. Bachman et al., 1996.
30. Golub et al., 2001.
31. SAMHSA, 2006a.
32. Johnston et al., 2005.
33. e.g., Maruna, 2001; Sampson and Laub, 1993; Shover, 1985.
34. Biernacki, 1986; Boeri, 2002; Esbensen and Elliot, 1994; Labouvie, Bates, and Pandina, 1997; Winick, 1962.
35. Chen and Kandel, 1995; Chen, White, and Pandina, 2001.
36. 1998; see Barnett, Blumstein, and Farrington, 1987.
37. Criminologists debate the study of desistance, since a lack of a clear definition of desistance from criminal behavior exists within criminological literature (Maruna, 2001). Common questions are what is the length of follow-up? Is it forever; a few days? For example, Farrington (1979) and Blumstein, Cohen, and Hsieh (1982) question if desistance could be assessed while the individual was still alive. Maruna (2001) suggests desistance be defined as "long-term abstinence from a lengthy span of persistent criminal behavior" (p. 26).
38. Cohen (1986) found that by the time offenders reach adulthood they de-escalate the seriousness of offense committed.
39. Laub and Sampson, 2001, p. 13; see also Sampson and Laub, 1993, 1997/ 2005, 2005.
40. e.g., Evans, Cullen, Velmer, Dunaway, and Benson, 1997; Horney, Osgood, and Marshall, 1995; Laub, Nagin, and Sampson; 1998; Laub, Sampson, and Allen; 2001; Wright, Caspi, Moffitt, and Silva, 1999.
41. Kerner, 2005, p. 267.
42. 2005, p. 34.
43. see also Horney et al., 1995; Laub et al., 1998.
44. Uggen, 2000.
45. Sampson and Laub, 1993, p. 156.
46. Labouvie, 1996.
47. Sampson and Laub, 2005.
48. 1993, 1997/2005.
49. e.g., Bennette, McCrady, Johnson, and Pandina, 1999; Decorte, 2000; Ter Bogt et al., 2002; Waldorf et al., 1991.
50. Loeber, Stouthamer-Loeber, Van Kammen, and Farrington, 1991; Sampson and Laub, 2003; Shover, 1985.
51. e.g., Biernacki, 1986; Hammersley et al., 2002; Hansen et al., 2001; Measham et al., 2001; Ter Bogt et al., 2002; Waldorf et al., 1991.
52. see also Decorte, 2000; Joe-Laidler, 2005; Waldorf et al., 1991.
53. Snow, 1973.
54. see Gove, 1985; Robins, 2005; Sampson and Laub, 1993; Shover, 1996.

55. 1997/2005, p. 183.
56. 2005, p. 61.
57. Cavacuiti, 2004; Esbensen and Elliott, 1994; Kandel and Davies, 1990; Latkin, Forman, and Knowlton, 2002; Labouvie, 1996; Yamaguchi and Kandel, 1997.
58. Matsueda and Heimer, 1997/2005.
59. see Adams, 1997/2005.
60. Osgood, Ruth, Eccles, Jacobs, and Barber, 2005, p. 343.
61. see also Horney, Osgood, and Marshall, 1995.
62. Adams, 2005; cf., Sampson and Laub, 2005.
63. Sampson and Laub, 2005, p. 34.
64. Matsueda and Heimer, 2005; Yamaguchi and Kandel, 1993.
65. see Hinchliff, 2001; Oliver and Sedikides, 1992; O'Sullivan, 1995; Parks and Scheidt, 2000; Sack, Keller, and Hinkle, 1981.
66. cf., Warr, 1998, 2002.
67. see Esbensen and Elliott, 1994; Labouvie, 1996.
68. Krohn and Thornberry, 2003.
69. 2003, p. 319.
70. e.g., Farrington, 2005, cf., Weisburd, Waring, and Chayet, 1993.
71. Sampson and Laub, 1997/2005; Thornberry, 1987.
72. cf., Robins, 2005.
73. 2001, p. 48; see also Osgood et al., 2005; Shanahan, 2000.
74. Bynner, 2005.
75. Laub and Sampson, 2001; Sullivan, 1989.
76. e.g., Sampson and Laub, 2005; Matsueda and Heimer, 1997/2005; Thornberry, 1987.
77. Sandefur, Eggerling-Boeck, and Park, 2005.
78. 1997/2005. See also Matsueda and Heimer, 1997/2005; Sampson and Laub, 1993.
79. e.g., Murphy and Rosenbaum, 1997.
80. 2001a, p. 3; emphasis in the original.
81. see Bourdieu, 1986.
82. Bourdieu, 1986, p. 242.
83. Lin, 2001a.
84. Bourdieu, 1986; cf., Messner and Rosenfeld, 2006.
85. 1997/2005, p. 168; emphasis added.
86. Burt, 2000; Lin, 2001a, 2001b.
87. 2001, 2004.
88. 1997/2005, p. 294.
89. Schoeni and Ross, 2005.
90. Furstenberg, Rumbaut, and Settersten, 2005, p. 19.
91. Le Blanc, 1997/2005; Thornberry, 1987.
92. 1987, p. 865.
93. 1991.

94. see Murphy and Rosenbaum, 1997.
95. e.g., Sullivan, 1996.
96. Krohn and Thornberry, 2005, p. 322.
97. 2005, p. 315.
98. e.g., Sandefur et al., 2005.
99. 2005, p. 177.
100. see Hagan, 1991; Sampson and Laub, 1993.
101. see Dunlap, Johnson, and Manwar, 1994; Murphy and Rosenbaum, 1997.
102. see Dunlap et al., 1994; Golub, Johnson, and Dunlap, 2007; Goode, 2002.
103. Beckett, Nyrop, and Pfingst, 2005; Beckett, Nyrop, Pfingst, and Bowen, 2005; Goode, 2002.
104. see Elder, 1985.
105. Arnett, 2000.
106. see Erikson, 1968/1994; 1970.
107. cf., Parker et al., 1998.
108. Arnett, 2000 and Furstenberg et al., 2005, respectively.
109. 2000.
110. 2005.
111. Bynner, 2005, p. 369.
112. Furstenberg et al., 2005, p. 5; see also Shanahan, 2000. While much evidence exists demonstrating the transitional shifts over the life-course, Bynner (2005) indicates that this does not cross all socio-economic classes. Rather, the structural difficulties within the lower classes cause their childhood stage to shrink and adulthood to extend. The emerging adulthood stage has occurred primarily among the advantaged, while "traditional accelerated routes to adult life" are still common among the disadvantaged (Bynner, 2005, p. 377). Among this group, "Early marriage, followed by divorce and single parenthood" is widespread (Bynner, 2005, p. 378). Therefore, in understanding transitions through the life course it is important to take into account structural factors.
113. 2005, p. 171.
114. see Castells, 2004; Fussell and Furstenberg, 2005; Giddens, 2003; Measham et al., 2001; Parker et al., 1998.
115. Furstenberg et al., 2005, p. 5.
116. e.g., Furstenberg et al., 2005.
117. Furstenberg et al., 2005, p. 20.
118. Osgood et al., 2005.
119. see e.g., Giddens, 1984; Laub and Sampson, 2003.
120. 2005, p. 40; see also Sullivan, 1996.
121. see Laub et al., 1998.
122. see also Bynner, 2005.
123. Kerner, 2005, p. 273.
124. e.g., Laub and Sampson, 2001; Maruna, 2001.
125. e.g., Biernacki, 1986; Waldorf et al., 1991.

126. 2001, p. 25; see also Trice and Roman, 1970.
127. Maruna, 2001, p. 25.
128. Giddens, 1984, p. 15.
129. cf., Bronfenbrenner, 1979; 1992.
130. e.g., Biernacki, 1986; Esbensen and Elliot, 1994; Glaser, 1969; Hammersley et al., 2002; Measham et al., 2001; Waldorf et al., 1991.
131. 1993.

7. DISCUSSION

Monica: I hope that you can convey that people can work and have recreation, ya know, do things on a recreational level, and still maintain a normal life. I hope you can get that out and convey that to people. Or, even if, like, say someone wasn't, was using it more than on a recreational level, know that, you can stop and . . . reduce . . . I'm a product of it.

The club kids' drug use patterns and drug experiences challenge many of the stereotypical images of drug users. Most of the literature on drug use focuses on adolescents, poor people, prisoners and those who are in drug treatment, as well as drug-related harms and the relationship of drug use to crime and violence. In contrast, most of the club kids studied here were White and relatively affluent drug-using adults who experienced little harm, avoided the criminal justice system, and engaged neither in crime (other than drug use) nor in violence. Certain aspects of the club kids' drug-using practices helped prevent them from incarnating the media's depictions of destructive drug users and allowed them to alleviate harmful experiences. Specifically, *drug, set, setting, timing* and *capital* are key factors for understanding how harm was both generated and mitigated. The immediate social situation (drug, set and setting) in which the drugs were used, together with the cultural, structural and institutional contexts of their lives, shaped the club kids' drug use, the nature of their drug experience, and drug-related harms. Through their access to capital and ties to conventional institutions (work, family and school), which (1) influenced their drug-using mindset, (2) determined drug-using settings, and (3) acted as informal social controls on their drug-using behaviors, the club kids engaged primarily in controlled drug use and employed harm-minimization methods.

The stress of everyday life, particularly in the stage of emerging adulthood, coupled with a highly commercialized culture of excess, produces strain and a desire to escape (Chapter 3). Delays in life transitions produce pressures of conflicting obligations, individual responsibilities, and achievement stressors. These burdens provoke individuals to desire places to experience release, engage in excess, transgress into different selves, and, as Michelle stated, "go nuts" on weekend nights. In a global, late capitalist, highly consumed and commercialized society, individuals are encouraged to seek pleasures and release through the consumption of commodities, including drugs (see Chapters 2 and 3). Within both the business and leisure spheres, individuals are continually persuaded to indulge and consume.

The club kids' choices for escape – consumption of drugs and clubbing – are both compatible with American cultural and capitalist ideals and outside of those ideals. Fitting within conventional norms, the club kids consume leisure commodities, such as clubbing on the weekends, for temporary pleasurable escapes. Moreover, their consumption of drugs, while illegal and socially disapproved, is undertaken for many of the same reasons that they and others consume legal substances. As Waldorf et al. state:[1] " . . . in our culture the consumption of drug commodities for entertainment and pleasure is not a big jump from the norms of society . . . [A]ll of us participate in and thus help constitute a culture in which the consumption of commodities for pleasure is so intrinsic that the consumption of drugs is commonplace." The consumption of mind-altering substances is widespread. For example, as many Americans consume alcohol to enhance social events, the club kids consumed GHB to heighten their clubbing experience. The proliferation of pharmaceutical and body-enhancement advertisements disseminated through media outlets demonstrates how in this society drugs are used routinely to maintain and to enhance lifestyles, performances, and physiques.[2] As many Americans ingest diet pills to produce ideal physical appearances, the club kids enjoy the weight-loss enhancing properties of ecstasy and crystal methamphetamine (see Chapter 2). Club kids George, MaryJane and Tina indicated how through the use of drugs, they and other individuals were able to look and feel better (see Chapter 2). Clearly, the club kids' "illicit drug use is 'rooted in legal drug use.'"[3]

The club kids sought to escape their commercialized and consumed everyday lives, only to enter a club culture that is equally, if not more, commodified, commercialized and globalized (see Chapter 4). The venues where the club kids chose to spend their leisure time are spaces for excess and transgression, in which themed-style outfits and the consumption of multiple substances help create a complete sensory experience. Often, venues are transformed from a dance club, restaurant, hotel pool area, or even a political forum into a carnival where the attendees enter a fantastical world to escape their everyday obligations. This world encourages and fosters capitalist ideals, maintains social hierarchies and encourages adherence to mainstream beauty images.

In these fantastical, carnivalesque settings, drug-use patterns, drug-use effects and folklore for preventing harms – all parts of the complete drug-induced experience – are learned and shared. Situational (drug, set and setting), cultural (consumption and commercialization), structural (globalization and capital), institutional (school and work), and developmental (stages within the life-course and life events) factors shape the use, effects and harms of drug use. The social context surrounding the use and the user both generates and mitigates harmful consequences associated with drugs.[4] Since most of these drug users seek, accumulate, and successfully maintain high levels of capital and conventional family ties and occupations, they make conscious efforts to avoid potential harms and stigmas associated with their use (see Chapter 6).

Socially and economically privileged drug users, such as the club kids, are better equipped to manage their clubbing and drug-using behaviors than are less privileged drug users. Their embeddedness in conventional institutions (work, family, and school) and access to resources help ensure that their escape does not conflict with the responsibilities and social bonds in their ordinary lives (see Chapters 3 and 6). While any drug user has the potential to experience drug-related harms, individuals like the club kids, who possess options for advancement and have a stake in conventional life, tend to have a greater capacity for controlling their drug use and minimizing the harms – even when their patterns of use are extreme (see Chapter 6). In contrast, when economically poor individuals begin using drugs, their attempts at being drug savvy are less likely to be successful. These users have fewer bonds to conventional society and fewer resources to cope with and avert drug-related harms (e.g., engaging in crime to purchase drugs). They are also more likely to be targeted by criminal justice tactics and subjected to criminal justice sanctions.[5] The war on drugs is disproportionately a war on poor people. Thus, White, middle-class users are more capable of concealing their drug use and escaping public and police detection than their lower-class counterparts.[6]

The club kids' social and economic privileges and the strength of their peer networks provide them with access to information about safer drug use and allow them to avoid arrest (see Chapter 5). The club kids take steps to avoid adverse reactions to drugs such as vomiting, passing out, and overdoses. By learning about the effects of drug combinations and sharing this knowledge through social networks, these users choose which drugs to use and when to use them (see Chapter 5). They often consume drugs of higher quality (i.e., increased purity), engage in drug use in private and protected settings beyond the scrutiny of police, and access resources that allow them to avoid harmful drug use.

The club kids' life responsibilities and obligations, both throughout the life-course and at the time of the drug-using events, prompt many of them to refrain increasingly and eventually desist from drug use as they grow older (see Chapter 6). If the club kids have important obligations to meet the following day, many restrain themselves from drug use. Most of these club kids desist from using certain drugs, such as ecstasy, when the time needed to recover from using those drugs begins to interfere with work and school responsibilities, or when new responsibilities arise that become priorities (e.g., work or family). Essentially, these users maintain controlled drug use with few harmful experiences.

The club kids, however, do not always follow their strategies for reducing negative consequences, and sometimes experience some short-term harm as a result of their use. Such incidents cannot be ignored (see Chapters 5 and 7). Two of the club kids awoke in emergency rooms as a result of GHB use, and Lucille's frequent panic attacks were a cause for concern. The increase in cocaine and crystal methamphetamine use within the club scene was also alarming. In 2004, approximately 4% of all emergency room visits involving illicit drugs were attributed to methamphetamine, and that proportion rose to 7.5% in 2005.[7] Even more strikingly, 19% of all emergency room visits for illicit drugs in 2004 involved cocaine, and this increased to 31% in 2005.[8] Clearly such drugs can be harmful, and some users are not able to avoid uncontrollable and destructive drug use.

The long-term negative health consequences that the club kids may experience as a result of their drug use are also unclear. Some literature indicates that MDMA is associated with cognitive impairment,[9] and some studies link methamphetamine use to cardiomyopathy, a condition in which the heart muscle is inflamed.[10] Moreover, intranasal cocaine and crystal methamphetamine use have been cited as sources of chronic sinus inflammation.[11] Some users of these drugs incur life-long health impairments.

The club kids studied here were aware of many of these harmful effects and took steps to avoid them. Many club kids engaged in behaviors to control their drug use. Their experiences demonstrate that through knowledge of the pharmacological properties of the drug and the appropriate set and the suitable setting for pleasurable drug experiences, some users can prevent harms associated with their use. With access to, and possession of, high levels of capital (economic, social, human, and cultural) and the appropriate timing of life-course transitions into conventional roles and activities, the club kids were able minimize harms associated with their drug use.

The club kids' drug-using trajectories further indicate that, for many, drug use is temporary, and that they can voluntarily shift patterns of, and desist from, drug use without treatment or criminal justice pressures. Drug users can also use large quantities and a variety of types of drugs over an extended period without failing out of school or losing employment. Most importantly, even when the club kids flirted with danger – engaging in excessive drug use or waking-up in emergency rooms – they continued to remain outside of the criminal justice system, which can potentially cause lasting problems for the users (e.g., job loss and stigma).

With criminal justice strategies dominating the approach to illicit drug use in the United States, many users face obstacles to controlling their drug use and minimizing drug-related harms. Many users are arrested and incarcerated, making it difficult for them to obtain employment and to maintain contact with social capital networks, such as family. Such criminal justice policies often dismantle the users' social support networks and reduce their economic opportunities, which these data show are necessary both for maintaining controlled drug use and avoiding drug harms.

Drug policies are crafted with a neglect of drug research, which indicates that people will continue to use drugs, and that reducing and ceasing use is most feasible when users are connected to mainstream institutions – school, family, employment (i.e., natural recovery).[12] The punitive nature of current drug policy disrupts the mechanisms that allow individuals to engage in controlled drug use and employ methods to reduce harms. Policing drug users and the spaces where drugs are used harms their social networks and hinders access to information that can permit controlled drug use.[13] Empirical studies show that, "official labeling and subsequent stigmatization generate negative consequences regarding social networks, jobs, and self esteem."[14] Many careers have regulations that formally preclude the hiring of ex-prisoners for example, electricians, billiards operators and plumbers.[15] As long as U.S. drug policy maintains this punitive focus, without incorporating alternative health-focused approaches, it will remain ineffective.

The findings of this study about the cultural aspect of drug use among non-stereotypical heavy drug users force us to confront our understanding of drug use. This study of the club kids challenges us to scrutinize how current drug policies affect (or fail to affect) the club kids and other users, and invites us to look at a wider spectrum of policy options for preventing drug-related harms. The findings should make us rethink the predominant criminal justice focus of our current drug policies, which do very little to avert drug harms. Rather than prevent harms, current policies actually produce harms by causing drug-using individuals to lose their ties to conventional institutions. Moreover, this study adds to the abundant evidence of racial and economic disparities in U.S. drug policies, and has produced racist and classist stereotypical images of drug users – as either Blacks or Latinos from inner city, poor communities or Whites from poor rural communities – who are in and out of drug treatment facilities, and are uneducated and unemployed. It is widely accepted that their drug use has kept them from becoming successful taxpaying members of society. In contrast, middle-class drug users, as shown in this study, remain successful taxpaying members of society, and experience few harms particularly harms resulting from criminal justice sanctions.

Arresting and incarcerating the club kids, and users like them, would cause great harm to their well-being and the overall health of our society. Such policies have the potential to dismantle networks and reduce levels of capital, which are critical to reducing harms associated with the use of drugs and discontinuing use. Such an approach would also contribute to the very large number of drug offenders already in our court and correction systems.[16] While there is some evidence that mandatory and coercive drug treatment may be effective,[17] the cost to the drug user of being swept up into the criminal justice system can also be serious and the source of additional long-term harm (loss of job and loss of access to social programs). In fact, at present, most people who are arrested or convicted for drug offenses do not get any treatment. Moreover, this study, as well as other research on drug users, shows that many can desist without treatment, especially without coerced treatment, and hence avoid the stigma and consequences of criminal justice sanctions. Drug users, their communities, and overall American society would be better served if all users, especially lower-class users, were treated like the club kids. Rather than arrest and punishment, all drug users should be helped to minimize the harms resulting from their use.

The war on drugs has been lost. The overreliance on criminal justice policies to address drug use in American society has been ineffective. The overall health and safety of drug users can be improved by shifting from an abstinence-only, criminal justice-based framework to a more balanced approach to addressing drug use. A better understanding of the cultural context of the users, and of the informal social control mechanisms that are developed and shared among drug users, can inform more effective drug policies and programs. In particular, health promotion initiatives – such as educating users on how drug, set and setting factors shape their experiences, and informing users about how to avoid harmful effects of their drug use – can influence their drug-using behaviors in a positive direction. A national drug policy that recognizes that a substantial number of substance users shift drug patterns and desist from use without treatment[18] can begin to destigmatize drug users. Furthermore, a drug policy that places less emphasis on the arrest and incarceration of drug users can mitigate much of the long-term damage to the life chances and well being of drug users. Clearly, the club kids' successes in life despite their drug-using patterns are evidence of that.

NOTES

1. 1991, p. 282.
2. see also Reinarman and Levine, 1997.
3. Waldorf et al., 1991, p. 343; see also Mugford, 1997.
4. see Parker and Auerhahn, 1998.
5. Mugford, 1997.
6. see Murphy and Rosenbaum, 1997.
7. SAMHSA, 2006b, 2007; respectively.
8. SAMHSA, 2006b, 2007; respectively.
9. Freese et al., 2002.
10. Wijetunga, Seto, Lindsay, and Schatz, 2003.
11. Banooni, Rickman, and Ward, 2000; Noskin and Kalish, 1991.
12. e.g., Granfield and Cloud, 2001.
13. e.g., Cooper, Moore, Gruskin, and Krieger, 2005.
14. Sampson and Laub, 1997/2005, p. 140; see also Clear, Rose, and Ryder, 2001; Link, Cullen, Struening, Shrout, and Dohrenwend, 1989.
15. Finn and Fontaine, 1985; Glaser, 1969.

16. Mauer and King, 2008.
17. e.g., Galloway and Drapela, 2006; Goldkamp, White and Robinson, 2001.
18. e.g., Biernacki, 1986; Granfield and Cloud, 2001; Waldorf et al., 1991.

APPENDIX A: DRUG SCHEDULES[1]

In 1970, the federal Comprehensive Drug Abuse Prevention and Control Act was passed into law. Title II of this law, the Controlled Substances Act, is the legal foundation of narcotics enforcement in the United States. The Controlled Substance Act regulates the manufacture and distribution of drugs, and places all drugs into one of five schedules.

SCHEDULE I

A: Drug has no medical uses.
B: Drug cannot be used safely even under medical supervision.
C: Not available for prescription.
D: Possession and Use is a felony.
Class examples: MDMA, LSD, GHB, heroin, psilocybin, marijuana, hashish.

SCHEDULE II

A: Drug has medical uses with restrictions. B: Drug has high potential for abuse leading to severe psychological or physical dependence.
C: Possession and use is a misdemeanor.
Class examples: ketamine, PCP, morphine, cocaine.

SCHEDULE III

A: Drug has current accepted medical use. B: Drug has medium potential for abuse leading to modest psychological or physical dependence.
Class examples: Rohypnol, opium, Vicodin, Tylenol with codeine.

SCHEDULE IV

A: Drug has medical uses. B: Drug has low potential for abuse.
Class examples: Xanax, Valium, Ambien, Ativan.

SCHEDULE V

A: Drug has medical uses. B: Drug has lowest potential for abuse.
Class examples: Lomotil, Phenergan, and liquid suspensions.
Class examples: Lomotil, Phenergan, and liquid suspensions.

NOTES

1. United States Government, Food and Drug Administration Codes: Title 21, Chapter 13, Subchapter I, Part B, Sec. 812 (or 21 USC § 812).

REFERENCES

Adams, K. (1997/2005). Developmental aspects of adult crime. In T. P. Thornberry (Ed.), *Advances in criminological theory: Developmental theories in crime and delinquency*, 7, 309–342. New Brunswick, NJ: Transaction Publishers.

Adler, P. A. (1993). *Wheeling and dealing: An ethnography of an upper-level drug dealing and smuggling community* (2nd ed.). New York: Columbia University Press.

Adorno, T. W., and Horkheimer, M. (2000). The culture industry: Enlightenment as mass deception. In J. B. Schor, and D. B. Holt (Eds.), *The consumer society reader* (pp. 3–20). New York: The New Press.

Agatston, A. (2003). *The South Beach diet: The delicious, doctor designed, foolproof plan for fast and health weight loss.* New York: Random House.

Akerlund, J. [Director]. (2002). *Spun* [Motion Picture]. Canada: Mongrel Media.

Akers, R. L. (1985). *Deviant behavior: A social learning approach* (3rd ed.). Belmont, CA: Wadsworth Publishing Company.

Alcedo, P. (2007). Sacred camp: transgendering faith in a Philippine festival. *Journal of Southeast Asian Studies*, 38, 1, 107–33.

Allaste, A. A., and Lagerspetz, M. (2002). Recreational drug use in Estonia: The context of club culture. *Contemporary Drug Problems*, 29, 183–200.

Altman, L. K. (2005, May 10). Cocaine users face greater risk of aneurysm. *The New York Times*, 154, 53210, F6.

American Society of Plastic Surgeons. (2005). *National Plastic Surgery Statistics.* Available at: http://www.plasticsurgery.org/public_education/2005Statistics.cfm

Anderson, E. (1994). The code of the streets. *The Atlantic Monthly*, 273, 80–94.

Arnett, J. J. (2000). Emerging adulthood: A theory of development from late teens through the early twenties. *American Psychologist*, 55, 5, 469–480.

Arnett, J. J. (2005). The developmental context of substance use in emerging adulthood. *The Journal of Drug Issues*, 35, 2, 235–251.

Appadurai, A. (1996). *Modernity at large: Cultural dimensions of globalization.* Minneapolis: University of Minnesota Press.

Asante, J. S. (1999). GHB: Grievous bodily harm. *FBI Law Enforcement Bulletin, 68,* 4, 21–25.

Associated Press. (2001, March 21). *"Ecstasy Selling Penalties Stiffened."* Available at: http://www.cbsnews.com/stories/2001/03/21/national/main 280539.shtml

Bachman, J. G., Johnston, L. D., O'Malley, M. P., and Schulenberg, J. (1996). Transition in drug use during late adolescence and youth adulthood. In J. A. Graber, J. Brooks-Gunn and A. C. Petersen (Eds.), *Transition through adolescence: Interpersonal domains and context* (pp. 111–140). Mahwah, NJ: Lawrence Erlbaum Associates.

Bailey, F. [Director], and Barbato, R. [Director]. (2003). *Party monster* [Motion Picture]. United States: Strand Releasing.

Bakhtin, M. M. (1968). *Rabelais and his world.* Translated by Helene Iswolsky. Cambridge, MA: MIT Press.

Banooni, P., Rickman, L. S., and Ward, D. M. (2000). Pott puffy tumor associated with intranasal methamphetamine. *The Journal of the American Medical Association, 283,* 10, 1293.

Barnett, A., Blumstein, A., and Farrington, D. P. (1987). Probabilistic models of youthful criminal careers. *Criminology, 25,* 83–107.

Baudrillard, J. (1975). *The mirror production.* Translated by Mark Poster. St. Louis: Telos Press.

Baudrillard, J. (1989). *America.* London: Verso.

Baudrillard, J. (1995). *Simulacra and simulation.* Translated by Sheila Faria Glaser. Ann Arbor: University of Michigan Press.

Baudrillard, J. (1998). *Consumer society: Myths and realities.* Translated by Chris Turner. Thousand Oaks: Sage Publications.

Bauman, Z. (1997). *Postmodernity and its discontents.* Cambridge, UK: Polity Press.

Bauman, Z. (1998). *Work, consumerism and the new poor.* Buckingham: Open University Press.

Beck, J., and Rosenbaum, M. (1994). *Pursuit of ecstasy: The MDMA experience.* Albany: State University of New York Press.

Becker, H. S. (1963). *Outsiders; studies in the sociology of deviance.* London: Free Press of Glencoe.

Becker, H. S. (1973). Consciousness, power and drug effects. *Trans-Action, 10,* 4, 26–31.

Becker, H. S. (1998). *Tricks of the trade: How to think about research while you're doing it.* Chicago, IL: The University of Chicago Press.

Beckett, K., Nyrop, K., and Pfingst, L. (2005). Race, drugs and policing: Understanding disparities in drug delivery arrests. *Criminology, 44,* 105–137.

Beckett, K. Nyrop, K., Pfingst, L., and Bowen, M. (2005). Drug use, drug possession arrests, and the question of race: Lessons from Seattle. *Social Problems, 52,* 419–441.

Bell, E. (1999). The negotiation of a working role in organizational ethnography. *International Journal of Social Research Methodology, 2,* 1, 17–37.

Bennette, M. E., McCrady, B. S., Johnson, V., and Pandina, R. J. (1999). Problem drinking from young adulthood to adulthood: Patterns, predictors and outcomes. *Journal of Studies on Alcohol, 60,* 605–614.

Benson, M. L. (2002). *Crime and the life course: An introduction.* Los Angeles: Roxbury Publishing Company.

Best, S. (1989). The commodification of reality and the reality of commodification: Jean Baudrillard and Post-Modernism. *Current Perspective in Social Theory, 9,* 11–51.

Biernacki, P. (1986). *Pathways from heroin addiction: Recovery without treatment.* Philadelphia: Temple University Press.

Biewend, J. (Producer). (2005). *Extreme makeover* [Television series]. Burbank, CA: ABC.

Blickman, T. (2004). *The ecstasy industry: Exploring the global market.* Amsterdam: Transnational Institute.

Blumstein, A., Cohen, J., and Hsieh, P. (1982 August). *The duration of adult criminal careers.* Final Report submitted to the U.S. Department of Justice, National Institute of Justice. Pittsburgh: Carnegie Mellon University.

Boeri, M. W. (2002). "I'm an addict, but I ain't no junkie": An ethnography analysis of the drug career of baby boomers. *Dissertation Abstracts International, 63,* 6, 2371-A–2372-A.

Bourdieu, P. (1984). *Distinction: A social critique of the judgment of taste.* Translated by Richard Nice. Cambridge, MA: Harvard University Press.

Bourdieu, P. (1986). The forms of capital. In J. G. Richardson (Ed.), *Handbook of theory and research for the sociology of education* (pp. 241–258). New York: Greenwood.

Brake, M. (1980). *The sociology of youth culture and youth subcultures: Sex and drugs and rock 'n' roll?* London: Routledge.

Brewer, N. T. (2003). The relation of internet searching to club knowledge and attitudes. *Psychology & Health, 18*, 387–401.

Bronfenbrenner, U. *(1979). The ecology of human development.* Cambridge, MA: Harvard University Press.

Bronfenbrenner, U. (1992). Ecological systems theory. In R. Vast (Eds.), *Six theories of child development: Revised formulations and current issues* (pp. 187–251). Philadelphia: Jessica Kingsley Publishers.

Bureau of Labor Statistics. (2006 March 24). *College enrollment and work activity of 2005 high school graduates.* News, USDL 06-514. Washington, DC: US Department of Labor. Available at: http://www.bls.gov/news.-release/archives/hsgec_03242006.pdf

Burr, A. (1984). The ideologies of despair: A symbolic interpretation of punks' and skinheads' usage of barbiturates. *Social Science & Medicine, 19*, 9, 929–938.

Burt, R. S. (2000). The network structure of social capital. *Research in Organizational Behavior: An annual series of analytical essays and critical reviews, 22*, 345–423.

Burt, R. S. (2001). Structural holes versus network closure as social capital. In N. Lin, K. Cook, and R. S. Burt (Eds.), *Social capital: Theory and research* (pp. 31–57). New York: Aldine De Gruyter.

Burt, R. S. (2004). Structural holes and good ideas. *The American Journal of Sociology, 110*, 2, 349–399.

Bynner, J. (2005). Rethinking the youth phase of the life-course: The case for emerging adulthood? *Journal of Youth Studies, 8*, 4, 367–384.

Carey, J. T., and Mandel, J. (1968). A San Francisco Bay area "Speed" scene. *Journal of Health and Social Behavior, 9*, 2, 164–174.

Carnoy, M. (2000). *Sustaining flexibility: Work, family and community in the information age.* Cambridge, MA: Cambridge University Press.

Caspi, A., and Moffitt, T. E. (1995). The continuity of maladaptive behavior: From description to understanding in the study of antisocial behavior. In D. Cicchetti, and D. J. Cohen (Eds.), *Manual of Developmental Psychology* (pp. 472–511). New York: John Wiley.

Castells, M. (2000). *The rise of the network society,* vol. 1 (2nd ed.). Cambridge, MA: Blackwell Publishers.

Castells, M. (2004). *The power of identity* (2nd ed.). Cambridge, MA: Blackwell Publishing.

Cavacuiti, C. A. (2004). You, me . . . and drugs – a love triangle: Important considerations when both members of a couple are abusing substances. *Substance Use & Misuse, 39*, 645–656.

Chatterton, P., and Hollands, R. (2003). *Urban nightscapes: Youth cultures, dance spaces and corporate power.* London: Routledge.

Chen, P. H., and Kandel, D. (1995). The natural history of drug use from adolescence to the mid-thirties in a general population. *American Journal of Public Health, 85*, 1, 41–47.

Chen, P. H., White, H. R., Pandina, R. J. (2001). Predictors of smoking cessation from adolescence into young adulthood. *Addictive Behaviors, 26*, 4, 517–529.

Clear, T. P., Rose, D. R., Ryder, J. A. (2001). Incarceration and the community: The problem of removing and returning offenders. *Crime & Delinquency, 47*, 3, 335–351.

Cleckner, P. (1979). Freaks and cognoscenti: PCP use in Miami. In H. W. Feldman, M. H. Agar, and G. M. Beschner, (Eds.), *Angel dust: An ethnographic study of PCP users* (pp. 183–211). Lexington, MA: Lexington Books.

Cloward, R. A., and Ohlin, L. E. (1960). *Delinquency and opportunity a theory of delinquent gangs.* Glencoe: Free Press.

Coffey, A. (1999). *The ethnographic self: Fieldwork and the representation of identity.* Thousand Oaks: Sage Publications.

Coffey, A. (2002). Sex in the field: Intimacy and intimidation. In T. Welland and L. Pugsley (Eds.), *Ethical dilemmas in qualitative research* (pp. 57–74). Burlington, VT: Ashgate.

Cohen, A. K. (1955). *Delinquent boys.* Glencoe: Free Press.

Cohen, J. (1986). Research on criminal careers: Individual frequency rates and offense seriousness. In A. Blumstein, J. Cohen, J. A. Roth, and C. A. Visher (Eds.), *Criminal careers and "career criminals"* (pp. 292–418). Washington, DC: National Academy Press.

Cohen, S. (1972/2002). *Folk devils and moral panics the creation of the Mods and Rockers* (3rd ed.). Oxford: M. Robertson.

Coleman, J. S. (1988). Social capital in the creation of human capital. *The American Journal of Sociology, 94* (Suppl. 95–120).

Community Epidemiology Work Group (CEWG). (2003). *Epidemiologic trends in drug abuse, Vol. I, highlights and executive summary.* Washington DC: National Institute on Drug Abuse, NIH Publication No. 04-5364.

Connell, J., and Gibson C. (2004). World music: Deterritorializing place and identity. *Progress in Human Geography, 28*, 3, 342–361.

Conrad, P., and Jacobson, H. T. (2003). Enhancing biology? Cosmetic surgery and breast augmentation. In S. J. Williams, L. Birke, and G. A. Bendelow (Eds.), *Debating biology: Sociological reflections on health, medicine and society* (pp. 223–234). London: Routledge.

Coomber, R., Morris, C., and Dunn, L. (2000). How the media do drugs: Quality control and the reporting of drug issues in the UK print media. *International Journal of Drug Policy, 11,* 217–225.

Cooper, H., Moore, L., Gruskin, S., and Krieger, N. (2005). The impact of a police drug crackdown on drug injectors' ability to practice harm reduction: A qualitative study. *Social Science & Medicine, 61,* 3, 673–684.

Crank, S., Dugdill, L., Peiser, B., and Guppy, A. (1999). *Moving beyond the drugs and deviance issues: Rave dancing as a health promoting alternative to conventional physical activity.* Conference paper, Club Health 2000. Amsterdam: Royal Tropical Institute.

Cullen, F. T., and Agnew, R. (2003). *Criminological theory: Past to present essential readings* (2nd ed.). Los Angeles: Roxbury Publishing Company.

Dalgarno, P., and Shewan, D. (2005). Reducing the risks of drug use: The case for set and setting. *Addiction Research & Theory, 13,* 3, 259–265.

Davies, C. A. (1999). *Reflexive ethnography: A guide to researching selves and others.* London: Routledge.

Davis, K. (1995). *Reshaping the female body: The dilemma of cosmetic surgery.* New York: Routledge.

Davis, F., and Munoz, L. (1970). Heads and freaks: Patterns and meanings of drug use among hippies. In J. D. Douglas (Ed.), *Observations of deviance* (pp. 301–313). New York: Random House.

Decorte, T. (2000). *The taming of cocaine: Cocaine use in Europe and American cities.* Belgium: VUB University Press.

Decorte, T. (2001a). Drug users' perceptions of 'controlled' and 'uncontrolled' use. *International Journal of Drug Policy, 12,* 297–320.

Decorte, T. (2001b). Quality control cocaine users: Underdeveloped harm reduction strategies. *European Addiction Research, 7,* 161–175.

Deery, J. (2004). Reality TV as advertisement. *Popular Communication, 2,* 1–19.

Denzin, N. K., and Lincoln, Y. S. (Eds.). (1994). *Handbook of qualitative research.* Thousand Oaks: Sage Publications.

Doblin, R. (2002). A clinical plan for MDMA (ecstasy) in the treatment of posttraumatic stress disorder (PTSD): Partnering with the FDA. *Journal of Psychoactive Drugs, 34,* 2, 185–194.

Douglas, J. D. (1973). Cooperative subcultures, deviant subcultures, and rebellious subcultures. In R. S. Denisoff, and C. H. McCaghy (Eds.), *Deviance, conflict, and criminality* (pp. 146–174). Chicago: Rand McNally.

Draut, T., and Silva, J. (2004). *Generation broke: The growth of debt among young Americans.* New York: Demos.

Drug Enforcement Administration. (2002). *"DEA to launch operation x-out" new club and predatory prevention initiative.* November 21, 2002. Available at: http://www.cbsnews.com/stories/2001/03/21/national/main 280539.shtml

Drummond, M. J. N. (2005). Men's bodies. *Men and Masculinities, 7,* 270–290.

Duncan, G. H., Dreyer, D. A., McKenna, T. M., and Whitsel, B. L. (1982). Dose and time-dependent effects of ketamine on SI neurons with cutaneous receptive fields. *Journal of Neurophysiology, 47,* 4, 647–699.

Dunlap, E., Johnson, B. D., and Manwar, A. (1994). A successful female crack dealer: Case study of a deviant career. *Deviant Behavior, 15,* 1, 1–25.

Durose, M. R., and Langan, P. A. (2001). *Bureau of Justice Statistics, State court sentencing of convicted felons, 1998 statistical tables.* Washington DC: US Department of Justice, available at: http://www.ojp.usdoj.gov/bjs/abstract/scsc98st.htm

Earleywine, M., and Martin, C. S. (1993). Anticipated stimulant and sedatives effects of alcohol vary with dosage and limp of the blood alcohol curve. *Alcoholism: Clinical and Experimental Research, 17,* 1, 135–139.

Ecstasydata.org, (2008). *Providing access to lab testing result for street ecstasy tablets.* Site sponsored by Erowid, Dancesafe, and MAPS. Last accessed August 1, 2008.

Elder, G. H., Jr. (1985). Perspectives on the life course. In G. H. Elder, Jr. (Ed.), *Life course dynamics: Trajectories and transitions, 1968–1980* (pp. 23–49). Ithaca, NY: Cornell University Press.

Erikson, E. H. (1968/1994). *Identity: Youth and crisis.* New York: W.W. Norton & Company.

Erikson, E. H. (1970). Reflections on the dissent of contemporary youth. *International Journal of Psycho-Analysis, 51,* 11–22.

Erickson, P. G., and Cheung, Y. W. (1999). Harm reduction among cocaine users: Reflections on individual intervention and community social capital. *International Journal of Drug Policy, 10,* 235–246.

Esbensen, F., and Elliot, D. S. (1994). Continuity and discontinuity in illicit drug use: Patterns and antecedents. *Journal of Drug Issues, 24,* 1–2, 75–97.

Evans, D. T., Cullen, F. T., Velmer, B. S., Jr., Dunaway, G., and Benson, M. L. (1997). The social consequences of self-control: Testing the general theory of crime. *Criminology, 35*, 475–500.

Eysenbach, G., and Till, J. E. (2001). Information in practice: Ethical issues in qualitative research on internet communities. *British Medical Journal, 323*, 1101–1105.

Farrington, D. P. (1979). Longitudinal research on crime and delinquency. In N. Morris and M. Tonry (Eds.), *Crime and Justice: A Review of Research, 1*, 289–348.

Farrington, D. P. (1986). Age and crime. In M. Tonry and N. Morris (Eds.), *Crime and Justice: A Review of Research, 7*, 189–250.

Farrington, D. P. (2005). Conclusions about developmental and life-course theories. In D. P. Farrington (Ed.), *Integrated development and life-course theory of offending* (pp. 247–257). New Brunswick, NJ: Transaction Publishers.

Farrington, D. P., and Maughan, B., (1999). Criminal careers of two London cohorts. *Criminal Behaviour and Mental Health, 9*, 91–106.

Featherstone, M. (1982). The body in consumer society. *Theory, Culture & Society, 1*, 18–33.

Feldman, H. W., Agar, M. H., and Beschner, G. M. (Eds.), (1979). *Angel dust: An ethnographic study of PCP users.* Lexington, MA: Lexington Books.

Fendrich, M., Wislar, J. S., Johnson, T. P., and Hubbell, A. (2003). A contextual profile of club drug use among adults in Chicago. *Addiction, 98*, 1693–1703.

Ferrell, J. (1995). Style matters: criminal identity and social control. In J. Ferrell and C. R. Sanders (Eds.), *Cultural criminology* (pp. 169–189). Boston: Northeastern University Press.

Fine, G. A., and Kleinman, S. (1979). Rethinking subculture: An interactionist analysis. *The American Journal of Sociology, 85*, 1–20.

Finestone, H. (1964). Cats, kicks and color. In H. S. Becker (Ed.), *The other side: Perspectives on deviance* (pp. 281–297). New York: Free Press of Glencoe.

Finn, R. H., and Fontaine, P. A. (1985). The association between selected characteristics and perceived employability of offenders. *Criminal Justice and Behavior, 12*, 353–365.

Fischer, C. S. (1975). Toward a subcultural theory of urbanism. *The American Journal of Sociology, 80*, 1319–1341.

Fiske, J. (2004). *Understanding popular culture.* London: Routledge.

Fitzgerald, J. L. (2002). A political economy of "Doves." *Contemporary Drug Problems, 29,* 1, 201–239.

Flicker, S., Haans, D., and Skinner, H. (2004). Ethical dilemmas in research on internet communities. *Qualitative Health Research, 14,* 124–134.

Flom, P. L., Friedman, S. R., Jose, B., and Curtis, R. (2001). Peer norms regarding drug use and drug selling among household youth in a low-income "drug supermarket" urban neighborhood. *Drugs: Education, Prevention & Policy, 8,* 219–232.

Forsyth, A. J. M. (1996). Places and patterns of drug use in the Scottish dance scene. *Addiction, 91,* 4, 511–521.

Frankel, M. S., and Siang, S. (1999). *Ethical and legal aspects of human subjects research on the internet.* Available at: http://www.aaas.org/spp/dspp/sfrl/projects/intres/main.htm

Freese, T. E., Miotto, K., and Reback, C. J. (2002). The effects and consequences of selected club drugs. *Journal of Substance Abuse Treatment, 23,* 2, 151–157.

Furstenberg, F. F., Jr., Rumbaut, R. G., and Settersten, R. A., Jr. (2005). On the frontier of adulthood: Emerging themes and new directions. In R. A. Settersten Jr., F. F. Furstenberg Jr., and R. G. Rumbaut (Eds.), *On the frontier of adulthood: Theory, research, and public policy* (pp. 3–24). Chicago: The University of Chicago Press.

Fussell, E., and Furstenberg, F. F., Jr. (2005). The transition to adulthood during the twentieth century: Race, nativity, and gender. In R. A. Settersten Jr., F. F. Furstenberg Jr., and R. G. Rumbaut (Eds.), *On the frontier of adulthood: Theory, research, and public policy* (pp. 29–76). Chicago: The University of Chicago Press.

Gaines, D. (1990). *Teenage wasteland: Suburbia's dead end kids.* Chicago: The University of Chicago Press.

Galloway, A. L., and Drapela, L. A. (2006). Are effective drug courts an urban phenomenon? Considering their impact on recidivism among a nonmetropolitan adult sample in Washington state. *International Journal of Offender Therapy and Comparative Criminology, 50,* 3, 280–293.

Gauthier, A. H., and Furstenberg, F. F., Jr. (2005). Historical trends in patterns of time use among young adults in developed countries. In R. A. Settersten Jr., F. F. Furstenberg Jr., and R. G. Rumbaut (Eds.), *On the frontier of adulthood: Theory, research, and public policy* (pp. 150–177). Chicago: The University of Chicago Press.

Gearing, J. (1995). Fear and loving in the West Indies: research from the heart (as well as the head). In D. Kulick, and M. Wilson (Eds.), *Taboo: Sex, identity, and erotic subjectivity in anthropological fieldwork* (pp. 186–219). New York: Routledge.

Giddens, A. (1984). *The constitution of society: Introduction of the theory of structuration.* Berkeley: University of California Press.

Giddens, A. (1990). *The consequences of modernity.* Stanford: Stanford University Press.

Giddens, A. (2003). *Runaway world: How globalization is reshaping our lives.* New York: Routledge.

Gilbert, J., and Pearson, E. (1999). *Discographies: Dance music, culture and the other politics of sound.* London: Routledge.

Gimlin, D. (2000). Cosmetic surgery: beauty as commodity. *Qualitative Sociology, 23,* 77–98.

Glaser, D. (1969). *The effectiveness of a prison and parole system* (abridged ed.). Indianapolis: Bobbs-Merrill Co.

Goffman, E. (1959). *The presentation of self in everyday life.* New York: Doubleday, Anchor Books.

Goldkamp, J. S., White, M. D., and Robinson, J. B. (2001). Do drug courts work? Getting inside the drug court black box. *Journal of Drug Issues, 31,* 27–73.

Golub, A., Johnson, B. D., Sifaneck, S. J., Chesluk, B., and Parker, H. (2001). Is the U.S experiencing an incipient epidemic of hallucinogen use? *Substance Use & Misuse, 36,* 12, 1699–1729.

Golub, A., Johnson B. D., and Dunlap, E. (2007). The race/ethnicity disparity in misdemeanor marijuana arrests in New York City. *Criminology & Public Policy, 6,* 1, 131–164.

Goode, E. (2002). Drug arrests at the millennium. *Society, 39,* 5, 41–46.

Gorman, E. M., Nelson, K. R., Applegate, T., and Scrol, A. (2004). Club drug and poly-substance abuse and HIV among gay/bisexual men: Lessons gleaned from a community study. *Journal of Gay and Lesbian Social Services, 16,* 2, 1–17.

Gotham, K. F. (2002). Marketing Mardi Gras: Commodification spectacle and the political economy of tourism in New Orleans. *Urban Studies, 39,* 10, 1735–1756.

Gottdiener, M. (2000a). Introduction. In M. Gottdiener (Ed.), *New forms of consumption: Consumers, culture and commodification* (pp. ix-xvii). London: Rowman & Littlefield Publishers.

Gottdiener, M. (2000b). Approaches to consumption: Classical and contemporary perspectives. In M. Gottdiener (Ed.), *New forms of consumption:*

Consumers, culture and commodification (pp. 3–33). London: Rowman & Littlefield Publishers.

Gottdiener, M. (2000c). The consumption of space and the spaces of consumption. In M. Gottdiener (Ed.), *New forms of consumption: Consumers, culture and commodification* (pp. 265–287). London: Rowman & Littlefield Publishers.

Gottfredson, M. R., and Hirschi, T. (1990). *A general theory of crime.* Palo Alto: Stanford University Press.

Gove, W. R. (1985). The effect of age and gender on deviant behavior: A biopsychosocial perspective. In A. S. Rossi (Ed.), *Gender and the life course* (pp. 115–155). New York: Adaline.

Gowing, L. R., Henry-Edwards, S. M., Irvine, R. J., and Ali, R. L. (2002). The health effects of ecstasy: A literature review. *Drug and Alcohol Review, 21,* 53–63.

Graham, J., and Bowling, B. (1995). *Young people and crime.* London: Home Office: A Research and Planning Unit.

Granfield, R., and Cloud, W. (2001). Social context and "natural recovery": The role of social capital in the resolution of drug-associated problems. *Substance Use & Misuse, 36,* 11, 1543–1570.

Gramsci, A. (1992). *Prison notebooks.* Translated by J. A. Buttigieg and A. Callari. New York: Columbia University Press.

Green, G. L. (2007). "Come to Life": Authenticity, value, and the carnival as cultural commodity in Trinidad and Tobago. *Identities: Global Studies in Culture and Power, 14,* 203–224.

Greenwald, R. [Director]. [2004]. *Outfoxed: Rupert Murdoch's war on journalism* [Documentary]. United States: Moveon.org.

Greer, C. (2004). Crime, media and community: Grief and virtual in late modernity. In J. Ferrell, K. Hayward, W. Morrison, and M. Presdee (Eds.), *Cultural criminology unleashed* (pp. 109–118). Portland: Cavendish Publishing.

Grinspoon, L., and Bakalar, J. B. (1997). *Psychedelic drugs reconsidered.* New York: The Lindesmith Center.

Grund, J. P. C. (1993). *Drug use as a social ritual: Functionality, symbolism and determinants of self-regulation.* Rotterdam: IVO Reeks Series.

Hagan, J. (1991). Destiny and drift: Subcultural preferences, status attainments, and the risks and rewards of youth. *American Sociological Review, 56,* 567–582.

Hagan, J., and Palloni, A. (1988). Crime as social events in the life course: Reconceiving a criminological controversy. *Criminology, 26,* 1, 87–100.

Hagan, J. (1997/2005). Crime and capitalization: Toward a developmental theory of street crime in America. In T. P. Thornberry (Ed.), *Advances in criminological theory: Developmental theories in crime and delinquency, 7,* 287–307. New Brunswick, NJ: Transaction Publishers.

Hamil-Luker, J., Land, K. C., and Blau, J. (2004). Diverse trajectories of cocaine use through early adulthood among rebellious and socially conforming youth. *Social Science Research, 33,* 300–321.

Hammersley, M., and Atkinson, P. (1995). *Ethnography: Principles in practice* (2nd ed.). New York: Routledge.

Hammersley, R., Ditton, J., Smith, I., and Short, E. (1999). Patterns of ecstasy use by drug users. *British Journal of Criminology, 39,* 4, (Spec. Issue), 625–647.

Hammersley, R., Khan, F., and Ditton, J. (2002). *Ecstasy and the rise of the chemical generation.* London: Routledge.

Hansen, D., Maycock, B., and Lower, T. (2001). "Weddings, parties, anything . . . ", A qualitative analysis of ecstasy use in Perth, Western Australia. *International Journal of Drug Policy, 12,* 181–199.

Hargreaves, D., and Tiggemann, M. (2003). The effect of "thin ideal" television commercials on body dissatisfaction and schema activation during early adolescence. *Journal of Youth and Adolescence, 32,* 367–373.

Harvey, D. (1990). *The condition of postmodernity.* London: Blackwell Publishing.

Hayward, K. J. (2004). *City limits: Crime, consumer culture and the urban experience.* London: Grasshopper Press.

Heather, N., and Robertson, I. (1981). *Controlled drinking.* London: Methuen.

Hebdige, D. (1979/2002). *Subculture: The meaning of style.* London: Routledge.

Henderson, S. (1993). *Young women, sexuality, and recreational drug use: A research and development project:* Final Report. Manchester: Lifeline.

Hill, E. (1985). Traditional figures in carnival: Their preservation, development, and interpretation. *Caribbean Quarterly, 31,* 2, 14–34.

Hinchliff, S. (2001). The meaning of ecstasy use and clubbing to women in the late 1990s. *International Journal of Drug Policy, 12,* 455–468.

Hirschi, T. (1969). *Causes of delinquency.* Berkeley: University of California Press.

Ho, C. G. T. (2000). Popular culture and the aestheticization of politics: Hegemonic struggle and postcolonial nationalism in the Trinidad carnival. *Transforming Anthropology, 9,* 3–18.

Home Box Office (HBO). (2002). *America undercover: Small town ecstasy.* [Documentary]. New York: HBO.

Holmes, B. (Producer). (2007). *Queer eye for the straight guy* [Television series]. Burbank, CA: Bravo.

Holt, D. B. (1998). Does cultural capital structure American consumption? *Journal of Consumer Research, 25,* 1–25.

Hoover, E. (2001). The lure of easy credit leaves more students struggling with debt. *Chronicle of Higher Education, 47,* 40, A35–A36.

Horney, J., Osgood, D. W., and Marshal, I. H. (1995). Criminal careers in the short-term: Intra-individual variability in crime and its relation to local life circumstances. *American Sociological Review, 60,* 655–673.

Howell, N. (1990). *Surviving fieldwork: a report of the advisory panel on health and safety in fieldwork.* Special Publication of the American Anthropological Association No. 26. Washington, DC: American Anthropological Association.

Hunt, G., and Evans, K. (2003). Dancing and drugs: A cross-national perspective. *Contemporary Drug Problems, 30,* 779–814.

Hunt, G., Evans, K., Wu, E., and Reyes, A. (2005). Asian American youth, the dance scene and club drugs. *Journal of Drug Issues, 35,* 4, 695–732.

Inciardi, J. A. (1993). Appendix A: Some considerations on the methods, dangers and ethics of crack-house research. In J. A. Inciardi, D. Lockwood, and A. E. Pettieger (Eds.), *Women and crack cocaine* (pp. 147–159). New York: Macmillan.

Inciardi, J. (2007). *The war on drugs IV: The continuing saga of the mysteries and miseries of intoxication, addiction, crime and public policy* (4th ed.). New York: Pearson.

Jackson-Jacobs, C. (2004). Hard drugs in a soft context: Managing trouble and crack use on a college campus. *The Sociological Quarterly, 45,* 4, 835–856.

Jacobs, B. A. (1998). Researching crack dealers: Dilemmas and contradictions. In J. Ferrell and M. S. Hamm (Eds.), *Ethnography at the edge: Crime, deviance, and field research* (pp. 166-177). Boston: Northeastern Press.

Jansen, K. (2001). *Ketamine: Dreams and realities.* Sarasota, FL: Multidisciplinary Association for Psychedelic Studies.

Jefferson, D. J. (2005, August 8). America's most dangerous drug. *Newsweek, 146,* 6, 40–48.

Jenkins, P. (1999). *Synthetic panics: The symbolic politics of designer drugs.* New York: New York University Press.

Joe-Laidler, K. A. (2005). The rise of club drug use in a heroin society: The case of Hong Kong. *Substance Use & Misuse, 40,* 1257–1278.

Johnson, B. D., Goldstein, P., Preble, E., Schmeidler, J., Lipton, D. S., Spunt, B., and Miller, T. (1985). *Taking care of business: The economics of crime by heroin users.* Lexington, MA: Lexington.

Johnston, L. D., O'Malley, P. M., and Bachman, J. G. (2003). *Monitoring the future: national survey result on drug use, 1975–2002.* Volume II. *College students and adults ages 19–40.* (NIH Publication No. 06-5884). Bethesda, MD: National Institute on Drug use.

Johnston, L. D., O'Malley, P. M., Bachman, J. G., and Schulenberg, J. E. (2005). *Monitoring the future: National result on adolescent drug use: Overview of key findings, 2004.* Washington DC: U.S. Department of Health and Human Services.

Jones, C. (2001). Suspicious death related to gamma-hydroxybutyrate (GHB) toxicity. *Journal of Clinical Forensic Medicine, 8,* 2, 74–76.

Jonville-Bera, A. P., Bera, F., and Autret-Leca, E. (2005). Are incorrectly used drugs more frequently involved in adverse drug reactions? A prospective study. *European Journal of Clinical Pharmacology, 61,* 3, 231–236.

Kandel, D. B., and Davies, M. (1990). Friendship networks of illicit drug users in adulthood: A comparison of two competing theories. *Criminology, 29,* 3, 441–469.

Kandel, D. B., and Yamaguchi, K. (1985). On the resolution of role incompatibility: A life event history analysis of family role and marijuana use. *The American Journal of Sociology, 90,* 6, 1284–1325.

Kates, S. M., and R. W. Belk. (2001). The meanings of Lesbian and Gay Pride Day: Resistance through consumption and resistance to consumption. *Journal of Contemporary Ethnography, 30,* 4, 392–429.

Kelly, B. C. (2006). Conceptions of risk in the lives of ecstasy using youth. In B. Sanders (Ed.), *Drugs, clubs and young people: Sociological and public health perspectives* (pp. 50–67). Aldershot: Ashgate.

Kerner, H. J. (2005). Book review essay: The complex dynamics of the onset, the development, and the termination of a criminal career: Lessons on repeat offenders to be drawn from recent longitudinal studies in criminology. In R. J. Sampson, and J. H. Laub (Eds.), *The Annals of the American Academy of Political and Social Science, 602,* 259–282.

King, R. (2008). *Disparity by geography: The war on drugs in America's cities.* Washington, DC: The Sentencing Project.

Klitzman, R. L., Greenberg, J. D., Pollack, L., and Dolezal, C. (2002). MDMA ("ecstasy") use and its association with high risk behaviors, mental health, and other factors among gay/bisexual men in New York City. *Drug & Alcohol Dependence, 66,* 115–126.

Kornhauser, R. R. (1978). *Social sources of delinquency: An appraisal of analytic models*. Chicago: University of Chicago Press.

Kozinets, R. V. (2002). Can consumers escape the market? Emancipatory illuminations from Burning Man. *Journal of Consumer Research, 29,* 1: 20–38.

Krebs, C. P., and Steffey, D. M. (2005). Club drug use among delinquent youth. *Substance Use & Misuse, 40,* 1363–1379.

Krohn, M. D., and Thornberry, T. P. (2003). Common themes, future directions. In T. P. Thornberry and M. D. Krohn (Eds.), *Taking stock in delinquency: An overview of findings from contemporary longitudinal studies* (pp. 313–326). New York: Kluwer Academic.

Kuhn, C., Swartzwelder, S., and Wilson, W. (1998). *Buzzed: The straight facts about the most used and abused drugs from alcohol to ecstasy*. New York: W.W. Norton Co.

Labouvie, E. (1996). Maturing out of substance use: Selection and self-correction. *Journal of Drug Issues, 26,* 2, 457–476.

Labouvie, E., Bates, M. E., and Pandina, R. J. (1997). Age of first use: Its reliability and predictive utility. *Journal of Studies on Alcohol, 58,* 638–643.

Lankenau, S., and Clatts, M. (2005). Patterns of polydrug use among keta-mine injectors in New York City. *Substance Use & Misuse, 40,* 1381–1398.

Langman, L. (2003). Part I. systematic comparisons across empirical case studies: Culture, identity and hegemony: The body in a global age. *Current Sociology, 51,* 223–247.

Latkin, C. A., Forman, V., and Knowlton, A. (2002). Concordance between drug users' and their network members' reported drug use and HIV status: Implications to HIV prevention. *Advances in Medical Sociology, 8,* 151–164.

Laub, J. H., and Sampson, R. J. (2001). Understanding desistance from crime. In M. Tonry (Ed.), *Crime and Justice: A Review of Research, 28,* 1–71.

Laub, J. H., and Sampson, R. J. (2003). *Shared beginnings, divergent lives: Delinquent boys to age 70*. Cambridge, MA: Harvard University Press.

Laub, J. H., Nagin, D. S., and Sampson, R. J. (1998). Trajectories of change in criminal offending: Good marriages and the desistance process. *American Sociological Review, 63,* 2, 225–238.

Laub, J. H., Sampson, R. J., and Allen, L. C. (2001). Explaining crime over the life course: Toward a theory of age-graded informal social control. In R. Paternoster and R. Bachman (Eds.), *Explaining criminals and crime: Essays in contemporary criminological theory* (pp. 97–112). Los Angeles: Roxbury Publishing Company.

Le Blanc, M. (1997/2005). A general control theory of the criminal phenomenon: The structural and dynamic statements of an integrated multilayered control theory. In T. P. Thornberry (Ed.), *Advances in criminological theory: Developmental theories in crime and delinquency, 7,* 215–287. New Brunswick, NJ: Transaction Publishers.

Le Blanc, M., and Fréchette, M. (1989). *Male criminal activity from childhood through youth: Multilevel and developmental perspectives.* New York: Springer.

Le Blanc, M., and Loeber, R. (1998). Developmental criminology updated. In M. Tonry (Ed.), *Crime and Justice: A Review of Research, 23,* 115–198.

Lee, D. (1997). Interviewing men: vulnerabilities and dilemmas. *Women's Studies International Forum, 20,* 4, 553–564.

Lenton, S., and Davidson, P. (1999). Raves, drugs, dealing and driving: Qualitative data from a West Australian sample. *Drug and Alcohol Review, 18,* 153–161.

Levy, K. B., O'Grady, K. E., Wish, E. D., and Arria, A. M. (2005). An in-depth qualitative examination of the ecstasy experience: Results of a focus group with ecstasy-using college students. *Substance Use & Misuse, 40,* 1427–1441.

Lewis, L. A., and Ross, M. W. (1995). *A selected body: The gay dance party Subculture and the HIV/AIDS pandemic.* New York: Cassell.

Liman, D. [Director]. (1999). *Go* [Motion Picture]. United States: Columbia Pictures, Sony Pictures, and Tristar Pictures.

Lin, N. (2001a). *Social capital: A theory of social structure and action.* New York: Cambridge University Press.

Lin, N. (2001b). Building a network theory of social capital. In N. Lin, K. Cook, and R. S. Burt (Eds.), *Social capital: Theory and research* (pp. 3–31). New York: Aldine De Gruyter.

Lincoln, Y. S., and Guba, E. G. (1985). *Naturalistic inquiry.* Newbury Park: Sage Publications.

Link, B., Cullen, F. T., Struening, E., Shrout, P., and Dohrenwend, B. (1989). A modified labeling approach to mental disorders: An empirical assessment. *American Sociological Review, 54,* 400–423.

Loeber, R., and Le Blanc, M. (1990). Toward a developmental criminology. In M. Tonry, and N. Morris (Eds.), *Crime and Justice: A Review of Research, 12,* 375–473.

Loeber, R., Stouthamer-Loeber, M., Van Kammen, W., and Farrington, D. P. (1991). Initiation, escalation and desistance in juvenile offending and their correlates. *Journal of Criminal Law and Criminology, 82,* 1, 36–82.

Logan, B. K. (2002). Methamphetamine-effects on human performance and behavior. *Forensic Science Review, 14,* 1–2, 133–151.

Lyttle, T., and Montagne, M. (1992). Drugs, music, and ideology: A social pharmacological interpretation of the acid house movement. *International Journal of the Addictions, 27,* 10, 1159–1177.

MacCoun, R. J., and Reuter, P. (2001). *Drug war heresies: Learning from other vices, times, and places.* New York: Cambridge University Press.

MacRae, R. (2004). Notions of 'us and them': Markers of stratification in clubbing lifestyles. *Journal of Youth Studies, 7,* 55–71.

Malbon, B. (1999). *Clubbing: Dancing, ecstasy and vitality.* London: Routledge.

Manning, R. D. (2000). *Credit card nation: The consequences of America's addiction to credit.* New York: Basic Books.

Martin, J. A., Hamilton, B. E., Sutton, P. D., Ventura, S. J., Menacker, F., Kirmeyer, S. (2006). Births: Final data for 2004. *National Vital Statistics Reports,* 55, 1.

Martin, J. A., Hamilton, B. E., Sutton, P. D., Ventura, S. J., Menacker, F., Kirmeyer, S. & Munson, M.L. (2007). Births: Final data for 2005. *National Vital Statistics Reports,* 56, 6.

Martins, S. S., Mazzotti, G., and Chilcoat, H. D. (2005). Trends in ecstasy use in the United States from 1995–2001: Comparison with marijuana users and association with other drug use. *Experimental and Clinical Psychopharmacology, 13,* 3, 244–252.

Markowitz, F. (1999). Sexing the anthropologist: implications for ethnography. In F. Markowitz, and M. Ashkenazi (Eds.), *Sex, sexuality, and the anthropologist* (pp. 161–174). Chicago: University of Illinois Press.

Maruna, S. (2001). *Making good: How ex-convicts reform and rebuild their lives.* Washington, DC: American Psychological Association.

Mauer, M., and King, R. S. (2008). *Drug war: The 25 year quagmire.* Washington, DC: The Sentencing Project.

Marx, K. (2000). The fetishism of the commodity and its secret. In J. B. Schor, and D. B. Holt (Eds.), *The consumer society reader* (pp. 360–375). New York: The New Press.

Matsueda, R. L., and Heimer, K. (1997/2005). A symbolic interactionist theory of role-transitions, role-commitments, and delinquency. In T. P. Thornberry (Ed.), *Advances in criminological theory: Developmental theories in crime and delinquency, 7,* 163–215. New Brunswick, NJ: Transaction Publishers.

Matza, D., and Sykes, G. M. (1961). Juvenile delinquency and subterranean values. *American Sociological Review, 26,* 5, 712–719.

Maxwell, J. A. (1996). *Qualitative research design: An interactive approach. Applied Social Research Methods Series, 41.* Thousand Oaks: Sage Publications.

Maxwell, J. C., and Spence, R. T. (2005). Profiles of club drug users in treatment. *Substance Use & Misuse, 40,* 1409–1426.

McElrath, K., and McEvoy, K. (2005). Negative experiences on ecstasy: The role of drug, set, and setting. In W. Palacios (Ed.), *Cocktails and dreams: Perspectives on drug use* (pp. 268–282). Upper Saddle River, NJ: Pearson Prentice Hall.

Measham, F. (2004). Play space: Historical and socio-cultural reflections on drugs, licensed leisure locations, commercialization and control. *International Journal of Drug Policy, 15,* 337–345.

Measham, F., Parker, H., and Aldridge, J. (2001). *Dancing on drugs risk, health and hedonism in the British club scene.* London: Free Association.

Melechi, A. (1993). The ecstasy of disappearance. In S. Redhead (Ed.), *Rave off politics and deviance in contemporary youth culture (Popular Cultural Studies, No. 1)* (pp. 28–40). Brookfield, VT: Avebury

Merton, R. K. (1938). Social structure and anomie. *American Sociological Review, 3,* 672–682.

Messner, S. F., and Rosenfeld, R. (2006). *Crime and the American dream* (4th ed.). Belmont, CA: Wadsworth Publishing Company.

Mignon, P. (1993). The end of the century party. In S. Redhead (Ed.), *Rave off politics and deviance in contemporary youth culture (Popular Cultural Studies, No. 1)* (pp. 175–192). Brookfield, VT: Avebury.

Miller, W. (1958). Lower class culture as a generating milieu of gang delinquency. *Journal of Social Issues, 14,* 5–19.

Mitchell, J. (2001). *The moral panic about Raves: Newspaper transmission and legislation.* Master of Arts in Sociology Thesis, Humboldt State University.

Moffitt, T. E. (1993). Adolescent-limited and life-course persistent antisocial behavior: A developmental taxonomy. *Psychological Review, 100,* 674–701.

Monaghan, L. F. (2003). Hormonal bodies, civilized bodies: Incorporating the biological into the sociology of health. In S. S. Williams, L. Birke, and G. A. Bendelow (Eds.), *Debating biology: Sociological reflections on health, medicine, and society* (pp. 145–234). New York: Routledge.

Moore, J. W. (1991). *Going down to the barrio: Homeboys and homegirls in change*. Philadelphia: Temple University Press.

Moreno, E. (1995). Rape in the field: reflections from a survivor. In D. Kulick, and M. Wilson, (Eds.), *Taboo: Sex, identity, and erotic subjectivity in anthropological fieldwork* (pp. 219–250). New York: Routledge.

Mugford, S. K. (1997). Crack in Australia: Why is there no problem? In C. Reinarman, and H. G. Levine (Eds.), *Crack in America: Demon drugs and social justice* (pp. 194–214). Berkeley, CA: University of California Press.

Muggleton, D. (2000). *Inside subculture: The postmodern meaning of style*. New York: Berg.

Murphy, P. L. (2000). The commodified self in consumer culture: A cross-cultural perspective. *The Journal of Social Psychology, 140*, 636–647.

Murphy, S. B., and Rosenbaum, M. (1997). Two women who used cocaine too much: Class, race, gender, crack and coke. In C. Reinarman, and H. G. Levine (Eds.), *Crack in America: Demon drugs and social justice* (pp. 98–113). Berkeley, CA: University of California Press.

Musto, D. F. (1999). *The American disease origins of narcotic control* (3rd ed.). New York: Oxford University Press.

National Institute on Drug Abuse. (2002). *Methamphetamine: Abuse and addiction. Research Report Series*. Washington, DC: National Institute of Health Publication # 02-4210.

National Survey on Drug Use and Health (NSDUH). (2005). *The NSDUH report: Substance use among past year ecstasy users*. Washington DC: U.S. Department of Health and Human Services.

Newman, R., Caras, J., and Dubin, L. (2006 December 28). *Safer nights, safer city: Recommendations of the NYC Council from the nightlife safety summit*. New York: New York City Council. Available at: http://www.nyccouncil.info/pdf_files/reports/nightlife_summit_rep ort_fin.pdf

Noskin, G. A., and Kalish, S. B. (1991). Pott's puffy tumor: A complication of intranasal cocaine abuse. *Reviews of Infectious Diseases, 13*, 606–608.

Noujaim, J. [Director]. (2004). *Control room* [Documentary]. United States: Magnolia Pictures.

Novoa, R. A., Ompad, D. C., Wu, Y., Vlahov, D., and Galea, S. (2005). Ecstasy use and its association with sexual behaviors among drug users in New York City. *Journal of Community Health, 30*, 5, 331–343.

Oh, M., and Arditi, J. (2000). Shopping and postmodernism: Consumption, production, identity and the Internet. In M. Gottdiener (Ed.), *New forms of consumption: Consumers, culture and commodification* (pp. 71–90). London: Rowman & Littlefield Publishers.

Oliver, M. B., and Sedikides, C. (1992). Effects of sexual permissiveness on desirability of partner as a function of low and high commitment to relationship. *Social Psychology Quarterly, 55,* 321–333.

Ompad, D. C., Galea, S., Fuller, C. M., Edwards, V., and Vlahov, D. (2005). Ecstasy use among Hispanic and black substance users in New York City. *Substance Use & Misuse, 40,* 1399–1407.

Osgood, W. D., Ruth, G., Eccles, J. S., Jacobs, J. E., and Barber, B. L. (2005). Six paths to adulthood: Fast starters, parents without careers, educated partners, educated singles, working singles, and slow starters. In R. A. Settersten Jr., F. F. Furstenberg Jr., and R.G. Rumbaut (Eds.), *On the frontier of adulthood: Theory, research, and public policy* (pp. 320–355). Chicago: The University of Chicago Press.

O'Sullivan, L. F. (1995). Less is more: Effects of sexual experience on judgments of men's and women's personality characteristics and relationship desirability. *Sex Roles, 33,* 159–181.

Owen, F. (2003). *Clubland: The rise and murderous fall of club culture.* New York: St. Martin's Press.

Panagopoulos, I., and Ricciardelli, L. A. (2005). Harm reduction and decision making among recreational ecstasy users. *International Journal of Drug Policy, 16,* 54–64.

Parker, H., and Williams, L. (2003). Intoxicated weekends: Young adults' work hard-play hard lifestyles, public health and public disorder. *Drugs: Education, Prevention and Policy, 10,* 345–367.

Parker, R. N., and Auerhahn, K. (1998). Alcohol, drugs, and violence. *Annual Review of Sociology, 24,* 291–311.

Parker, H., Aldridge, J., and Measham, F. (1998). *Illegal leisure: The normalization of adolescent recreational drug use.* London: Routledge.

Parks, K. A., and Scheidt, D. M. (2000). Male bar drinkers' perspective on female bar drinkers. *Sex Roles, 43,* 927–941.

Patton, M. Q. (1990). *Qualitative evaluation methods.* Thousand Oaks: Sage Publications.

Pedersen, W., and Skrondal, A. (1999). Ecstasy and new patterns of drug use: A normal population study. *Addiction, 94, 11,* 1695–1706.

Perrone, D. P. (2006). New York City club kids: A contextual understanding of club drug use. In B. Sanders (Ed.), *Drugs, clubs and young people: Sociological and public health perspectives* (pp. 26–50). Aldershot: Ashgate.

Perrone, D. P. (in press). Gender and sexuality in the field: A female ethnographers experience researching drug use in dance clubs. *Substance Use and Misuse*.

Peters, J. (2002). *Going through it. On Live with Jonathan Peters* [CD]. New York: Groovilicious.

Piquero, A. R., Farrington, D. P., and Blumstein A. (2003). The criminal career paradigm. In M. Tonry (Ed.), *Crime and Justice: A Review of Research, 30*, 359–506.

Pittenger, D. J. (2003). Internet research: An opportunity to revisit classic ethical problems in behavioral research. *Ethics & Behavior, 13*, 45–60.

Polsky, N. (1967/1998). *Hustlers, beats and others*. New York: The Lyons Press.

Presdee, M. (2000). *Cultural criminology and the carnival crime*. London: Routledge.

Public Broadcasting System (PBS). (2001). *In the mix: Ecstasy* [funded by the National Institute of Drug Abuse]. Washington, DC: PBS.

Pulse Check (2004). *Trends in drug abuse: Advanced report December 2003*. Washington DC: Executive Office of the President, Office of National Drug Control Policy.

Quetelet, A. (1831/1984). *Research on the propensity for crime at different ages*. Translated by Sawyer F. Sylvester. Cincinnati: Anderson.

Ram, U. (2004). Glocommodification: How the global consume the local – McDonald's in Israel. *Current Sociology, 52*, 11–31.

Rea, W. (1998). Rationalising culture: Youth, elites and masquerade politics. *Africa, 86*, 1, 98–117.

Redhead, S. (1993a). The end of the century party. In S. Redhead (Ed.), *Rave off politics and deviance in contemporary youth culture (Popular Cultural Studies, No. 1)* (pp. 1–6). Brookfield, VT: Avebury.

Redhead, S. (1993b). The politics of ecstasy. In S. Redhead (Ed.), *Rave off politics and deviance in contemporary youth culture (Popular Cultural Studies, No. 1)* (pp. 7–27). Brookfield, VT: Avebury.

Redhead, S. (1997). *Subculture to clubcultures: An introduction to popular cultural studies*. Oxford, UK: Blackwell Publishers.

Redman, D. (2003). Playful deviance as an urban leisure activity: Secret selves, self-validation, and entertaining performance. *Deviant Behavior, 24*, 1, 27–51.

Reighley, K. B. (2000). *Looking for the perfect beat: The art and the culture of the DJ*. New York: Pockets Books.

Reinarman, C., and Levine, H. G. (1997). The cultural contradictions of punitive prohibition. In C. Reinarman, and H. G. Levine. (Eds.), *Crack in America: Demon drugs and social justice* (pp. 334–345). Berkeley, CA: University of California Press.

Rietveld, H. (1993). Living the dream. In S. Redhead (Ed.), *Rave off politics and deviance in contemporary youth culture (Popular Cultural Studies, No. 1)* (pp. 41–90). Brookfield, VT: Avebury.

Riley, S. C., and Hayward, E. (2004). Patterns, trends, and meanings of drug use by dance-drug users in Edinburgh, Scotland. *Drugs: Education, Prevention and Policy, 11*, 243–262.

Ritzer, G., and Ovadia, S. (2000). The process of McDonaldization is not uniform, nor are its settings, consumers, or the consumption of its goods and services. In M. Gottdiener (Ed.), *New forms of consumption: Consumers, culture and commodification* (pp. 33–51). London: Rowman & Littlefield Publishers.

Roberts, J. M. and Sanders, T. (2005). Before, during and after: Realism, reflexivity and ethnography. *The Sociological Review, 53*, 2, 294–313.

Robins, L. N. (2005). Explaining when arrests end for serious juvenile offenders: Comments on the Sampson and Laub study. In R. J. Sampson, and J. H. Laub (Eds.), *The Annals of the American Academy of Political and Social Science, 602*, 57–73.

Robins, L. N., Davis, D. H., and Goodwin, D. W. (1974). Drug use in U.S. army enlisted men in Vietnam: A follow-up on their return home. *American Journal of Epidemiology, 99*, 235–249.

Rojek, C. (2000). Mass tourism or the re-enchantment of the world? Issues and contradictions in the study of travel. In M. Gottdiener (Ed.), *New forms of consumption: Consumers, culture and commodification* (pp. 51–71). London: Rowman & Littlefield Publishers.

Ross, M. W., Mattison, A. M., and Franklin, D. R. (2003). Club drugs and sex on drugs are associated with different motivations for gay circuit party attendance in men. *Substance Use & Misuse, 38*, 1173–1184.

Sabol, W. J.,Couture, H., and Harrison, P. M. (2007). *Bureau of Justice Statistics, Prisoners in 2006.* Washington, DC: U.S. Department of Justice.

Sack, A. R., Keller, J. F., and Hinkle, D. E. (1981). The sexual double standard: How prevalent today? *College Student Journal, 15*, 47–52.

Salasuo, M., and Seppälä, P. (2004). Drug use within the Finnish club culture as markers of distinction. *Contemporary Drug Problems, 31*, 2, 213–230.

Sampson R. J., and Laub, J. H. (1993). *Crime in the making: Pathway and the turning points through life.* Cambridge, MA: Harvard University Press.

Sampson, R. J., and Laub, J. H. (1997/2005). A life course theory of cumulative disadvantage and the stability of delinquency. In T. P. Thornberry (Ed.), *Advances in criminological theory: Developmental theories in crime and delinquency, 7,* 133–163. New Brunswick, NJ: Transaction Publishers.

Sampson, R. J., and Laub, J. H. (2005). A life course view of the development of crime. In R. J. Sampson and J. H. Laub (Eds.), *The Annals of the American Academy of Political and Social Science, 602,* 12–45.

Sandefur, G. D., Eggerling-Boeck, J., and Park, H. (2005). Off to a good start? Postsecondary education and early adult life. In R. A. Settersten Jr., F. F. Furstenberg Jr., and R.G. Rumbaut (Eds.), *On the frontier of adulthood: Theory, research, and public policy* (pp. 292–320). Chicago: The University of Chicago Press.

Sanders, B. (2005). In the club: ecstasy use and supply in a London nightclub. *Sociology, 39,* 241–258.

Schoeni, R. F., and Ross, K. E. (2005). Material assistance from families during the transition to adulthood. In R. A. Settersten Jr., F. F. Furstenberg Jr., and R. G. Rumbaut (Eds.), *On the frontier of adulthood: Theory, research, and public policy* (pp. 396–417). Chicago: The University of Chicago Press.

Schulenberg, J., O'Malley, P. M., Bachman, J. G., and Johnston, L. D. (2005). Early adult transitions and their relations to well-being and substance use. In R. A. Settersten Jr., F. F. Furstenberg Jr., and R. G. Rumbaut (Eds.), *On the frontier of adulthood: Theory, research, and public policy* (pp. 417–453). Chicago: The University of Chicago Press.

Seiler, C. (2000). The commodification of rebellion: Rock culture and consumer capitalism. In M. Gottdiener (Ed.), *New forms of consumption: Consumers, culture and commodification* (pp. 203–227). London: Rowman & Littlefield Publishers.

Sellin, T. (1938). Culture conflict and crime. *The American Journal of Sociology, 44,* 97–103.

Sferios, E. (2001). Introduction. In J. J. Jansen (Ed.), *Ketamine: Dreams and realities.* (pp. 9–11). Sarasota, FL: Multidisciplinary Association for Psychedelic Studies.

Shanahan, M. J. (2000). Pathways to adulthood in changing societies: Variability and mechanisms in life course perspective. *Annual Review of Sociology, 26,* 667–692.

Shaw, C., and McKay, H. (1942). *Delinquency and urban areas.* Chicago: Chicago University Press.

Sherlock, K., and Conner, M. (1999). Patterns of ecstasy use amongst club-goers on the UK 'dance scene'. *International Journal of Drug Policy,* *10,* 117–129.

Shewan, D., and Dalgarno, P. (2005). Reducing the risks of drug use: The case for set and setting. *Addiction, Research & Theory, 13,* 3, 259–265.

Shewan, D., Dalgarno, P., and Reith, G. (2000). Perceived risk and risk reduction among ecstasy users: The role of drug, set, and setting. *International Journal of Drug Policy, 10,* 431–453.

Shover, N. (1985). *Aging criminals.* Thousand Oaks: Sage Publications.

Shover, N. (1996). *Great pretenders: Pursuits and careers of persistent thieves.* Boulder: Westview Press.

Shukla, R. K. (2003). A rational choice analysis of decision-making and desistance from marijuana use. *Dissertation Abstracts International, 64,* 4, 1417–A.

Sifaneck, S. J., Kaplan, C. D., Dunlap, E., and Johnson, B. D. (2003). Blunts and blowtjes: Cannabis use practices in two cultural settings and their implications for secondary prevention. *Free Inquiry in Creative Sociology, 31,* 1, 3–14.

Sifaneck, S. J. and Neaigus, A. (2001). The ethnographic accessing, sampling and screening of hidden populations: Heroin sniffers in New York City. *Addiction Research & Theory, 7,* 519–543.

Silcott, M. (1999). *Rave America: New culture dancescapes.* Toronto, Ontario: ECW Press.

Slotar, D. (Producer). (2007). *What not to wear* [Television series]. Burbank, CA: Discovery Channel.

Smith, K. M., Larive, L. L., and Romanelli, F. (2002). Club drugs: methylenedioxymethamphetamine, flunitrazepam, ketamine hydrochloride, and gamma-hydroxybutyrate. *American Journal of Health-System Pharmacy, 59,* 1067–1076.

Snow, M. (1973). Maturing out of narcotic addiction in New York City. *International Journal of the Addictions, 8,* 921–938.

Southgate, E., and Hopwood, M. (2001). The role of folk pharmacology and lay experts in harm reduction: Sydney gay drug using networks. *International Journal of Drug Policy, 12,* 321–335.

Spradley, J. P. (1979). *The ethnographic interview.* Fort Worth: Harcourt Brace Jovanovich College Publishers.

Spruit, I. P. (1999). Ecstasy use and policy responses in the Netherlands. *Journal of Drug Issues, 29,* 3, 653–678.

Strauss, A. (1987). *Qualitative analysis for social scientists.* Cambridge, England: Cambridge University Press.

Stout, D. (1999, August 22). New drug can induce coma or death, FDA Warns. *The New York Times, 148,* 51410, A23.

Student Monitor®. (2008). *Student monitor converts data to insight: Financial services – Spring 2008.* Ridgewood, NJ: Student Monitor, LLC.

Substance Abuse and Mental Health Services Administration [SAMHSA]. (2003). *Results from the 2002 National Survey on Drug Use and Health: National findings.* Rockville, MD: Office of Applied Studies, NHSDA Series H-22, DHHS Publication No. SMA 03-3836.

Substance Abuse and Mental Health Services Administration [SAMHSA]. (2006a). *Results from the 2005 National Survey on Drug Use and Health: National findings.* Rockville, MD: Office of Applied Studies, NSDUH SERIE H-30, DHHS Publication No. SMA 06-4194.

Substance Abuse and Mental Health Services Administration [SAMHSA], Office of Applied Studies. (2006b). *Drug Abuse Warning Network, 2004: National estimates of drug-related emergency department visits.* DAWN Series D-28, DHHS Publication No. (SMA) 06-4143, Rockville, MD.

Substance Abuse and Mental Health Services Administration [SAMHSA], Office of Applied Studies (2007). *Drug Abuse Warning Network, 2005: National estimates of drug-related emergency department visits.* DAWN Series D-28, DHHS Publication No. (SMA) 07-4256, Rockville, MD.

Sullivan, M. L. (1989). *"Getting paid." Youth crime and work in the inner city.* Ithaca: Cornell University Press.

Sullivan, M. L. (1996). Developmental transition in poor youth: Delinquency and crime. In J. A. Graber, J. Brooks-Gunn, and A. C. Petersen (Eds.), *Transition through adolescence: Interpersonal domains and context* (pp. 141–164). Mahwah, NJ: Lawrence Erlbaum Associates.

Summer, D., Moroder, G., and Bellotte, P. (1997). I feel love [Record by Donna Summer]. *On I remember yesterday* [album]. California: Casablanca.

Sutherland, E. H., and Cressey, D. R. (1966). *Principles in criminology* (7th ed.). Philadelphia, PA: J. B. Lippincott.

Ter Bogt, T., Engels, R., Hibbel, B., Van Wel, F., and Verhagen, S. (2002)."Dancestasy": Dance, youth and MDMA use in Dutch youth culture. *Contemporary Drug Problems, 29,* 157–181.

Thick, D. (D.J.). (2004). Tweakin'. *On Tweakin'* [12" single album]. New Jersey: Sondos.

Thomas, H. (2003). *The body, dance and cultural theory.* New York: Palgrave Macmillan.

Thornberry, T. P. (1987). Toward an interactional theory of delinquency. *Criminology, 25,* 863–891.

Thornberry, T. P. (2005). Explaining multiple patterns of offending across the life course and across generations. In R. J. Sampson, and J. H. Laub (Eds.), *The Annals of the American Academy of Political and Social Science, 602,* 156–196.

Thornton, S. (1996). *Club cultures: Music, media and subcultural capital.* Hanover, England: Wesleyan University Press.

Tittle, C. R. (1989). Urbanness and unconventional behavior: A partial test of Claude Fischer's subcultural theory. *Criminology, 27,* 273–306.

Tonry, M. (2008). Crime and human rights—how political paranoia, protestant fundamentalism, and constitutional obsolescence combined to devastate Black America: The American Society of Criminology 2007 Presidential Address. *Criminology, 46,* 1, 1–34.

Topp, L., Hando, J., Dillon, P., Roche, A., and Solowij, N. (1999). Ecstasy use in Australia: Patterns of use and associated harm. *Drug and Alcohol Dependence, 55,* 105–115.

Trice, H. M., and Roman, P. M. (1970). Delabeling, relabeling and Alcoholics Anonymous. *Social Problems, 17,* 538–546.

Twitchell, J. (1999). Two cheers for materialism. *Wilson Quarterly, 23,* 16.

Uggen, C. (2000). Work as a turning point in the life course of criminals: A duration model of age, employment and recidivism. *American Sociological Review, 67,* 529–546.

U.S. Census Bureau. (2005, March). *Current Population Survey.* Washington, DC: Bureau of the Census.

United States Government, Food and Drug Administration Code, TITLE 21: Food and drugs, CHAPTER 13: Drug abuse prevention and control, SUBCHAPTER I: Control and enforcement, PART B: Authority to control; Standards and schedules, SECTION 812: Schedules of controlled substances (21 USC § 812).

van de Wijngaart, R. B., Braam, R., De Bruin, D., Fris, M., Maalste, N. J. M., and Berbraeck, H. T. (1999). Ecstasy use at large-scale dance events in the Netherlands. *Journal of Drugs Issues, 29,* 679–702.

van der Rijt, G., d'Haenens, L., and van Straten, P. (2003). Subcultural grounding of teenage smoking, drinking, and use of drugs. *Communications, 28*, 1–15.

Van Koningsbruggen, P. (1997). *Trinidad carnival: A quest for national identity.* London: Macmillan.

Veblen, T. (1994/1899). *The theory of the leisure class.* New York: Penguin Books.

Viser, V. J. (1994). Commodification as a system of signs in the contemporary historical bloc. *Dialectical Anthropology, 19,* 1, 109–127.

Wachowski, A. (Writer/Director), and Wachowski, L. (Writer/Director), (1999). *The Matrix* [Motion Picture]. United States: Warner Bros. Pictures.

Waldorf, D., Reinarman, C., and Murphy, S. (1991). *Cocaine changes: The experience of using and quitting.* Philadelphia: Temple University Press.

Warner, J., Room, R., and Adlaf, E. M. (1999). Rules and limits in the use of marijuana among high-school students: The results of a qualitative study in Ontario. *Journal of Youth Studies, 2,* 59–76.

Warr, M. (1998). Life-course transitions and desistance from crime. *Criminology, 36,* 2, 183–216.

Warr, M. (2002). *Companions in crime: The social aspects of criminal conduct.* Cambridge, UK: Cambridge University Press.

Weil, A., and Rosen, W. (2004). *From chocolate to morphine: Everything you need to know about mind-altering substances* (rev. ed.). New York: Houghton Mifflin.

Weir, E. (2000). Raves: A review of the culture, the drugs and the prevention of harm. *Canadian Medical Association Journal, 162,* 13, 1843–1850.

Weisburd, D., Waring, E., and Chayet, A. (1993 July). *White collar crime and career criminals. A final report submitted to the U.S. Department of Justice.* National Institute of Justice.

Whiteacre, K. W. (2005). Criminal constructions of drug users. In W. Palacios (Ed.), *Cocktails and dreams: Perspectives on drug use* (pp. 268–282). Upper Saddle River, NJ: Pearson Prentice Hall.

Whyte, W. F. (1993). *Street corner society: The social structure of an Italian slum* (4th ed.). Chicago: University of Chicago Press.

Wijetunga, M., Seto, T., Lindsay, J., and Schatz, I. (2003). Crystal methamphetamine-associated cardiomyopathy: Tip of the iceberg? *Journal of Toxicology. Clinical Toxicology, 41,* 7, 981–986.

Williams, T. (1996). Exploring the cocaine culture. In C. D. Smith and W. Kornblum (Eds.), *In the field: Readings on the field research experience* (2nd. ed., pp. 27–32). Westport, CT: Praeger.

Williams, T., Dunlap, E., Johnson, B. D., and Hamid, A. (1992). Personal safety in dangerous places. *Journal of Contemporary Ethnography, 21,* 3, 343–374.

Winick, C. (1962). Maturing out of narcotic addiction. *Bulletin on Narcotics, 14,* 1, 1–7.

Winterbottom, M. [Director]. (2002). *24 hour party people* [Motion Picture]. United Kingdom: Pathé Distribution Ltd.

Wolfgang, M., and Ferracuti, F. (1982). *The subculture of violence.* Thousand Oaks: Sage Publications.

Wright, B. R. E., Caspi, A., Moffitt, T. E., and Silva, P. A. (1999). Low self-control, social bonds, and crime: Social causation, social selection, or both? *Criminology, 37,* 479–514.

Wright, R. T., and Decker, S. H. (1994). *Burglars on the job: Streetlife and residential break-ins.* Boston, MA: Northeastern University Press.

Wright, S., Grogan, S., and Hunter, G. (2001). Body-builders' attitudes toward steroid use. Drugs: education, prevention and policy, *8,* 91–95.

Yacoubian, G. S., Jr., Boyle, C., Hardin, C. A., and Loftus, E. A. (2003). It's a rave new world: Estimating the prevalence and perceived harm of ecstasy and other drug use, among club rave attendees. *Journal of Drug Education, 33,* 2, 187–197.

Yamaguchi, K., and Kandel, D. (1993). Marital homophily on illicit drug use among young adults: Assortative mating or marital influence? *Social Forces, 72,* 2, 505–528.

Yamaguchi, K., and Kandel, D. (1997). The influence of spouses' behavior and marital dissolution on marijuana use: Causation or selection. *Journal of Marriage and Family, 59,* 22–36.

Zavitz, A. L., and Allaher, A. L. (2002). Racial politics and cultural identity in Trinidad's carnival. *Identity: An International Journal of Theory and Research, 2,* 2, 125–145.

Zinberg, N. E. (1984). *Drug, set, and setting: The basis for controlled intoxicant use.* New Haven: Yale University Press.

Zinberg, N. E., and Harding, W. M. (1982). Introduction – Control and intoxicant use: A theoretical and practical overview. In N. E. Zinberg, and W. M. Harding (Eds.), *Control over intoxicant use: Pharmacological, psychological and social considerations* (pp. 13–37). New York: Human Services Press.

Index[1]

---

[1]Pseudonyms assigned to informants in this study are listed in italics.